Florida Scholarships
Seventh Edition

Executive Editor
John L. Adams

Editor
Shawn Liu

Florida Funding Publications
A John L. Adams Company
Miami, FL
2004

2
Florida Scholarships

CONTRIBUTING STAFF

Publisher and Executive Editor   John L. Adams

Editor   Shawn Liu

Sales and Distribution Manager   Mariha Oliveira

Florida Funding Publications, Inc.
A John L. Adams Company
8925 S.W. 148th Street, Suite 110
Miami, FL 33176
(305) 251-2203
Fax: (305) 251-2773
Email: info@floridafunding.com
www.floridafunding.com

TABLE OF CONTENTS

INTRODUCTION

Florida Scholarships is the most comprehensive listing available for scholarship funding opportunities for students in Florida. It is our desire that students, parents, teachers, and financial aid administrators will read this book and understand the world of scholarship opportunities that exist for Florida students.

The seventh edition contains more than 400 private foundations that specifically fund scholarships. Florida Funding Publications staff researched a variety of public records, including 990-PF's (IRS records), annual reports, newsletters, and other published information about Florida foundations to compile the list found in this book. Entries were mailed to potential foundations to ensure accurate, up-to-date information. Florida Funding Publications is the only publisher in the state of Florida to publish this information exclusively for Florida students.

Readers will be pleased to discover many scholarship opportunities found in the seventh edition have an Internet website included to facilitate and expedite the application process. Included are also sample application letters to give students an edge when applying for scholarships.

It is important to note that many of the federal and state scholarship opportunities have deadlines. Paying close attention to them is essential. If you are considering applying for a scholarship that specifies a summer deadline, you should make contact with the administering agency several months in advance.

Keep in mind that in the game of scholarship hunting, it pays not only to apply early, but to research early, as well.

It is our sincere hope that this book will be the catalyst in your quest to finance your education. Good luck and best wishes,

Shawn Liu
Editor

CHAPTER ONE

FEDERAL FINANCIAL AID ASSISTANCE RESOURCES

FEDERAL FINANCIAL AID ASSISTANCE RESOURCES

Federal Student Financial Aid is one of the more popular resources available to students in need of financial assistance. The federal government annually sets aside about $50-$60 billion to the United States Department of Education, which in turn administers and operates programs that touch every area and level of education.

The Department's elementary and secondary programs annually serve 15,000 school districts and more than 53 million students attending over 92,000 public schools and more than 27,000 private schools.

Department programs also provide grant, loan, and work-study assistance to more than 10 million postsecondary students. In the federal fiscal year of 2005, more than ten million college students will receive more than $33 billion in federal grants, loans (excluding consolidation loans) and campus-based programs. Nearly 420,000 students will receive close to $13 billion in federal Pell Grants each year, which serve the neediest students.

Federal Financial Assistance Programs

Applying for financial aid requires three important virtues:

1. *Planning ahead,*
2. *Establishing financial need,*
3. *Gathering all important and required records and forms.*

The U.S. Department of Education administers the following financial aid programs:

Pell Grants

Pell grants are for undergraduate students who have yet to receive a bachelor's or professional degree. The grants are awarded based on financial need as demonstrated by the student's family income. The amount of the Pell grant a student receives is based on financial need displayed, and how much of an entitlement your school receives. Entitlements are based on various criteria set by the federal government each year. Annual awards usually range from $200 to $4,000.

College Work Study Program (CWS)

College Work Study allows students to gain work experience and earn additional funds working in various positions in school. The program provides students with supplemental income that facilitates funding throughout the college years. Wages earned via the College Work Study Program meet the federal minimum wage requirements, but may be higher in some cases depending on the skills needed for the position. Students are allowed to earn as much as possible, provided the amount does not surpass the student's financial need.

Stafford Loans

Stafford Loans are federally guaranteed, low interest loans available to students who have been approved for federal financial aid assistance. Once a student is approved, the loan is processed by the school's financial aid office, which in turn sends the application form to a bank that disburses it, although some schools disburse the funds themselves. Depending on the student's needs, the loans are given in subsidized or unsubsidized interest terms. A **subsidized loan** is a loan for where the interest is paid by the government as long as the student is actively seeking a degree. An **unsubsidized loan** is a loan for which the interest is not paid by the government, and thus accrues. Undergraduate and graduate students are eligible to apply for Stafford loans.

Perkins Loans

Perkins Loans are federally subsidized loans, but unlike Stafford loans, are processed, awarded, and distributed by the school. Upon graduation the student must repay the school, instead of a lending institution. These low interest loans are available to both graduate and undergraduate students.

Federal Supplemental Education Opportunity Grant (FSEOG)

A Federal Supplemental Educational Opportunity Grant (FSEOG) is for undergraduates with exceptional financial need--that is, students with the lowest Expected Family Contributions (EFCs)--and gives priority to students who receive Federal Pell Grants. An FSEOG does not have to be paid back. Students can receive **between $100 and $4,000 a year,** depending on when they apply, their level of need, the funding level of the schools attended, and the policies of the individual financial aid offices.

Consolidated Loans

Consolidated loans are low interest loans that allow students to combine various types of federal student loans to simplify repayment. There are two types of loans currently available. The Direct Consolidated Loans and FFEL Consolidation Loans. For information about Direct Consolidated Loans, call 800/557-7392. Students should consult with their respective financial aid advisors for consolidation options and loan repayment options.

Federal Parents Loans for Undergraduate Students (PLUS)

PLUS loans are low interest loans available to parents of students that are ineligible for other federal loan programs. PLUS loans have variable interest rates, and which usually do not exceed 9%. Students should consult their school's financial aid office for application requirements and procedures.

Applying for Federal Financial Aid

Completing a Free Application for Federal Student Aid form (FAFSA)

What is the FAFSA?

The *Free Application for Federal Student Aid*, or FAFSA, is used to apply for federal student financial aid, including grants, loans, and work-study. In addition, it is used by most states and schools to award nonfederal student financial aid.

How does it work?

Completing the FAFSA is the first step in the financial aid process. Once you submit it, it is processed and a copy of your information is electronically sent to the schools you listed in the application. The Department of Education then mails a report, called a *Student Aid Report*, or SAR, to you. It is important to review your SAR when you receive it to make sure all of your information is correct and to provide any necessary corrections or additional information.

Your information is entered into a formula from the Higher Education Act of 1965, as amended, and the result is your Expected Family Contribution, or **EFC**. This represents the amount your family is expected to contribute towards the cost of your education (although this amount may not exactly match the amount you and your family end up contributing). If your information is complete, your SAR will contain your EFC.

The schools you list receive your EFC along with the rest of your information. They use the EFC to prepare a financial aid package to help you meet your financial need. **Financial need** is the difference between your EFC and your school's **cost of attendance** (which can include living expenses), as determined by the school. If you believe that you have special circumstances that should be taken into account, such as unusual medical or dental expenses or a significant change in income from one year to the next, contact the financial aid administrator at the schools to which you are applying. Any financial aid you are eligible to receive will be paid to you through your school. Typically, your school will first use the aid to pay tuition, fees, and room and board (if provided by the school). Any remaining funds are paid to you for your other expenses.

The Free Application for Federal Student Aid (FAFSA) is available from the following resources:

1. FAFSA on the Web: http://www.fafsa.ed.gov
2. The Financial Aid Office Located in Your School
3. Contact the Federal Student Aid Information Center at:

800/433-3243
Hearing Impaired: 800/730-8913
http://studentaid.ed.gov

Things to Remember:

Read the form

Many questions on the FAFSA are straightforward, like your social security number or your date of birth. However, many require you to read the instructions to make sure you answer the question correctly. Words like "household," "investments," and even "parent" all have common meanings, but are specifically defined for purposes of financial aid. Be sure to read all instructions.

Apply early

Deadlines for aid from your state, from your school, and from private sources tend to be much earlier than deadlines for federal aid. To make sure that any financial aid package your school offers will contain aid from as many sources as possible, apply as soon as you can after January 1, 2004. The U.S. Department of Education will process your 2004-2005 FAFSA right up until June 20, 2005. However, to actually receive aid, your school must have your correct, complete information before your last day of enrollment in the 2004-2005 school year. It is important to apply early to make sure you leave enough time for your school to receive your information and to make any necessary corrections.

Federal Scholarships

The federal government administers scholarships based on factors that are NOT based on financial need. Instead, they are administered on the basis of scholastic excellence, specialized areas of study, and other criteria. Students who wish to apply for these scholarships should do so at the earliest possible time as some programs have application deadlines.

Americorps Program

The Americorps Program closely resembles the Peace Corps, with the exception that it is a domestic program. Americorps volunteers earn educational benefits in exchange for one or two years of service in the Americorps program. Americorps are made up of hundreds community service programs all across the country. Upon completion, volunteers are entitled to a portion of their student loan debt forgiven. For more information, contact: 202/606-5000.
www.americorps.org

Barry M. Goldwater Scholarship Program

The Barry M. Goldwater Program was designed to honor former Senator Barry Goldwater through the operation of an education scholarship program. Financed by a permanent trust fund endowment, it is designed to encourage outstanding students to excel in engineering and the natural sciences. Eligible applicants include undergraduate, sophomore-, and junior-level students at two and four year colleges and universities who are nominated by their respective institution. Awards range up to $7500 per annum. Application deadline is February 1 yearly. For more information, contact the Barry M. Goldwater Scholarship and Excellence in Education Foundation, Gerald J. Smith, President, 6225 Brandon Avenue, Suite 315, Springfield, VA 22150-2519. Telephone: 703/756- 6012. E-Mail: goldh2o@erols.com. www.act.org/goldwater

Educational Exchange for Graduate Students

The aim of the Educational Exchange for Graduate Students is to improve and strengthen international relations of the United States by promoting better understanding among cultures of the world through educational exchanges. To be eligible, students must be U.S. citizens at the time of application, must hold a Bachelor's degree before the date of the grant, not hold a doctoral degree at the time of application, and be proficient in English. Scholarship amounts range from $1,200 to $35,000. Applications are accepted beginning May 1. Enrolled applicants must submit applications to the campus Fulbright program adviser by the date established. For more information, contact your school's Fulbright program, or write to: Institute of International Education, 809 United Nations Plaza, New York, NY 10017.
exchanges.state.gov

Harry S. Truman Scholarship Program

The objective of the Harry S. Truman program is to honor former President Harry S. Truman through a scholarship, financed by a permanent trust fund endowment, to create increased opportunities for students preparing for pursue careers in public service. To be eligible, students must be undergraduate junior-level students at 4-year colleges and universities. Nominating colleges and universities must be accredited and recognized by the Department of Education. Students receive financial assistance ranging from $3,000 to $13,500 per annum. For more information, contact the Harry S. Truman Scholarship Foundation, Louis Blair, Executive Secretary, 712 Jackson Place, NW, Washington, DC 20006. Telephone: 202/395-4831.
www.truman.gov

National Security Education Scholarships

Students who participate are encouraged to equip themselves with an understanding of less commonly taught languages and culture and to help build a critical base of future leaders both in the marketplace and in government service. Students enrolled in accredited 2- or 4-year public or private colleges or universities are eligible to apply. Scholarship amounts are up to $8,000 per academic term, not to exceed two terms per year. Application deadlines are specified in the annual application materials, but are usually in January or February. For more information regarding undergraduate scholarships, contact: Institute of International Education (NSEP), 1400 K Street, N.W., Suite 650, Washington, D.C. 20005-2403. Phone: 1-800-618-6737. Email: nesp@iie.org. For more information on graduate fellowships, contact Academy for Educational Development (NSEP), 1875 Connecticut Avenue, N.W., Suite 900, Washington, D.C. 20009-1202. Telephone: 800/498-9360. Email: nsep@aed.org.
www.ndu.edu/nsep

Undergraduate Scholarship Program for Individuals from Disadvantaged Backgrounds

Scholarships are available to students aspiring to pursue academic study, where prepares them for selected professions as established by the National Institutes of Health (NIH). Eligible applicants include undergraduate full time students enrolled in 4-year colleges and universities. Students will receive a dollar amount determined by the school. For more information, contact The National Institutes of Health, Office of Loan Repayment and Scholarship, 2 Center Drive, Room 2E24, Bethesda, MD 20892-0230. Telephone: (800) 528-7689. Facsimile: (301) 480-5481. Email: ugsp@nih.gov.
ugsp.info.nih.gov

Armed Forces R.O.T.C. Scholarships

These scholarships are offered through the Air Force, Army, Marines, and Navy. Program awards range from 2- to 5-year scholarships that pay for tuition, books, and fees in return for commitments to reserve or active duty service. Your local military recruiter can provide you with more information about colleges with ROTC programs and appointments to the military academies; the latter generally requiring endorsement from your Congressional representative and other requirements. You may write to the U.S. military academies and ROTC programs at the following addresses:

Service	Academy	ROTC
Army	Director of Admissions United States Military Academy West Point, NY 10996-1797 www.usma.edu	Army ROTC Scholarship Program HQ-Cadet Command Building 56/Scholarship Branch Fort Monroe, VA 23651 www.armyrotc.com
Navy-Marines	Dean of Admissions U.S. Naval Academy Leahy Hall Annapolis, MD 21402 www.usna.edu	Navy-Marine Corps NROTC Scholarship Program Chief of Naval Education Code N-1/081 Naval Air Station Pensacola, FL 32508-5100 www.nrotc.navy.mil
Air Force	Director of Admissions U.S. Air Force Academy Colorado Springs, CO 80840-500 www.usafa.af.mil	Air Force ROTC Four-Year Scholarship Program Maxwell Air Force Base Montgomery, AL 36112-5001
Coast Guard	Director of Admissions U.S. Coast Guard Academy New London, CT 06320-4195 www.cga.edu	None
Merchant Marine (not a military service)	Director of Admissions U.S. Merchant Marine Academy Steamboat Road Kings Point, NY 11024 www.usmma.edu	None

CHAPTER TWO

STATE OF FLORIDA FINANCIAL ASSISTANCE RESOURCES

STATE OF FLORIDA FINANCIAL ASSISTANCE RESOURCES

The State of Florida offers students various types of financial assistance programs. Each program determines eligibility requirements. Students who are eligible to be claimed on a parent's income tax return when the parent lives out of state, and independent students whose domicile in the state of Florida is temporary or merely incidental to enrollment in a Florida institution of higher education, are generally not eligible for Florida state aid. All other Florida students are eligible.

Most high school guidance offices and all financial aid offices at state colleges and universities have application forms, guidelines and general information for the following programs:

- Children of Deceased or Disabled Veterans or Children of Servicemen Classified as Prisoners of War or Missing in Action Scholarship Program

- Critical Teacher Shortage Student Loan Forgiveness Program

- Critical Teacher Shortage Tuition Reimbursement Program

- Ethics in Business Scholarship Program

- Florida Bright Futures Scholarship Program

- Florida Prepaid College Program

- Florida Student Assistance Grant Program

- Florida Work Experience Program

- Jose Marti Scholarship Challenge Grant

- Mary McLeod Bethune Scholarship Program

- Robert C. Byrd Honors Scholarship Program

- Rosewood Family Scholarship Program

- William L. Boyd, IV, Florida Resident Access Grant

A brief synopsis of each program follows. For more information, or to contact the programs directly, visit on the Internet: **http://www.firn.edu/doe/bin00065/splist.htm**

Or write to:
Office of Student Financial Assistance
Florida Department of Education
1940 North Monroe Street, Suite 70
Tallahassee, Florida 32303-4759
888/827-2004

State Financial Assistance Programs

Children of Deceased or Disabled Veterans or Children of Servicemen Classified as Prisoners of War or Missing in Action Scholarship Program

Florida provides scholarships to dependent children of Florida veterans or servicemen who died in action or from diseases directly correlated to service, disabilities verified from the state of Florida. Students whose parents are deemed missing in action (MIA) are also eligible for educational financial aid. Applications are due April 1 annually. Award amounts are the maximum cost of attending any public university in the state of Florida.
www.firn.edu/doe/bin00065/cddvfactsheet.htm

Critical Teacher Shortage Forgiveness Loan Program

This program was created to encourage qualified individuals to seek employment in Florida schools, and to pursue careers in critical teacher shortage subject areas in Florida. The loan program gives awards for upper division undergraduate and graduate students enrolled in teacher preparation programs leading to certification in a critical teacher shortage subject area. Eligible students include individuals who are fully admitted to Florida colleges and universities and, pursuing a degree in teaching. Applications must be received by the March 15 deadline.
www.firn.edu/doe/bin00065/ctsflfactsheet.htm

Critical Teacher Shortage Tuition Reimbursement Program

This program was created to improve skills and knowledge of certified, full-time, publicly funded school employees currently teaching or preparing to teach in a Pre K-12 teacher shortage area. Awards can range up to $78 per semester hour. The program operates on a first-come, first-served basis. Deadline is July 15.
www.firn.edu/doe/bin00065/ctslffactsheet.htm

Ethics in Business Scholarship Program

This Ethics in Business Scholarship Program gives assistance to undergraduate college students currently enrolled in community colleges and eligible Florida colleges and universities. Funding for the program is provided by private and state contributions. Awards are dependent on private, matching funds. Eligible students are current students enrolled in colleges and universities. Students should contact the financial aid office for further information. For more information, or to apply, visit:
www.firn.edu/doe/bin00065/ethicfactsheet.htm

Florida Bright Futures Scholarship Program

The Bright Futures Scholarship Program was created by the Florida Legislature to create a comprehensive scholarship program based on three scholarship programs (Florida Scholars, Vocational Gold Seal Endorsement and Florida Merit Scholars). This award was made available for the first time in 1997. Bright Futures Scholarships can be used to attend on a full or part-time basis at any public or private Florida college, university, community college, or other postsecondary institution. **Important! You must apply during your last year in high school or you will forfeit all future eligibility for a Bright Futures Scholarship.** Students should apply as soon as possible to be considered. For more information, students should consult with their school's financial aid officer.
www.firn.edu/doe/brfutures/bffactsheet.htm

Florida Prepaid College Program

The Prepaid College Program allows families to prepay the cost of their children's education expenses at a fixed rate. For more information, call 1-800-552-GRAD, or visit:
www.floridaprepaidcollege.com

Florida Student Assistance Grant Program

This program is for undergraduate students attending Florida colleges or universities (public or private) and is need-based. Awards are based on information submitted to the Free Application for Student Aid (FAFSA). Interested students must inform the Florida Department of Education by marking a box that allows their FAFSA information to be released to the State of Florida. For more information, contact the financial aid office at eligible colleges and universities, or visit:
www.firn.edu/doe/bin00065/fsagfactsheet.htm

Florida Work Experience Program

As the name suggests, this program allows students to earn money while gaining valuable work experience. Eligible students based on FAFSA have the opportunity to work either on-campus or in other approved environments, while earning income toward tuition costs. Interested students should contact the financial aid advisor at their college or university.
www.firn.edu/doe/bin00065/fwepfactsheet.htm

Jose Marti Scholarship Challenge Grant

Hispanic Americans currently attending a Florida college or university (undergraduate and graduate) are eligible for the grant. Awards can be as much as $2,000 per year. High school students should apply during their last year of school, while gradate students must apply prior to their first year of study. Applications are due April 1.
www.firn.edu/doe/bin00065/jmfactsheet.htm

Mary McLeod Bethune Scholarship program

The Mary McLeod Bethune Scholarship is a need-based scholarship grant of $3,000 per academic year that is administered for a maximum of eight semesters or twelve quarters. Outstanding seniors who plan to attend Florida Agricultural & Mechanical University, Bethune-Cookman College, Edward Waters College or Florida Memorial College are encouraged to apply. Participating universities set application deadlines. Students should request an application from the address or phone number at the beginning of this section. www.firn.edu/doe/bin00065/mmbfactsheet.htm

Robert C. Byrd Honors Scholarship Program

This program is administered by the state of Florida, but it is federally funded. Students who achieve a 3.8 GPA while in grades 9 through 12 are eligible for this award and their respective public or private high school nominates students. To apply, interested students should consult with their high school advisor or financial aid representative. www.firn.edu/doe/bin00065/byrdfactsheet.htm

Rosewood Family Scholarship Program

A total of 25 people who are direct descendants of the African-American families affected by the tragedy that occurred in 1923 in Rosewood, Florida are eligible for this scholarship. Awards are $4,000 per academic year. Students must have completed a Free Application for Federal Student Aid, and the corresponding Rosewood scholarship application. Application deadline is May 15. For more information, students should contact their academic advisor. www.firn.edu/doe/bin00065/rosewoodfactsheet.htm

William L Boyd, IV, Florida Resident Access Grant

This program provides tuition assistance to Florida undergraduates attending eligible private, non-profit Florida colleges or universities. The Florida Resident Access Grant (FRAG) award is not based on financial need and can be used for undergraduate tuition and expenses. Awards amounts typically amount to $2,100. Deadlines are revolving. www.firn.edu/doe/bin00065/fragfactsheet.htm

CHAPTER THREE

PRIVATE FOUNDATION SCHOLARSHIPS

PRIVATE FOUNDATION SCHOLARSHIPS

Private Florida foundations' financial strength represents over $13.4 billion in assets and $897 million in contributions to nonprofit organizations, with a significant amount awarded in the form of scholarships. Many students don't realize that the same foundations that give to local non-profit organizations also sponsor scholarship programs. The resources available are substantial; financial assistance available to students has never been greater.

This chapter contains the complete list of Florida-based foundations that offer students financial assistance. The information contained in this chapter was obtained through review of thousands of IRS 990-PF forms filed each year by private foundations. *Florida Funding Publications* maintains close ties to Florida foundations, as they supply us with yearly updates on changes and additional funds available for disbursement. Here are some tips that will make your scholarship search an easy, seamless process:

- Write the foundations you are interested in. Many foundations are small, and thus processing times may take longer than larger foundations.

- Increase your chances of a response by **always** including a self-addressed stamped envelope when writing to any foundation. Performing this simple act of courtesy will greatly increase your chances of receiving a response.

- Focus on important details. If a foundation requires specifications like a grade point average (GPA) or a geographic preference, make certain to include this information in your letter of initial inquiry.

- Do not overload the foundation with information. Do not send the foundation your transcripts, letters of recommendation or any other credentials unless the foundation explicitly requests it, or if the foundation's official application guidelines specify them. It is perfectly fine, however, to mention an outstanding GPA or any other exceptional awards of achievement in your initial letter of inquiry.

- Do not overlook corporations. If you already have decided on a field you want to study, many companies in a given field provide scholarships. Make an effort to do research on those companies, as many of them provide students with a variety of financial support.

Types of Foundations

There are several types of foundations. Understanding the difference between them can help you better understand their mission and goals.

Independent Foundations

Independent foundations are private organizations that are funded by of an individual, family, or group of close associates. Foundations in this category often have mandates that dictate who will receive funding, often focusing their resources to specific charities, religious organizations, and educational purposes.

Corporate Foundations

Corporate foundations are also private organizations, but with a difference. These foundations are established through the contributions of a profit-making company or corporation. Corporate foundations are separate entities of the sponsoring corporation and usually provide funding to various areas of interest. Corporate giving also tends to be in interest areas that are common with those of the business itself.

Community Foundations

Community foundations are based in a community and usually limit contributions to a predetermined geographic area form community foundations. Most community foundations administer some type of scholarship program through a memorial or trust fund. Community foundations are the easiest to approach in terms of funding. They are typically well staffed, respond well to phone inquiries, and have standard procedures for requesting scholarships and funds.

Most foundation profiles contain contact information, funding activity, asset information, and contact information. Unless otherwise specified, the best way to approach a foundation is to send an initial query letter, accompanied by a self-addressed, stamped envelope.

Foundation Profile Map

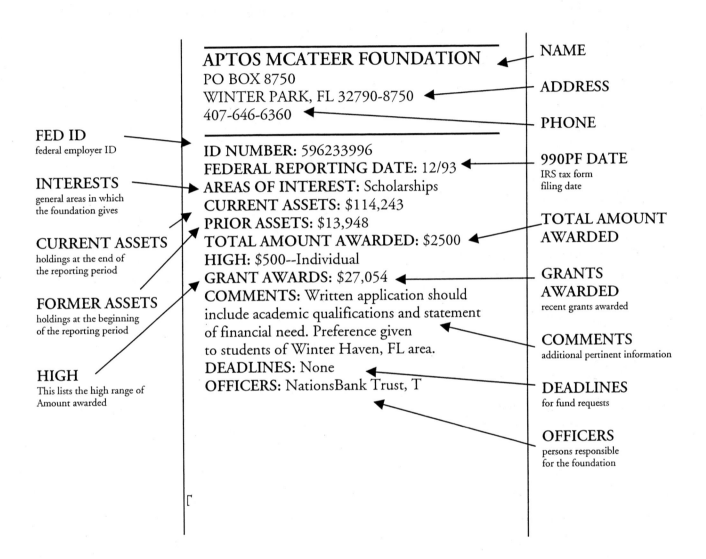

FED ID
federal employer ID

INTERESTS
general areas in which
the foundation gives

CURRENT ASSETS
holdings at the end of
the reporting period

FORMER ASSETS
holdings at the beginning
of the reporting period

HIGH
This lists the high range of
Amount awarded

APTOS MCATEER FOUNDATION
PO BOX 8750
WINTER PARK, FL 32790-8750
407-646-6360

ID NUMBER: 596233996
FEDERAL REPORTING DATE: 12/93
AREAS OF INTEREST: Scholarships
CURRENT ASSETS: $114,243
PRIOR ASSETS: $13,948
TOTAL AMOUNT AWARDED: $2500
HIGH: $500--Individual
GRANT AWARDS: $27,054
COMMENTS: Written application should
include academic qualifications and statement
of financial need. Preference given
to students of Winter Haven, FL area.
DEADLINES: None
OFFICERS: NationsBank Trust, T

NAME

ADDRESS

PHONE

990PF DATE
IRS tax form
filing date

**TOTAL AMOUNT
AWARDED**

**GRANTS
AWARDED**
recent grants awarded

COMMENTS
additional pertinent information

DEADLINES
for fund requests

OFFICERS
persons responsible
for the foundation

Foundation Profile Terms

Name

The name of the foundation is listed as it appears on its annual report or tax return. However, this name may be inverted in the listing for alphabetical purposes.

Address

The address is taken from the most recently filed IRS Form 990-PF or annual report.

Phone

The telephone number is taken from the most recently filed IRS Form 990-PF or annual report. This number may be for the foundation's office, legal counsel, principal manager, or their contact person.

Fed ID

The federal employer identification number is taken from the IRS Form 990-PF.

Comments

These provide additional information that may be relevant to the application process.

Deadlines

These are dates set by the foundation for receiving applicant information for consideration.

Current Assets

These are total assets listed on the Form 990-PF or annual report as of the latest reporting period.

Former Assets

These are total assets listed on the Form 990-PF or annual report as of the beginning of the reporting period.

Officers

These names and titles are listed as per the most recent IRS Form 990-PF.

Total Amount Awarded

This is the total amount awarded during a given period.

High

This is the highest reported award.

ABBOTT, CLAUDE A. & BLANCHE MCCUBBIN CHARITABLE TRUST

3495 PINETREE ST.
PT. CHARLOTTE, FL 33952-7976
941-743-7228

ID NUMBER: 237213934
FEDERAL REPORTING DATE: 07/01
AREAS OF INTEREST: Arts & Culture, Education, Medicine, Religion, Research, Scholarships, Social Services, Other
CURRENT ASSETS: $241,107 PRIOR ASSETS: $140,862
TOTAL AMOUNT AWARDED: $11,468
HIGH: $1,500--Children's Cancer Foundation
MID: $1,000--Muscular Dystrophy
LOW: $100--American Cancer Society
GRANTS AWARDS: Catholic Charities--$500, Chesepeake Search & Rescue--$1,500, Diocese of Venice--$500, Florida Studio Theatre--$1,000, Maryvale Prep School--$500
SERVICE AREA: SW FL, MD, CT
COMMENTS: No required form. Submit to William D. Wells, P.O. Box 694, Hampstead, MD 2174.
DEADLINES: None
OFFICERS: Wells, William D., T

AINGER, L. A. JUNIOR HIGH SCHOOL FOUNDATION, INC.

LEMON BAY HIGH SCHOOL
2201 PLACIDA RD.
ENGLEWOOD, FL 34224
941-474-7702

ID NUMBER: 650108396
FEDERAL REPORTING DATE: 03/00
AREAS OF INTEREST: Scholarships
CURRENT ASSETS: $53,147 PRIOR ASSETS: $51,563
TOTAL AMOUNT AWARDED: $1,500
HIGH: $500--Individual
MID: $500--Individual
LOW: $500--Individual
GRANTS AWARDS: N/A
SERVICE AREA: Charlotte County, FL
COMMENTS: Application format requires completion of "Local Scholarship Application". Required content includes, name, add., phone #, ss#, educational data, SAT and/or ACT scores and post secondary school selection info. Must be: grad. of LA Ainger M.S., grad. of any H.S. in Charlotte Cty, FL, and pr. of accept. to post-secondary sch
DEADLINES: N/A
OFFICERS: Schmidt, Dr. Max L., TR; Stickland, William, TR; Sullivan, Charles, TR; Horton, Mac, TR

ALBERTANI, TEYA FOUNDATION FOR INVOLVMENT, INC.

5128 BRYWILL CIR.
SARASOTA, FL 34234

ID NUMBER: 592981976
FEDERAL REPORTING DATE: 08/01
AREAS OF INTEREST: Scholarships
CURRENT ASSETS: $111,728 PRIOR ASSETS: $101,076
TOTAL AMOUNT AWARDED: $5,000
HIGH: $2,500--Individual
LOW: $2,500--Individual

GRANTS AWARDS: N/A
SERVICE AREA: National
DEADLINES: 1/15
OFFICERS: Houchins, Doris, D; Wacholder, Barry L., D

ALLEN, R.E. & JOAN S. FOUNDATION, INC.

C/O ALLEN INVESTMENTS, INC.
2400 S. FEDERAL HWY., STE. 200
STUART, FL 34994-4531
561-288-9800

ID NUMBER: 650225533
FEDERAL REPORTING DATE: 05/01
AREAS OF INTEREST: Scholarships
CURRENT ASSETS: $975,878 PRIOR ASSETS: $1,055,347
TOTAL AMOUNT AWARDED: $169,850
HIGH: $2,000--Individual
MID: $750--Individual
LOW: $500--Individual
GRANTS AWARDS: N/A
SERVICE AREA: Kenton, OH only
COMMENTS: Send applications to Dr. Karen Allen 2400 S. Federal Highway, STuart, FL. 34994. Grants only for residents of Kenton, Ohio and/or employees of Imperial Cup Corp. .
DEADLINES: None
OFFICERS: Allen, R.E., P; Allen, Richard, VP; Allen, Rex, VP; Allen, Karen, S; First Union National Bank, TR

ALPERT, RUTH SEYMOUR & HARRIET CHARITABLE FOUNDATION

2546 N.W. 63RD LN.
BOCA RATON, FL 33496
561-989-8690

ID NUMBER: 650541337
FEDERAL REPORTING DATE: 06/01
AREAS OF INTEREST: Community, Environment, Health, Religion, Scholarships, Social Services, Sports & Athletics
CURRENT ASSETS: $42,740 PRIOR ASSETS: $46,123
TOTAL AMOUNT AWARDED: $5,200
HIGH: $2,500--North American Conference on Ethiopia
MID: $1,500--Fund to Cure Asthma
LOW: $50--National Wild Life Federation
GRANTS AWARDS: Temple Shaaray Tefila--$500, Special Olympics New Jersey--$250, SOLEIF--$50
SERVICE AREA: NJ
COMMENTS: Gives to preselected organizations. Awards were made to students in NJ.
DEADLINES: None
OFFICERS: Alpert, Seymour, P; Alpert, Harriet, S; Alpert, Joseph, D; Alpert, Marc, D

AMERICAN LEGION MEMORIAL SCHOLARSHIP FUND, INC.

255 S. COUNTY RD.
PALM BEACH, FL 33480
561-655-4305

ID NUMBER: 596151027
FEDERAL REPORTING DATE: 11/01

AREAS OF INTEREST: Education, Scholarships
CURRENT ASSETS: $780,955 PRIOR ASSETS:
$831,533
TOTAL AMOUNT AWARDED: $29,800
HIGH: $2,000--Individual
MID: $2,000--Individual
LOW: $1,000--Individual
GRANTS AWARDS: N/A
SERVICE AREA: Palm Beach Co.
COMMENTS: Use form provided by American Legion
Scholarship Funds, Inc. Applicant must be a Palm Beach Co.,
Fl. resident.
DEADLINES: 05/01
OFFICERS: Eassa, Jack, P; Kuehnel, Louise M., VP; Kramer,
R. K., S/T; Minsky, Howard, D; Zern, William Jr., D; Gurton,
Christy, D

AMIN, C.M. FOUNDATION

1802 NOTTINGHAM LN.
CLEARWATER, FL 33764

ID NUMBER: 593475679
FEDERAL REPORTING DATE: 01/02
AREAS OF INTEREST: Scholarships
CURRENT ASSETS: $39,641 PRIOR ASSETS: $30,127
TOTAL AMOUNT AWARDED: $1,480
HIGH: $325--Individual
LOW: $90--Individual
GRANTS AWARDS: N/A
SERVICE AREA: India
COMMENTS: Gives to preselected organizations.
DEADLINES: None
OFFICERS: Amin, Vanlila, P,S; Patel, Anjni, D; Amin,
Mahesh, D

AMS FOUNDATION FOR THE ARTS SCIENCES HUMANITIES

C/O CHOPIN & MILLER
505 S. FLAGLER DR., STE. 300
WEST PALM BEACH, FL 33401
561-655-9500

ID NUMBER: 521188804
FEDERAL REPORTING DATE: 05/01
AREAS OF INTEREST: Arts & Culture, Education,
Scholarships
CURRENT ASSETS: $2,595,132 PRIOR ASSETS:
$2,568,563
TOTAL AMOUNT AWARDED: $82,021
HIGH: $30,000--American Film Institute
MID: $14,350--American Assoc. Royal Academy
LOW: $124--Connecticut Grand Opera
GRANTS AWARDS: Marilyn Horne Foundation--$5,000,
Washington Opera--$10,000, Versailles Foundation--$15,000,
Individual--$6,890
SERVICE AREA: National
COMMENTS: Submit written material regarding how funds
will be utilized.
DEADLINES: None
OFFICERS: Sackler, Gillian, P; Cutter, Curtis, D; Tully,
Doris Q., VP; Tully, B.K., D

ANDERSEN, MARTIN & GRACIA FOUNDATION

P.O. BOX 547918
ORLANDO, FL 32854-7918
407-647-5654

ID NUMBER: 596166589
FEDERAL REPORTING DATE: 03/02
AREAS OF INTEREST: Arts & Culture, Community,
Education, Environment, Health, Medicine, Religion,
Research, Scholarships, Social Services, Sports & Athletics
CURRENT ASSETS: $54,779,451 PRIOR ASSETS:
$1,288,908
TOTAL AMOUNT AWARDED: $517,625
HIGH: $50,000--Women Playing for Time
MID: $25,000--West Orange Health Alliance
LOW: $160--Veterans of Foreign Affairs
GRANTS AWARDS: Florida Hospital Fdn.--$36,570, Alco-
An Club, Inc.--$25,000, American Cancer Society--$1,000,
Boggy Creek Gang--$16,000, American Red Cross Disaster
Relief Fund--$25,000, Bach Festival Society, Inc.--$6,000, Boy
Scouts of America, Central FL--$10,500, Edgewood Children's
Ramch--$1,000, Festival of Orchestras--$2,500, Fellowship of
Christian Athletes--$500, Coalition for the Homeless--$500,
Bok Tower Gardens--$500, DePugh Nursing Home--$1,000,
Downtown Orlando Fdn.--$500, Atlantic Salmon Federation--
$500
SERVICE AREA: Orlando, NC
COMMENTS: Send letter requesting application to Thomas
P. Warlow III, President.
DEADLINES: None
OFFICERS: Warlow, Whomas P., III, P; Sessions, Gail
Warlow, D; Trismen, Richard F., S; Barr, L. Graham, Jr., VP;
Hames, Clifford M., TR; Brown, Majorie A., S

ANGELIS-HERO FOUNDATION, INC.

7873 AFTON VILLA CT.
BOCA RATON, FL 33433-7402
561-487-4746

ID NUMBER: 112539613
FEDERAL REPORTING DATE: 04/02
AREAS OF INTEREST: Education, Religion, Scholarships,
Social Services
CURRENT ASSETS: $533,558 PRIOR ASSETS:
$626,963
TOTAL AMOUNT AWARDED: $19,250
HIGH: $6,000--Florida Culinary Institute
MID: $2,000--Senior Meals Program
LOW: $250--American Red Cross
GRANTS AWARDS: Johnson & Wales University--$5,000,
The Soup Kitchen, Inc.--$1,000, Ruth Ralfs Family Service--
$5,000, Senior Healing Program--$2,000
SERVICE AREA: FL
COMMENTS: Grants are made only to accredited colleges to
further education in culinary arts as well as as approved charities
for food distribution.
DEADLINES: None
OFFICERS: Daniels, Theodore, Esq., P; Siegal, Milton, CPA,
VP

ANSBACHER, L & S FAMILY FOUNDATION, INC.

5151 BELFORT RD., BLDG. 100
JACKSONVILLE, FL 32255-6010
904-296-0100

ID NUMBER: 592610689
FEDERAL REPORTING DATE: 01/01
AREAS OF INTEREST: Arts & Culture, Community, Education, Religion, Scholarships
CURRENT ASSETS: $213,298 PRIOR ASSETS: $223,236
TOTAL AMOUNT AWARDED: $20,200
HIGH: $5,700--Jacksonville Jewish Ctr.
MID: $2,500--National Jewish Fund
LOW: $1,000--We Care JAX, Inc.
GRANTS AWARDS: Jewish Family & Comm. Srvs.--$5,000, Jewish National Fund--$2,500
SERVICE AREA: FL, GA, NY
COMMENTS: Gives to preselected organizations.
DEADLINES: None
OFFICERS: Ansbacher, Lewis, P/T; Ansbacher, Sybil, S/TR/T; Ansbacher, Lawrence, TR; Ansbacher, Richard, TR; Ansbacher, Barry, TR

APPLE CORPS

741 GERHARDT DR.
PENSACOLA, FL 32503-3216
850-432-1163

ID NUMBER: 593075454
FEDERAL REPORTING DATE: 08/01
AREAS OF INTEREST: Arts & Culture, Education, Health, Religion, Scholarships, Social Services
CURRENT ASSETS: $402,046 PRIOR ASSETS: $342,526
TOTAL AMOUNT AWARDED: $22,000
HIGH: $2,500--Pensacola Children's Chorus
MID: $1,000--Ronald McDonald House
LOW: $100--Pensacola Rotary Club
GRANTS AWARDS: Miracle Camp--$500, Salvation Army--$2,000, Hospice--$1,000, Habatit for Humanity--$500, American Red Cross--$500, Nas Museum Camp--$650, United Way of Escambia County--$1,000, Pensacola Junior College--$2,000
SERVICE AREA: Escambia County, Pensacola
COMMENTS: Submit written requests only.
DEADLINES: None
OFFICERS: Applegard, John H., P/D; Applegard, Eleanor K., S/T; Applegard, Diane, D; Applegard, Kate, D

ARCHIBALD FOUNDATION, INC

7100 ROBERTS RD.
TALLAHASSEE, FL 32308
850-893-8884

ID NUMBER: 593414615
FEDERAL REPORTING DATE: 05/02
AREAS OF INTEREST: Community, Environment, Health, Scholarships, Social Services
CURRENT ASSETS: $3,494,880 PRIOR ASSETS: $3,416,664
TOTAL AMOUNT AWARDED: $150,000
HIGH: $50,000--Children's Home Society
MID: $16,000--John G. Riley House Museum
LOW: $5,000--Southern Scholarship
GRANTS AWARDS: The Nature Conservancy--$8,000, The Mary Brogan Museum of Arts and Science--$5,000, Goodwood Museum & Gardens--$10,000, Tall Timbers Research--$8,000, Tallahassee Memorial Healthcare Fdn.--$10,000, Trust for Public Land--$8,000, Apalachee Land Conservancy--$10,000, Ochlockonee River--$10,000, Duchess Outreach, Inc.--$5,000
SERVICE AREA: Tallahassee, FL.
COMMENTS: Gives to preselected organizations.
DEADLINES: None
OFFICERS: Archibald, Delbert M., D; Archibald, Katty, D; Archibald, Kenneth C, D; Archibald, Daniel I., D

ARNOLD FOUNDATION

P. O. BOX 568
PALM BEACH, FL 33480
561-833-6118

ID NUMBER: 596152134
FEDERAL REPORTING DATE: 03/02
AREAS OF INTEREST: Arts & Culture, Community, Education, Environment, Health, Medicine, Religion, Scholarships, Social Services
CURRENT ASSETS: $426,132 PRIOR ASSETS: $379,680
TOTAL AMOUNT AWARDED: $29,393
HIGH: $6,650--Norton Gallery Palm Beach Atlantic College
MID: $3,000--Royal Poinciana Chapel
LOW: $50--Ann Norton Sculpture Garden
GRANTS AWARDS: Athen Academy--$1,000, Blue Ridge School--$500, Brunswick School--$500, Cardinal Newman High School--$2,003, Colorado Community Church--$500, First Church Of Round Hill--$2,000, Greenwich Academy Benefit--$500, Holy Trinity Deacon Diverstona--$3,000, Junior League of Palm Beach--$50, March of Dimes--$1,500
SERVICE AREA: National
COMMENTS: Gives to preselected organizations.
DEADLINES: None
OFFICERS: Arnold, James Y. Jr., TR; Arnold, F. Brooks, TR; Benjamin, Paige A. TR

ARVIDA REALITY FOUNDATION, INC.

300 S. PARK PLACE BLVD., STE. 150
CLEARWATER, FL 33759
727-538-5468

ID NUMBER: 593242513
FEDERAL REPORTING DATE: 04/02
AREAS OF INTEREST: Arts & Culture, Community, Education, Environment, Health, Medicine, Religion, Research, Scholarships, Social Services, Sports & Athletics, Other
CURRENT ASSETS: $233,547 PRIOR ASSETS: $273,775
TOTAL AMOUNT AWARDED: $421,464
HIGH: $10,000--J. Colin English Elementary
MID: $4,000--Beaux Arts Festival
LOW: $190--Handy, Inc.
GRANTS AWARDS: American Cancer Society--$1,000, God's Little Acres--$5,000, Hospoce of Northwest Florida--$500, Restore Orlando, Inc.--$1,000, Project Lakw Worth--$500, CASA--$300, Police Athletic League of Manatee County--$500, Project Yes--$2,500, Melissa Institute--$1,000, Infinity--$200, Education Partnership of Palm Beach County--$10,000
SERVICE AREA: National
COMMENTS: Gives to preselected organizations.

DEADLINES: None
OFFICERS: Cope, Richard W., P/C; Sticco, Lewis A., S/T; Tooke, Edwin C., VP

ASARCH FAMILY CHARITABLE FOUNDATION, INC.
7140 LIONS HEAD LN.
BOCA RATON, FL 33496

ID NUMBER: 650710107
FEDERAL REPORTING DATE: 09/01
AREAS OF INTEREST: Medicine, Religion, Scholarships, Social Services
CURRENT ASSETS: $117,958 PRIOR ASSETS: $122,794
TOTAL AMOUNT AWARDED: $10,807
HIGH: $4,000--Jewish Fed. of South Palm Beach Co.
MID: $1,035--Anti Defamation League
LOW: $100--Lukemia Society of America
GRANTS AWARDS: Norton Museum--$250, American Society for Yad Vashew--$250, American Red Cross--$1,000, --$100
SERVICE AREA: FL, National
COMMENTS: Gives to preselected organizations.
DEADLINES: None
OFFICERS: Asarch, Steven J., D; Asarch, Gail, D; Gilmore, Rhonda, D

AURORA MINISTRIES, INC.
P. O. BOX 1848
BRADENTON, FL 34206
941-748-4100

ID NUMBER: 237178299
FEDERAL REPORTING DATE: 11/01
AREAS OF INTEREST: Arts & Culture, Scholarships, Other
CURRENT ASSETS: $2,990,239 PRIOR ASSETS: $2,832,131
TOTAL AMOUNT AWARDED: $3,168,503
HIGH: $3,165,753-Various Individuals
MID: $2,000--ICEVI
LOW: $750--Audio Scriptures International
GRANTS AWARDS: N/A
SERVICE AREA: PA, CA
COMMENTS: Requests should contain evidence that the applicant is visually handicapped. Grants of cassette recordings of the Bible made to the visually handicapped. Send applications to: Aurora Ministries, Inc., P. O. Box 1848, Bradenton, Fl. 34206. (941)748-4100.
DEADLINES: None
OFFICERS: Aleppo, Joseph A., P/D; Johnson, Phillip R., VP/D; Aleppo, Georgia, D; Madison, Daniel Q., S/D; Hines, Richard, T/D; Rossi, Sanna, D

BACHELLER, KENNETH G. CHARITABLE FOUNDATION
P. O. BOX 998
DELRAY BEACH, FL 33447
561-276-2613

ID NUMBER: 656234551
FEDERAL REPORTING DATE: 05/02
AREAS OF INTEREST: Education, Scholarships
CURRENT ASSETS: $423,416 PRIOR ASSETS: $429,302

TOTAL AMOUNT AWARDED: $40,000
HIGH: $20,000--Univ. of Miami College of Engineering
LOW: $20,000--Wentworth Institute of Technology, MA
GRANTS AWARDS: N/A
SERVICE AREA: FL, MA
COMMENTS: Send applications to Kenneth G. Bacheller at P.O. Box 998 Delray Beach, FL. 33447.
DEADLINES: None
OFFICERS: Bacheller, Kenneth G., TR; Bacheller, Ann J., TR; Bacheller, Kay, TR; Bacheller, Suzanne, TR

BANK OF AMERICA CLIENT FOUNDATION
P. O. BOX 4275
SARASOTA, FL 34230
941-952-2711

ID NUMBER: 596142753
FEDERAL REPORTING DATE: 05/02
AREAS OF INTEREST: Arts & Culture, Community, Education, Health, Medicine, Religion, Scholarships, Social Services
CURRENT ASSETS: $5,696,399 PRIOR ASSETS: $5,265,992
TOTAL AMOUNT AWARDED: $501,838
HIGH: $35,000--Florida Studio Theatre
MID: $1,500--Friends of Oscar Scherer Park
LOW: $100--United Way of Sarasota County
GRANTS AWARDS: Boy Scouts of America--$298, Boys and Girls Club--$15,750, Child Protection Center--$15,736, Circus Sarasota--$10,000, Crowley Museum and Nature Center--$15,000, Easter Seal Society--$13,540, Education Fdn.--$25,000, First Congregational Church--$26,393, Florida Sheriff's Youth Ranches--$6,261, Florida Studio Theatre--$35,000, Girls Inc. of Sarasota County--$10,000, Habitat for Humanity--$10,140
SERVICE AREA: FL
COMMENTS: Send letter with purpose, amount asking, and specifications to organization.
DEADLINES: None
OFFICERS: NationsBank Trust, T

BAPTIST FOUNDATION OF FT. MYERS
1279 LAVIN LN.
NORTH FT. MYERS, FL 33917-5341
941-656-0196

ID NUMBER: 591947687
FEDERAL REPORTING DATE: 05/01
AREAS OF INTEREST: Scholarships, Social Services
CURRENT ASSETS: $353,764 PRIOR ASSETS: $362,989
TOTAL AMOUNT AWARDED: $75,656
HIGH: $1,900--Individual
MID: $1,380--Individual
LOW: $500--Ridgecrest Summer Camp
GRANTS AWARDS: Individual--$1,000, Individual--$800, Individual--$1,000, Individual--$800, Individual--$600
SERVICE AREA: Ft. Myers, FL, NC
COMMENTS: Submit written letter requesting an education loan or grant including specific needs such as tuition, books, housing, etc. or requesting other charitable, benevolent, or religious works as needed, to: James T. Humphrey, Baptist Fdn. of Ft. Myers, FL Inc., P.O. Box 2449, Ft. Myers, FL 33902-2449; 941-334-2722
DEADLINES: None

OFFICERS: Humphrey, James T., P/D; Cornwell, Nat S., VP/D; Nychyk, Andrew J., Sr., T/D; Miller, T. Wayne, D; Hogan, Dilmus, S/D; Decarlo, Paul, D

BARBOUR, WILLIAM & MARY FOUNDATION

8211 COLLEGE PARKWAY
FORT MYERS, FL 33919
941-482-5522

ID NUMBER: 222231677
FEDERAL REPORTING DATE: 06/01
AREAS OF INTEREST: Arts & Culture, Education, Health, Medicine, Religion, Research, Scholarships, Social Services, Other
CURRENT ASSETS: $245,614 PRIOR ASSETS: $232,614
TOTAL AMOUNT AWARDED: $21,305
HIGH: $15,200--Wycliffe Bible Translators
MID: $600--T.E.A.M.
LOW: $10--U.S.O.
GRANTS AWARDS: Christ of the Island World--$25, Evelyn Davis Scholarship--$100, Grace Church--$1,200, Mission Avaiation--$15, Shell Point Village Pavilion--$50, Shell Pt. Village Library--$25, The Village Church--$2,825, S.I.L. Translation Centers--$1,000
SERVICE AREA: National
COMMENTS: Submit amount and purpose of gift or grant.
DEADLINES: None
OFFICERS: Barbour, William R., Jr., P; Barbour, Mary M., VP; Barbour, Bruce, TR; Barbour, Hugh, TR

BARFIELD MOCK FOUNDATION, INC.

1143 HOLMESDALE RD.
JACKSONVILLE, FL 32207
904-306-9083

ID NUMBER: 593195041
FEDERAL REPORTING DATE: 12/01
AREAS OF INTEREST: Education, Scholarships
CURRENT ASSETS: $250 PRIOR ASSETS: $250
TOTAL AMOUNT AWARDED: $700
HIGH: $700--Tallahassee Community College Fdn.
GRANTS AWARDS: N/A
SERVICE AREA: FL
DEADLINES: None
OFFICERS: Mock, Margarette E.; Mock, David B.; Buzbee, Melanie M.; Mock, Janet E.

BAROVICK, JOAN B. & RICHARD L. FAMILY TRUST

2840 LE BATEAU DR.
PALM BEACH GARDENS, FL 33410
212-759-6556

ID NUMBER: 137074075
FEDERAL REPORTING DATE: 05/02
AREAS OF INTEREST: Arts & Culture, Community, Education, Environment, Health, Medicine, Religion, Scholarships, Social Services
CURRENT ASSETS: $779,184 PRIOR ASSETS: $997,366
TOTAL AMOUNT AWARDED: $134,000
HIGH: $30,000--Jewish Museum

MID: $8,000--Orpheus Chamber Orchestra
LOW: $125--Central Park Conservancy
GRANTS AWARDS: WPFT Frenchman's Creek--$1,000, 2000-2001 Trinity Fund--$1,000, Together We Care--$500, Animal Rescue Force--$100, Adams Walsh Fdn.--$400, Museum of Modern Art--$120, Children's Blood Fdn.--$250, WPBT--$175, First Serve for Charity--$1,000, Metropolitan Museum of Art--$225, CT. College--$250, Inner City Scholarship Fund--$6,000, Artista for Breast Cancer--$5,000, Women Playing for TIMC--$150, Kids in Crisis--$1,000
SERVICE AREA: National
COMMENTS: Gives to preselected organizations.
DEADLINES: None
OFFICERS: Barovick, Richard, D; Barovick, Joan, D

BAYLOR, CHESTER & RUTH FAMILY FOUNDATION

5731 FIRESTONE CT.
SARASOTA, FL 34233
941-923-7994

ID NUMBER: 650540821
FEDERAL REPORTING DATE: 05/01
AREAS OF INTEREST: Community, Religion, Scholarships, Social Services
CURRENT ASSETS: $178,323 PRIOR ASSETS: $101,756
TOTAL AMOUNT AWARDED: $10,420
HIGH: $4,750--Methodist Church
MID: $1,540--Ripley County Fdn
LOW: $130--Milan Scholarship Fund
GRANTS AWARDS: Milan Volunteer Fire--$2,000, Milan Rescue Sqaud--$2,000
SERVICE AREA: IN
COMMENTS: Gives to preselected organizations.
DEADLINES: None
OFFICERS: Baylor, Chester R.; Baylor, Ruth R.; Baylor, Robert R.; Hammond, Bonnie B.; Baylor, Stephen C.; Williams, James F.

BAYNARD, ROBERT & MILDRED CHARITABLE TRUST

669 1ST AVE., N.
ST. PETERSBURG, FL 33701
727-894-0676

ID NUMBER: 597049328
FEDERAL REPORTING DATE: 05/01
AREAS OF INTEREST: Education, Religion, Scholarships
CURRENT ASSETS: $3,723,450 PRIOR ASSETS: $3,746,210
TOTAL AMOUNT AWARDED: $166,157
HIGH: $50,000--St. Thomas Episcopal Church
MID: $20,000--University of Florida Foundation
LOW: $1,000--Prison Fellowship
GRANTS AWARDS: Delta Gamma Fdn.--$2,500, Alpha Tau Omega Fdn.--$5,000,500, St. Petersburg Junior College Fdn.--$18,527, Florida National Assn. Prevent Blindness--$5,000, Crystal Cathedral Ministries--$1,500, Cedars Home for Children--$6,630, Liberty University--$1,000, Prison Fellowship--$1,000, Resurection House--$35,000, Tampa Bay Research Institute--$10,000
SERVICE AREA: National
COMMENTS: Gives to preselected organizations.
DEADLINES: None
OFFICERS: Baynard, Lester B., TR; Lang, Joseph H., TR; Norris, Anita, TR; Christian, Mary B., TR; Corvell, Ettie, TR

BEALL, BEVERLY & R. KEMP REICHMAN FOUNDATION

1806 38TH AVE., E.
BRADENTON, FL 34208
941-744-4309

ID NUMBER: 650808807
FEDERAL REPORTING DATE: 04/02
AREAS OF INTEREST: Education, Scholarships, Other
CURRENT ASSETS: $2,005,340 PRIOR ASSETS: $250,314
TOTAL AMOUNT AWARDED: $51,114
HIGH: $5,000--Individual
MID: $2,500--Individual
LOW: $284--Individual
GRANTS AWARDS: N/A
SERVICE AREA: FL
COMMENTS: (941) 747-2355 ext. 309 Provides funding for teachers to design and implement classroom projects and/or activities. Call for application forms.
DEADLINES: None
OFFICERS: Beall, Beverly, TR; Riechmann, R. Kemp, TR; Beall, Robert M., II, TR

BEALL, R.M. SR. CHARITABLE FOUNDATION

1806 38TH AVE.,E.
BRADENTON, FL 34208
941-744-4309

ID NUMBER: 592851924
FEDERAL REPORTING DATE: 06/02
AREAS OF INTEREST: Arts & Culture, Community, Education, Medicine, Scholarships, Social Services, Sports & Athletics
CURRENT ASSETS: $1,656,852 PRIOR ASSETS: $1,569,095
TOTAL AMOUNT AWARDED: $327,341
HIGH: $277,176--Individual Scholarships
MID: $12,500--University of Florida
LOW: $100--St. Martha School
GRANTS AWARDS: Cardinal Mooney High School--$7,000, Congressional Classroom--$1,000, Fortune Education Fdn., Inc.--$1,500, St. Steven's Episcopal School--$10,000, Bradenton Christian School--$250, Bradenton Country Club--$1,500, East Manatee Youth Football Assn.--$500, Habitat for Humanity Sarasota--$250, Junior Achievement--$315, GROWTH Manatee High School--$100, Sarasota Family YMCA--$400
SERVICE AREA: FL
COMMENTS: Write to John Nicholas, Foundation Administrator, 1806 38th Avenue, East, Bradenton, FL 34208 for prescribed application for scholarships.
DEADLINES: None
OFFICERS: Beall, R.M. II, TR; Beall, Beverly, TR; Szymanski, Betty B., TR; Walters, Clifford L., TR

BEALL, ROBERT & ALDONA FAMILY FOUNDATION

1806 38TH AVE., E.
BRADENTON, FL 34208
941-747-2355

ID NUMBER: 650545213

FEDERAL REPORTING DATE: 04/02
AREAS OF INTEREST: Scholarships
CURRENT ASSETS: $211,637 PRIOR ASSETS: $234,847
TOTAL AMOUNT AWARDED: $22,667
HIGH: $3,000--Individual
MID: $1,250--Individual
LOW: $117--Individual
GRANTS AWARDS: N/A
SERVICE AREA: FL
COMMENTS: Accepts applications only from members of the Palmetto Youth Center of Palmetto, FL. Submit applications to Foundation Administrator, Robert & Aldona Beall Family Foundation, P.O. Box 25207, Bradenton, FL 34206-5207.
DEADLINES: None
OFFICERS: Beall, Robert M. II, TR; Beall, Aldona K., TR; Knopik, Stephen M., TR

BELL, JAMES E. & CONSTANCE L. FOUNDATION

167 GOMEZ ROAD
HOBE SOUND, FL 33455
561-546-3708

ID NUMBER: 592473417
FEDERAL REPORTING DATE: 11/01
AREAS OF INTEREST: Arts & Culture, Community, Education, Health, Medicine, Religion, Research, Scholarships, Social Services
CURRENT ASSETS: $5,052,885 PRIOR ASSETS: $5,337,533
TOTAL AMOUNT AWARDED: $286,439
HIGH: $194,000--Luzerne Fdn.
MID: $25,000--Town of Jupiter Island
LOW: $100--International Crane Fdn.
GRANTS AWARDS: E.W.S. Development--$500, Toys for Kids--$500, US Olympic Committee--$800, AmeriCares--$1,000, Trinity Episcopal School for Ministry--$1,000, Wyoming Seminary--$5,000, St. Anne's Episcopal School--$5,000, Salvation Army of Martin County--$1,000, American Red Cross--$1,000, Canterbury School--$2,500, Memorial Sloan Kettering--$500, Ctr. for the Theology of Childhood--$2,500, Univ. of Pennsylvania--$5,000, Choate Rosemary Hall--$2,000, Cimarron Volunteer Ambulance Service--$1,000
SERVICE AREA: National
COMMENTS: Gives to preselected organizations.
DEADLINES: None
OFFICERS: Bell, James, D/P/T; Bell, Constance, D/VP; Bell, Stuart, D/S

BENDON FAMILY FOUNDATION

P.O. BOX 14728
FORT LAUDERDALE, FL 33302
954-765-7400

ID NUMBER: 650631534
FEDERAL REPORTING DATE: 11/01
AREAS OF INTEREST: Arts & Culture, Community, Education, Environment, Religion, Scholarships
CURRENT ASSETS: $1,966,574 PRIOR ASSETS: $1,521,858
TOTAL AMOUNT AWARDED: $102,400
HIGH: $35,000--Maui Community College
MID: $10,000--Second Presbyterian Church
LOW: $400--Maui Academy Of Performing Arts
GRANTS AWARDS: Friends of Children's Advocacy--$5,000, Hawaii Public Radio--$1,000, Hawaii Public

Television--$1,000, Lowell Whitman School--$5,000, Maui
Committe for the Humanities--$1,000, Maui Community
Food Bank--$5,000, Maui Family YMCA--$5,000, Maui
United Way--$20,000, Pacific Primate Sanctuary--$5,000,
Salvation Army--$3,000, Seabury Hall--$6,000
SERVICE AREA: Hawaii
COMMENTS: Gives to preselected organizations.
DEADLINES: None
OFFICERS: Bendon, James A., P; Bendon, Susan Kaylor,
S; Bendon, John James, D

BENJAMIN, BENNIE & MARTHA
FOUNDATION, INC.

C/O JACK ALBERT
7500 BONDSBERRY CT.
BOCA RATON, FL 33434-3229
561-479-3606

ID NUMBER: 133555717
FEDERAL REPORTING DATE: 09/01
AREAS OF INTEREST: Health, Medicine, Scholarships,
Other
CURRENT ASSETS: $2,223,471 PRIOR ASSETS:
$1,992,038
TOTAL AMOUNT AWARDED: $113,681
HIGH: $26,500--St. Croix Benjamin Scholarship Program
MID: $12,181--Univ. of Virgin Islands
LOW: $8,000--Mt. Sinai School of Med.
GRANTS AWARDS: Wright St. Univ. School of Med.--
$10,000, Florida A&M College--$24,000, Temple Univ.--
$10,000, Univ. of Puerto Rico--$8,000, Midwestern Univ.--
$15,000
SERVICE AREA: National
COMMENTS: Gives to preselected organizations.
DEADLINES: None
OFFICERS: Albert, Jack, D; Beale, David A., D; Braun,
Seymour, Esq., D

BERRY EDUCATIONAL TRUST

C/O CAROLYN BERRY
1465 GULF OF MEXICO DR.
LONGBOAT KEY, FL 34228

ID NUMBER: 650533522
FEDERAL REPORTING DATE: 05/01
AREAS OF INTEREST: Arts & Culture, Education,
Scholarships, Other
CURRENT ASSETS: $304,009 PRIOR ASSETS:
$308,251
TOTAL AMOUNT AWARDED: $22,604
HIGH: $20,000--West Virginia Univerity Foundation, Inc.
LOW: $2,604--Mathew Cruthers
GRANTS AWARDS: N/A
SERVICE AREA: Morgantown, WV, Honolulu, HI
COMMENTS: Gives to preselected organizations.
DEADLINES: None
OFFICERS: Berry, Carolyn, TR; Anderson, Rebecca A., TR;
Berry, David E., TR; Berry, Brian, TR

BICKEL, KARL A. CHARITABLE
TRUST

P.O. BOX 267
SARASOTA, FL 34230
941-361-5807

ID NUMBER: 596515937
FEDERAL REPORTING DATE: 09/01
AREAS OF INTEREST: Education, Scholarships
CURRENT ASSETS: $4,658,677 PRIOR ASSETS:
$3,937,457
TOTAL AMOUNT AWARDED: $190,905
HIGH: $63,665--Stanford Univ.
MID: $63,665--Univ. of Tennessee
LOW: $63,575--Univ. of Florida
GRANTS AWARDS: N/A
SERVICE AREA: FL, TN, CA
COMMENTS: No specified form. Send applications to: First
Union National Bank of Florida, P.O.Box 267, Sarasota,
Sarasota, Fl., 34230. (941)361-5813. Schools of Journalism.
DEADLINES: None
OFFICERS: First Union National Bank, TR

BICKLEY, E. J. MEMORIAL TRUST

8640 SEMINOLE BLVD.
SEMINOLE, FL 33772
727-397-5571

ID NUMBER: 596685618
FEDERAL REPORTING DATE: 09/01
AREAS OF INTEREST: Scholarships
CURRENT ASSETS: $475,216 PRIOR ASSETS:
$459,648
TOTAL AMOUNT AWARDED: $44,
HIGH: $11,214--St. Joseph's School
MID: $11,213--Florida Sheriff's Youth
LOW: $11,213--St. Francis Xavier Chu
GRANTS AWARDS: St. Jude's Cathed
COMMENTS: Gives to preselected orga
DEADLINES: None
OFFICERS: DeLoach, Dennis R. Jr., TR   Peter T.,
TR

BLANK FAMILY FOUND   ,
INC.

3455 N.W. 54TH ST.
MIAMI, FL 33142
305-663-8587

ID NUMBER: 650060771
FEDERAL REPORTING DATE: 08/01
AREAS OF INTEREST: Arts & Culture, Community,
Education, Environment, Health, Medicine, Religion,
Scholarships, Social Services, Sports & Athletics, Other
CURRENT ASSETS: $21,721,615 PRIOR ASSETS:
$20,303,603
TOTAL AMOUNT AWARDED: $1,098,450
HIGH: $200,000--UM - Comprehensive Pain and Rehab Ctr.
MID: $50,000--Temple Emanu-El
LOW: $150--Performing Art Center
GRANTS AWARDS: Abraham Fund--$15,000, American
Cancer Society--$700, Anti-Defamation League--$10,000,
Hope Center--$15,250, Camillus House--$3,000, Buffalo Bill
Historical Center--$5,000, Hospice of Woodriver Valley--
$1,000, Mount Sinai Medical--$50,000, Children's
Bereavement Center--$5,000, March of Dimes--$1,750, Daily

Bread Food Bank--$10,000, Miami City Ballet--$2,000, FIU -
Art Museum--$1,000, Goodwill Industries--$20,000, Hands
On Atlanta, Inc.--$2,500
SERVICE AREA: Miami, FL, National
COMMENTS: Applications should be addressed to Andy
Blank, Blank Family Foundation, Inc., 3455 N.W. 54th Street
Miami, Fl. 33142. (305) 633-8587
DEADLINES: None
OFFICERS: Blank, Jerome, D/P; Blank, Andrew, D/VP;
Blank, Tony, D/VP; Blank, Mark, D/VP

BLANTON CHARITABLE FOUNDATION, INC.
200 LAKE MORTON DR.
LAKELAND, FL 33801
863-688-7611

ID NUMBER: 593162785
FEDERAL REPORTING DATE: 04/02
AREAS OF INTEREST: Education, Scholarships
CURRENT ASSETS: $237,141   PRIOR ASSETS:
$451,431
TOTAL AMOUNT AWARDED: $53,500
HIGH: $16,000--Florida Southern College
MID: $10,000--Imperial Symphony
LOW: $1,000--Bartow High School Band
GRANTS AWARDS: Junior Achievement of West Coast
Central FL--$5,000, Southeastern College--$8,500, Charleston
Southern University--$8,000
SERVICE AREA: Lakeland, FL
COMMENTS: Scholarships are available for educational
funding to pursue fields of organ music; church music. Req.
incl: statement of proposed study, complete biographica record,
explanation of plans and commitments after scholarsh
references and recommendations, details of academic career,
explanation of financial needs.
DEADLINES: None
OFFICERS: Blanton, Hilda Sutton, P/D; Withers, Mettie,
S/T/D; Mason, Beth, D; Martin, E. Snow Jr., VP/D

BLOGOSLAWSKI FAMILY FOUNDATION, INC.
C/O WALTER BLAKE
P.O. BOX 177
VERO BEACH, FL 32961
561-778-3254

ID NUMBER: 650668962
FEDERAL REPORTING DATE: 06/02
AREAS OF INTEREST: Community, Education,
Environment, Scholarships, Social Services
CURRENT ASSETS: $747,346   PRIOR ASSETS:
$709,698
TOTAL AMOUNT AWARDED: $12,700
HIGH: $10,000--Boston College
MID: $1,000--YMCA
LOW: $200--Taft School
GRANTS AWARDS: NY Firefighters Relief Fund--$1,500
SERVICE AREA: National
COMMENTS: Gives to preselected organizations.
DEADLINES: None
OFFICERS: Blake, Walter D., P; Sullivan, Brenda, TR;
Blogoslawski, Cheryl S., TR; Hoerle, Patricia, M

BLUM, ROBERT B. FOUNDATION
225 COMMODORE DR.
JUPITER, FL 33477
561-743-4622

ID NUMBER: 236670879
FEDERAL REPORTING DATE: 05/01
AREAS OF INTEREST: Arts & Culture, Education, Religion,
Scholarships
CURRENT ASSETS: $128,650   PRIOR ASSETS:
$128,744
TOTAL AMOUNT AWARDED: $7,000
HIGH: $2,500--St. Andrews School
MID: $1,000--Philadelphia Scholars
LOW: $500--Seamens Church Institute
GRANTS AWARDS: Denworth Memorial Fund--$1,000,
Free Library of Philadelphia Foundation--$1,000, Landmark-
Powel House--$1,000
SERVICE AREA: DE, FL
COMMENTS: Gives to preselected organizations.
DEADLINES: None
OFFICERS: Blum, Robert B., TR; Blum, Leslie, TR

BODMAN FAMILY FOUNDATION
C/O COX & NICI, ATTORNEYS AT LAW
3001 TAMIAMI TR., N., STE. 100
NAPLES, FL 34103
239-430-8544

ID NUMBER: 656321705
FEDERAL REPORTING DATE: 05/02
AREAS OF INTEREST: Arts & Culture, Community,
Education, Health, Medicine, Religion, Research, Scholarships,
Social Services
CURRENT ASSETS: $754,807   PRIOR ASSETS:
$471,758
TOTAL AMOUNT AWARDED: $103,270
HIGH: $25,000--Intercollegiate Studies Institute, Inc.
MID: $2,500--Massachusettes Institute of Technology
LOW: $100--Young Singers Foundation
GRANTS AWARDS: St. Matthew's House--$250, Henry H.
Kessler Foundation--$2,125, Immaculate Conception School--
$250, Philharmonic Center for the Arts--$1,000, Recording for
the Blind & Dyslexic--$20,000, Children's Hospital
Foundation--$100, Shelter for Abused Women--$1,925,
Harmony Foundation--$20,000, WETA Leadership Circle--
$14,820, Boys & Girls Club of Collier County--$15,000
SERVICE AREA: National
COMMENTS: Gives to preselected organizations.
DEADLINES: None
OFFICERS: Bodman, Richard S., TR; Bodman, Karna S., TR

BOGAN, R. CHAD SCHOLARSHIP FOUNDATION
2456 VIA SIENNA
WINTER PARK, FL 32789-1381
407-645-0749

ID NUMBER: 311584418
FEDERAL REPORTING DATE: 05/02
AREAS OF INTEREST: Education, Scholarships
CURRENT ASSETS: $25,107   PRIOR ASSETS: $29,229
TOTAL AMOUNT AWARDED: $8,000
MID: $1,000--Individual
GRANTS AWARDS: N/A
SERVICE AREA: FL, IL
COMMENTS: Academic: 3.5 GPA, 1170 SAT, 26 ACT.

DEADLINES: May 15
OFFICERS: Bogan, R. Van, TR

BRADISH MEMORIAL SCHOLARSHIP TRUST UNDER WILL

C/O BANK OF AMERICA, TRUSTEE
P. O. BOX 40200
JACKSONVILLE, FL 32203-0200
877-446-1410

ID NUMBER: 596161559
FEDERAL REPORTING DATE: 11/01
AREAS OF INTEREST: Education, Scholarships, Other
CURRENT ASSETS: $1,730,140   PRIOR ASSETS:
$1,778,188
TOTAL AMOUNT AWARDED: $118,048
HIGH: $16,370--Washington Univ.
MID: $8,967--Lawrence Univ.
LOW: $31--Darius Viet Wall Street Journal for Econ. Class
GRANTS AWARDS: Winneshiek Co. Memorial Hospital--
$300, Winter Park Health Fdn.--$50, Bowling Green Univ.--
$9,432, Northwestern Univ.--$10,673, Darius Viet Ironcad
Prog. Engineering Software--$200, Aaron Bauhs Bradish
Memorial Scholarship Award--$200, Braham Ketcham Bradish
Memorial Scholarship Aw.--$200, Iowa State Univ.--$562
COMMENTS: Send applications to: Jeffrey Seward, C/o Bank
of America 250 Park Avenue South, Suite 400, Winter Park,
FL 32489 Restricted to male, unmarried graduates of Decorah
High School, Decorah, IA. Execelent academic record,
intellectual and in need of financial assistance.
DEADLINES: None
OFFICERS: Bank of America, TR

BRANCH FAMILY FOUNDATION, INC.

P. O. BOX 940
OCALA, FL 34478-0940
352-732-4143

ID NUMBER: 593516536
FEDERAL REPORTING DATE: 10/01
AREAS OF INTEREST: Education, Scholarships, Social
Services, Other
CURRENT ASSETS: $456,583   PRIOR ASSETS:
$415,691
TOTAL AMOUNT AWARDED: $12,000
HIGH: $9,500--Central Florida Community College Fdn.
MID: $1,000--Monroe Regional Development Fdn.
LOW: $500--Interfaith Emergency Services, Inc.
GRANTS AWARDS: Arnette House, Inc.--$1,000
COMMENTS: Gives to preselected organizations.
DEADLINES: None
OFFICERS: Branch, Gregory C., P/D; Branch, Mary C.,
VP/D; Branch, Diane, S/D; Allen, Gregory S., T/D; Branch,
Overby C., D/C

BRANDON ROTARY SCHOLARSHIP FUND, INC.

777 W. LUMSDEN RD.
BRANDON, FL 33511
813-685-1832

ID NUMBER: 593329005

FEDERAL REPORTING DATE: 10/01
AREAS OF INTEREST: Scholarships
CURRENT ASSETS: $130,973   PRIOR ASSETS:
$127,407
TOTAL AMOUNT AWARDED: $2,000
HIGH: $2,000--Individual
GRANTS AWARDS: N/A
SERVICE AREA: FL
COMMENTS: Gives to preselected organizations. Send
applications to: Brandon Rotary Club, P. O. Box 303,
Brandon, Fl. 33509-0303.
DEADLINES: None
OFFICERS: Glass, Marshall, P; Sellars, John, VP; Curry,
Derrell, S/T

BRASWELL, ALLEN & CASSIE FOUNDATION, INC.

TWO SEASIDE LN., STE. 102
BELLEAIR, FL 33756
727-441-8470

ID NUMBER: 593505793
FEDERAL REPORTING DATE: 06/01
AREAS OF INTEREST: Arts & Culture, Health, Religion,
Scholarships, Social Services
CURRENT ASSETS: $526,111   PRIOR ASSETS:
$614,756
TOTAL AMOUNT AWARDED: $76,790
HIGH: $25,000--First United Methodist Church
MID: $10,000--United Way of Haywood
LOW: $80--Trinity Presbyterian Church
GRANTS AWARDS: Haywood Regional Hospital
Foundation--$2,500, Peachtree Road UMC--$5,000, Religous
Community Services--$200, Pinson Methodist--$150,
Salvation Army--$800, Smyrna Baptist Church--$100
SERVICE AREA: GA, NC, FL, National
COMMENTS: Gives to preselected organizations.
DEADLINES: None
OFFICERS: Braswell, Allen S., D; Braswell, Cassie, D;
Braswell, Bruce A., D

BREDE & WILKINS SCHOLARSHIP FUND

C/O BANK OF AMERICA
P. O. BOX 40200, MC FL9-100-10-19
JACKSONVILLE, FL 32203-0200
877-446-1410

ID NUMBER: 592911979
FEDERAL REPORTING DATE: 10/01
AREAS OF INTEREST: Education, Scholarships
CURRENT ASSETS: $912,670   PRIOR ASSETS:
$904,828
TOTAL AMOUNT AWARDED: $122,000
HIGH: $53,000--Office of Student Financial AFF Brede
Wilikins
MID: $25,500--FSU Student Financial Services
LOW: $500--American Travel Institute-(Individual Grant)
GRANTS AWARDS: N/A
SERVICE AREA: FL
COMMENTS: Send applications to: Amy Bock, Bank of
America, P. O. Box 8888, Winter Park, Fl. 32790 in written
form. Applicants must exhibit need for financial assistance,
have sufficient academic ability, character & motivation
necessary to succeed in completing their education.
DEADLINES: None
OFFICERS: Bank of America, TR

BREHM, C.E. FOUNDATION

C/O SYLVIA BREHM NEAL
425 DOCKSIDE DR., STE. 405
NAPLES, FL 34110-3657
941-566-9941

ID NUMBER: 376044243
FEDERAL REPORTING DATE: 06/01
AREAS OF INTEREST: Community, Education, Health,
Scholarships
CURRENT ASSETS: $147,208 PRIOR ASSETS:
$128,395
TOTAL AMOUNT AWARDED: $6,205
HIGH: $2,500--Individual
MID: $1,000--Brehm Preparatory School
LOW: $100--Girl Scout Little House
GRANTS AWARDS: Individual--$830, Condell Health Care
Foundation--$1,000, The American Cancer Society--$425,
North Suburban Library Foundation--$350
SERVICE AREA: IL, FL
COMMENTS: Applicants should submit a written
correspondence in letter form stating reason for request.
DEADLINES: None
OFFICERS: Hinrichsen, Karen, D

BREVARD HEART FOUNDATION

1901 S. HARBOR CITY BLVD.
STE. #806
MELBOURNE, FL 32901
321-725-2292

ID NUMBER: 596150538
FEDERAL REPORTING DATE: 06/01
AREAS OF INTEREST: Scholarships
CURRENT ASSETS: $463,920 PRIOR ASSETS:
$483,713
TOTAL AMOUNT AWARDED: $21,500
HIGH: $3,000--Individual
MID: $1,500--Individual
LOW: $500--Individual
GRANTS AWARDS: N/A
COMMENTS: Contact foundation and complete application
form.
DEADLINES: 6/15
OFFICERS: Jones, Bonnie B., D; Ploeger, Emest, D; Preston,
G. Merritt, D; Sietsma, Larry, D; Stoms, James T., D; Von
Thron, Dr. Joe, D

BROAD, SHEPARD FOUNDATION

801 BRICKEL AVE., STE. 2350
MIAMI, FL 33131
305-372-5790

ID NUMBER: 590998866
FEDERAL REPORTING DATE: 05/02
AREAS OF INTEREST: Arts & Culture, Community,
Education, Environment, Health, Medicine, Religion,
Scholarships, Social Services
CURRENT ASSETS: $5,358,247 PRIOR ASSETS:
$5,483,143
TOTAL AMOUNT AWARDED: $399,758
HIGH: $100,000--St. Joseph College
MID: $25,000--Univ. of Miami
LOW: $118--Temple Beth Shalom

GRANTS AWARDS: Miami City Ballet--$1,000,
Philharmonic Mathcing Funds--$1,000, Mexican American Bar
Fdn.--$2,500, Camillus House--$2,500, Fairchild Tropical
Gardens--$500, LA Police Historic Society--$1,500, Greater
Miami Jewish Federation--$2,000, Temple B'nai Horn--$500,
City of Hope--$1,000, Duke Univ. Medical Ctr.--$2,000,
American Heart Assn.--$500, Baptist Health System of S. FL.--
$5,000, Florida State Univ.--$100,000, WPBT--$750,
Southern Scholarship Fdn.--$3,000
SERVICE AREA: National
COMMENTS: Send applications to John Bussel at 801
Brickell Avenue, Suite 2350, Miami, FL. 33131. Applicants
must state details supporting request made and justify merit of
same as it concerns the advancement of applicat's activity be it
health, education, or welfare. Must be a nonprofit under IRS
rules and regulations.
DEADLINES: None
OFFICERS: Bussel, Ann B., VP; Bussel, Deborah L., S;
Berman, Karen A.B., D; Bussel, Daniel, D

BRONNER FOUNDATION

C/O MAX BRONNER, TOWER OF KEY BISCAYNE
1121 CRANDON BLVD.
KEY BISCAYNE, FL 33149

ID NUMBER: 136158665
FEDERAL REPORTING DATE: 01/02
AREAS OF INTEREST: Arts & Culture, Community,
Education, Medicine, Religion, Research, Scholarships, Social
Services
CURRENT ASSETS: $340,734 PRIOR ASSETS:
$513,917
TOTAL AMOUNT AWARDED: $24,792
HIGH: $5,300--Individual
MID: $2,800--KMZ Foundation
LOW: $10--Memorial Sloan Cancer
GRANTS AWARDS: Jewish United Fund--$7,020, Moadow
Kel--$300, Latin School of Chicago--$2,300, Amherst College-
-$2,500, CCFA--$100, Lane Shore Synagogue--$1,367, Croius
Colitis Fund--$100, Lynn Sage Cancer Research--$250,
American College of Cardiology--$500
SERVICE AREA: Miami, National
COMMENTS: Gives to preselected organizations.
DEADLINES: None
OFFICERS: Bronner, Max, TR; Bronner, Frances, TR

BRONSON, R. CARLYLE SCHOLARSHIP FOUNDATION, INC.

2375 SUE DR.
KISSIMMEE, FL 34741
407-788-0250

ID NUMBER: 593392431
FEDERAL REPORTING DATE: 04/02
AREAS OF INTEREST: Scholarships
CURRENT ASSETS: $0 PRIOR ASSETS: $0
TOTAL AMOUNT AWARDED: $20,000
HIGH: $2,000--Individual
MID: $1,000--Individual
LOW: $1,000--Individual
GRANTS AWARDS: N/A
SERVICE AREA: FL
COMMENTS: Forms available upon request. Osceola County,
FL residents only.
DEADLINES: Prior to beginning of school year

OFFICERS: Overstreet, Charlie Mac, Ch/D; Overstreet, Dorine, P/D; Grissom, Edward C. III, D; Larson, Iris, VP/D; Smith, Vianne, S/T/D; Bronson, Vincent, D

BROWN, ALBERT LEROY FOUNDATION

P.O. BOX 491227
LEESBURG, FL 34748
352-787-7963

ID NUMBER: 593332046
FEDERAL REPORTING DATE: 01/02
AREAS OF INTEREST: Education, Scholarships
CURRENT ASSETS: $665,708 PRIOR ASSETS: $665,564
TOTAL AMOUNT AWARDED: $46,500
HIGH: $7,500--Florida Memorial College
MID: $3,000--Bethel Baptist Assn.
LOW: $500--State Board of Community Colleges
GRANTS AWARDS: Rollins College--$5,000, Bethune Cookman College--$5,000, FL A & M University--$3,000, Rimes Elementary School--$2,000, Lake County Boys & Girls Club--$2,000, Lake Sumter Community College--$1,500, Seminole Community College--$6,500, United Negro College Fund--$4,500, Univ. of Central Florida--$3,000, Univ. of South Florida--$3,000
SERVICE AREA: FL
COMMENTS: Gives to preselected organizations.
DEADLINES: None
OFFICERS: Hamilton, Christyne B., P/T; Brown, Jana M., S/D; Brown, Albert L. Jr., VP/D

BRUNS, LINDA S. SCHOLARSHIP TRUST

4400 N. HWY A1A, STE. 1201
NORTH HUTCHINSON ISLAND, FL 34949
217-942-5244

ID NUMBER: 376355491
FEDERAL REPORTING DATE: 04/01
AREAS OF INTEREST: Scholarships
CURRENT ASSETS: $25,741 PRIOR ASSETS: $25,704
TOTAL AMOUNT AWARDED: $1,000
HIGH: $500--Individual
LOW: $500--Individual
GRANTS AWARDS: N/A
COMMENTS: To recieve scholarship must be graduate of Alton High School IL , major foreign language at college/university.
DEADLINES: 5/1 prior to graduation
OFFICERS: Burnett, Marjorie, TR

BUCK, BLANCHE S. CHARITABLE FOUNDATION

2780 E. OAKLAND PARK BLVD.
FORT LAUDERDALE, FL 33306
954-566-9990

ID NUMBER: 650123180
FEDERAL REPORTING DATE: 08/01
AREAS OF INTEREST: Scholarships, Social Services
CURRENT ASSETS: $315,426 PRIOR ASSETS: $336,878
TOTAL AMOUNT AWARDED: $32,500
HIGH: $11,500--Kids in Distress, Inc.

MID: $11,000--Jack & Jill Nursery, Inc.
LOW: $10,000--So. Scholarship Fdn.Inc.
GRANTS AWARDS: N/A
SERVICE AREA: National
COMMENTS: Must be a 501(c)(3) IRS approved organization. Gives to preselected organizations.
DEADLINES: None
OFFICERS: Dow, Alex, D/P; Buck, Blanche S., D; SunTrust Bank, South Florida, D/S/T; Gundlach, William, D/VP

BURNETT, AL CHARITABLE FOUNDATION, INC.

1025 ANCHORAGE CT.
WINTER PARK, FL 32789
407-628-1194

ID NUMBER: 592620060
FEDERAL REPORTING DATE: 01/02
AREAS OF INTEREST: Religion, Research, Scholarships
CURRENT ASSETS: $2,384,639 PRIOR ASSETS: $1,029,123
TOTAL AMOUNT AWARDED: $50,125
HIGH: $15,000--Penobscot Boy YMCA
MID: $1,000--Heart of Florida United Way
LOW: $625--United Cerebral Palsy
GRANTS AWARDS: Orlando Museum of Art--$1,000, Freedom Ride--$5,000, Florida Hospital Fund--$500, Campus Crusade for Christ--$1,000, Make a Wish Foundation--$1,000
COMMENTS: Gives to preselected organizations.
DEADLINES: None
OFFICERS: Burnett, J.A.; Burnett, N.L.; Steale, Mindy

BURROUGHS FAMILY FOUNDATION

500 RIVER DR.
VERO BEACH, FL 32963
561-231-1424

ID NUMBER: 46151877
FEDERAL REPORTING DATE: 04/01
AREAS OF INTEREST: Arts & Culture, Community, Education, Health, Medicine, Religion, Research, Scholarships, Social Services
CURRENT ASSETS: $183,554 PRIOR ASSETS: $186,107
TOTAL AMOUNT AWARDED: $11,305
HIGH: $2,000--Friends Grace Church
MID: $1,000--Atlantic Classical Orchestra
LOW: $25--Indian River Ambulance
GRANTS AWARDS: Vero Beach for Arts--$60, Milwaukee Art Museum--$100, American Cancer Society--$100, WPBT Channel 2--$100, Planned Parenthood--$100, American Red Cross--$100, Junior League Sneaker Fund--$25, Grace Opportunity Program--$500, Riverside Theater--$500, Vero Beach Concert Assn.--$500, African Film Festival--$250, Center Reproductive Life--$250, Englewood Public Library--$100, Friends Boerner Garden--$200, Green Tree Garden Club--$110
SERVICE AREA: National
COMMENTS: Gives to preselected organizations.
DEADLINES: None
OFFICERS: Burroughs, S. Roy, TR; Burroughs, Pamela, TR; Burroughs, Diana, TR

BUSH, MAX O. TRUST UNDER WILL

C/O BANK OF AMERICA
P.O. BOX 40200
JACKSONVILLE, FL 32203-0200
904-464-3664

ID NUMBER: 596622713
FEDERAL REPORTING DATE: 07/
AREAS OF INTEREST: Education, Sc
CURRENT ASSETS: $637,477 PRIO
$627,839
TOTAL AMOUNT AWARDED: $25,5
HIGH: $23,509--Morton College
LOW: $2,000--Morton High School
GRANTS AWARDS: N/A
SERVICE AREA: IL
COMMENTS: Gives to preselected organizatio
DEADLINES: None
OFFICERS: Bank of America, T

C S R AMERICA COMPANIES FOUNDATION

1501 BELVEDERE RD.
WEST PALM BEACH, FL 33406
561-833-5555

ID NUMBER: 596139266
FEDERAL REPORTING DATE: 03/01
AREAS OF INTEREST: Arts & Culture, Community,
Education, Environment, Scholarships, Social Services, Sports
& Athletics
CURRENT ASSETS: $7,950,581 PRIOR ASSETS:
$7,966,472
TOTAL AMOUNT AWARDED: $0
HIGH: $100,000--United Way of Palm Beach County
MID: $5,000--Univ of Nevada Las Vegas
LOW: $1,500--Granite Falls Educationl Fdn.
GRANTS AWARDS: H. Council on Economic Education--
$2,500, Seminole Community College--$32,000, Florida State
University Fdn.--$1,000, Alpena Community College-
Masonry--$26,786, Alpena Community College Fdn.--
$50,000, Univ. of Nevada at Las Vegas--$5,000, Bellingham
Technical College--$2,500, Univ. of Missouri-Rolla
Scholarship Comm.--$20,000, Palm Beach Atlantic College--
$40,000, University of Florida--$100,000
SERVICE AREA: FL, WH, MO, NV
COMMENTS: No required form. Contact Frank S. LaPlaca
for application procedures. Scholarships to Florida residents
majoring in business/construction.
DEADLINES: None
OFFICERS: Clarke, David, P; Driver, Adrian; Watson, Karl
H. Sr.; Watson, Karl H., Jr.; Failkow, Ira

CADE, ROBERT & MARY FOUNDATION, INC.

529 N.W. 58TH ST.
GAINESVILLE, FL 32607-2139
352-332-3093

ID NUMBER: 592938184
FEDERAL REPORTING DATE: 02/02
AREAS OF INTEREST: Arts & Culture, Education, Health,
Medicine, Scholarships
CURRENT ASSETS: $45,342 PRIOR ASSETS: $127,619
TOTAL AMOUNT AWARDED: $259,937

HIGH: $174,054--University of Florida Foundation
MID: $8,660--HELP
LOW: $500--University of Beijing
GRANTS AWARDS: University of Orlo--$10,000, Bucholz
Highschool--$2,500, Hospice of N. Central FL--$5,000,
Individual--$6,000, Individual--$2,000, Individual--$1,000,
Individual--$2,000, Individual--$6,000, Individual--$8,000
SERVICE AREA: FL, National
COMMENTS: Awards are based on financial need. Submit to
Arnold Zimmerman, 1106 NW 57th Street, Gainesville, FL
32605; 352-332-5549. Include details of income and college
costs.
DEADLINES: None
OFFICERS: Cade, J. Robert MD, P; Cade, Mary S., VP;
Zimmerman, Arnold, S/T

CAMICCIA-ARNAUTOU CHARITABLE FOUNDATION

C/O BILL T. SMITH
980 N. FEDERAL HWY., STE. 402
BOCA RATON, FL 33432
561-368-5757

ID NUMBER: 650610686
FEDERAL REPORTING DATE: 06/02
AREAS OF INTEREST: Arts & Culture, Education, Health,
Scholarships, Social Services
CURRENT ASSETS: $1,297,820 PRIOR ASSETS:
$1,228,140
TOTAL AMOUNT AWARDED: $97,500
HIGH: $25,000--St. John of Arc Catholic Church Fdn.
MID: $10,000--Migrant Assn. of So. Fla
LOW: $1,000--Project Graduation
GRANTS AWARDS: St. Jude Catholic Church--$9,000, Our
Lady of Perpetual Help Mission--$5,000, St. Joan of Arc
Catholic Church--$1,000, National Society of Arts & Letters--
$7,500, American Cancer Society--$1,000, American Heart
Assn.--$1,000, Barton's Boosters--$5,000, F tic
Univ.--$3,000, Florida Prepaid College Fdn
Hospice by the Sea--$3,000, Pope John Pau :hool--
$9,000
SERVICE AREA: FL
COMMENTS: Gives to preselected organ
DEADLINES: None
OFFICERS: Arnautou, Lena M., P/TR; !   Γ.,
S/T/TR; D'elia, , Maxine, TR; Gesner, C

CANTONIS, MICHAEL FOUNDATION, INC.

P.O. BOX 4989
CLEARWATER, FL 33758-4989
727-937-3222

ID NUMBER: 592214565
FEDERAL REPORTING DATE: 05/01
AREAS OF INTEREST: Arts & Culture, Community,
Education, Health, Medicine, Religion, Research, Scholarships,
Social Services, Sports & Athletics
CURRENT ASSETS: $1,047,625 PRIOR ASSETS:
$886,082
TOTAL AMOUNT AWARDED: $58,550
HIGH: $19,500--St. Michaels The Archangel
MID: $5,000--U.S. Ski Foundation, CO
LOW: $100--Tarpon Springs Public Library
GRANTS AWARDS: Berkley Preparatory School--$3,000,
Hellenic Times Scholarshio Fund, NY--$1,000, Ahepa
Centennial Foundation--$1,000, CCFA Chrons Disease

Assoc.--$1,000, Hanna, Inc., NY--$1,000, Moffit Cancer Research Center--$500, Olympic Village Foundation--$1,000
SERVICE AREA: FL, NY
DEADLINES: None
OFFICERS: Cantonis, Michael G., P/D; Cantonis, Anastasia H., VP/D; Cantonis, George H., VP/D

CAPE CORAL COMMUNITY FOUNDATION

P. O. BOX 32
CAPE CORAL, FL 33910
941-542-2194

ID NUMBER: 237410312
FEDERAL REPORTING DATE: 06/98
AREAS OF INTEREST: Scholarships
CURRENT ASSETS: $285,808 PRIOR ASSETS: $173,146
TOTAL AMOUNT AWARDED: $1,200
HIGH: $800--Edison Community College Fund
LOW: $400--University of St. Francis
GRANTS AWARDS: N/A
SERVICE AREA: FL, IL
DEADLINES: 1/15, 8/15
OFFICERS: Tabor, Elmer W., P; Biggs, Robert, VP; Warchol, Martha, S/T; Swift, M.T., D; Hafer, Richard, D

CAPITAL CITY GROUP FOUNDATION, INC.

217 N. MONROE ST.
TALLAHASSEE, FL 32301
850-671-0598

ID NUMBER: 592276367
FEDERAL REPORTING DATE: 05/02
AREAS OF INTEREST: Arts & Culture, Community, Education, Environment, Health, Medicine, Scholarships, Social Services
CURRENT ASSETS: $1,559,007 PRIOR ASSETS: $1,620,604
TOTAL AMOUNT AWARDED: $348,873
HIGH: $101,600--Economic Devel Council
MID: $50,000--United Way of the Big Bend
LOW: $500--March of Dimes (Julian V. Smith contribution)
GRANTS AWARDS: Capital Cultural Center/Odyssey--$5,000, City of Tallahassee-Community Neighborhood--$4,000, City of Valley Capital Project Fund--$10,000, Community Foundation of North Florida--$5,000, Education Foundation of Gilchrist County--$2,000, FAMU Booster--$1,000, Florida Tax Wach--$2,500, FSU Seminal Booster--$26,800, Southeastern Community Blood Center--$3,333, Take Stock in Children -Gadsden County--$1,250, Tallahasee Memorial hospital Foundation--$8,200, Tallahassee Urban League--$1,000, Taxwatch 2000--$1,000, Tree House--$1,500, United Way of Macon--$5,000
SERVICE AREA: Only Local Capital City Bank Communities, National
COMMENTS: Send applications to P.O. Box 11248, Tallahassee, FL 32302. Only gives to 501(c)(3) tax-exempt organization's in Capital City Bank Communities. Does not give to individuals.
DEADLINES: None
OFFICERS: Smith, William G., Jr., P; Barron, Thomas A., VP; Ruggiero, Donald L., S/T

CASEY FAMILY FOUNDATION

330 S. BEACH RD.
HOBE SOUND, FL 33455

ID NUMBER: 26013556
FEDERAL REPORTING DATE: 05/01
AREAS OF INTEREST: Arts & Culture, Education, Environment, Health, Medicine, Religion, Scholarships, Social Services
CURRENT ASSETS: $1,133,043 PRIOR ASSETS: $1,169,805
TOTAL AMOUNT AWARDED: $76,311
HIGH: $77,581--Phillip Exeter Academy
MID: $5,000--Landmark School
LOW: $25--Marblehead Arts
GRANTS AWARDS: 1000 Friends of FL--$500, American Heart Association--$500, Yale University--$790, Appalachian Mountain Club--$75, Boys and Girls Club--$300, College of Charleston--$250, First Baptist Church of Big Bear Lake--$500, Christ Memorial Chapel--$3,000, Tower School--$6,500, Taber Academy--$450, St. Andrew's Church--$1,300, Spring Lake Ranch--$2,500, WGBH--$100, WCOS--$500, WHOI--$200
SERVICE AREA: National
COMMENTS: Gives to preselected organizations.
DEADLINES: None
OFFICERS: Casey, E. Paul, TR

CASH, J.B. FOUNDATION, INC.

P.O. BOX 4556
PRINCETON, FL 33092
305-245-5923

ID NUMBER: 650764220
FEDERAL REPORTING DATE: 05/02
AREAS OF INTEREST: Education, Medicine, Scholarships, Social Services
CURRENT ASSETS: $2,700,724 PRIOR ASSETS: $2,711,208
TOTAL AMOUNT AWARDED: $69,800
HIGH: $10,000--Woman's Club of Homestead
MID: $5,000--Sunrise Community Inc.
LOW: $300--Miss Homestead Scholarship
GRANTS AWARDS: Florida State University--$1,000, Florida International University--$1,000, University of South Florida--$1,000, Leukemia & Lymphoma Society--$2,000, Brooke Langston/Rollins College--$1,000, Woman's Club of Homestead--$1,500, Charles Castello/Florida International U.--$1,000
SERVICE AREA: FL
COMMENTS: Submit application in writing to Gloria C. Lawler, 17901 S. 288th Street, Princeton, FL 33030. Include background of organization and purpose of request.
DEADLINES: None
OFFICERS: Lawler, Gloria C., P/D; Lawler, E. Roy, V.P./T

CATALINA MARKETING CHARITABLE FOUNDATION

200 CARILLON PKWY.
ST. PETERSBURG, FL 33716
727-579-5000

ID NUMBER: 330489905
FEDERAL REPORTING DATE: 03/02
AREAS OF INTEREST: Arts & Culture, Community, Education, Environment, Health, Medicine, Research, Scholarships, Social Services

CURRENT ASSETS: $413,851 PRIOR ASSETS:
$504,495
TOTAL AMOUNT AWARDED: $91,902
HIGH: $40,000--Pinellas County Education Fund
MID: $14,000--City of Hope
LOW: $25--National Multiple Sclerosis Society
GRANTS AWARDS: American Heart Assn.--$5,000, Bames
Jewish Hospital Fdn.--$10,000, Assns. of Small Foundations--
$300, Friends of Bovd Hill Nature Park--$75, Connecticut
College--$25, Douglass Annual Fund, Douglas College--$25,
USF Fdn.--$100, Big Brothers, Big Sisters--$100, Pinellas Assn.
for Retarded Citizens--$500, Alpha House of Tampa--$500,
FL. Education Fund--$100, St. Petersburg Free Clinic--$100,
SPCA of St. Petersburg--$500, National Parkinson's Fdn.--
$250, Neighborly Senior Services--$250
SERVICE AREA: National
COMMENTS: Send Applications to Bill Protz at 200 Carillon
Pkwy, St. Petersburg, FL. 33716.
DEADLINES: None
OFFICERS: Off, George W., C/D; Bechtol, Michael, D;
Agostino, Stephen, D; Wolf, Chris, S; Port, Joseph P., CFO;
Groe, Gerald, S

CETRINO, CHERYL ANN FISH
SCHOLARSHIP FUND
C/O SANDRA CETRINO
640 GLORIOSA DR.
VENICE, FL 34293-6918
941-492-3717

ID NUMBER: 43167141
FEDERAL REPORTING DATE: 09/01
AREAS OF INTEREST: Scholarships
CURRENT ASSETS: $34,051 PRIOR ASSETS: $32,633
TOTAL AMOUNT AWARDED: $850
HIGH: $850--Individual
GRANTS AWARDS: N/A
DEADLINES: N/A
OFFICERS: Cetrino, Vinicenzo, TR; Cetrino, Sandra, TR

CHILDREN'S FOUNDATION OF
LAKE WALES
P. O. BOX 990
LAKE WALES, FL 33859-0990
863-676-7981

ID NUMBER: 596137951
FEDERAL REPORTING DATE: 07/01
AREAS OF INTEREST: Scholarships
CURRENT ASSETS: $71,618 PRIOR ASSETS: $71,542
TOTAL AMOUNT AWARDED: $3,650
HIGH: $550--Individual
MID: $550--Individual
LOW: $450--Individual
GRANTS AWARDS: N/A
COMMENTS: Send applications to: David M. Rockness, 16
North 3rd st, Lake Wales, Fl. 33853.
DEADLINES: None
OFFICERS: Wilson, David (deceased), P; Matteson, John,
VP; Hurst, Michelle, S/T

CHRISTIAN FOUNDATION
121 LAKE HOLLINGSWORTH DR.
LAKELAND, FL 33801
941-683-2581

ID NUMBER: 566067052
FEDERAL REPORTING DATE: 05/02
AREAS OF INTEREST: Arts & Culture, Community,
Education, Medicine, Religion, Research, Scholarships, Social
Services
CURRENT ASSETS: $188,491 PRIOR ASSETS:
$198,604
TOTAL AMOUNT AWARDED: $14,125
HIGH: $5,000--Moldovan Children's Audiology Foundation,
Inc.
MID: $1,000--St. Michael's Episcopal Church
LOW: $25--Florida Elks Children's
GRANTS AWARDS: American Bible Society--$250,
American Lung Assoc. of Gulf Coast, Inc.--$100, Boys & Girls
Club of Lakeland--$500, Christian Appalachian Project--$500,
Girl Scouts - Heart of Florida Council--$250, Goodwill
Suncoast Foundation--$100, Help Hospitalized Veterans--
$200, Juvenile Diabetes Research Foundation--$200, Von
Ministries--$750
SERVICE AREA: National
COMMENTS: Requires concise letter format stating name of
organization, purpose and benefits of grant. Do not phone.
DEADLINES: None
OFFICERS: Miller, Truman W., P; Miller, Marie M., T

CHURCH, LOU EDUCATIONAL
FOUNDATION, INC.
1700 N.E. 26 ST.
WILTON MANORS, FL 33062
954-563-5861

ID NUMBER: 592761512
FEDERAL REPORTING DATE: 05/02
AREAS OF INTEREST: Education, Scholarships
CURRENT ASSETS: $2,739,353 PRIOR ASSETS:
$3,109,438
TOTAL AMOUNT AWARDED: $330,000
HIGH: $35,000--Hillsdale College
MID: $15,000--Westminster Academy
LOW: $10,000--Pine Crest Prep School
GRANTS AWARDS: Ludwig Von Mieses Institution--
$30,000, Goal Incorporated--$20,000, Foundation for Eco
Education--$30,000, Grove City College--$30,000
SERVICE AREA: National
DEADLINES: None
OFFICERS: Helmholdt, Robert, DDS, P; Bigelow, Arthur L.;
Drury, Jack; Johnson, D. Allen; Meehan, Edward

CLEMENTINE ZACKE
FOUNDATION
2400 S.E. FEDERAL HWY.
STE. 400
STUART, FL 34994
561-286-1700

ID NUMBER: 656270436
FEDERAL REPORTING DATE: 05/01
AREAS OF INTEREST: Medicine, Religion, Scholarships
CURRENT ASSETS: $1,516,370 PRIOR ASSETS:
$1,488,776
TOTAL AMOUNT AWARDED: $85,233

HIGH: $39,208--Immanuel Lutheran Church
MID: $23,525--Hospice of Martin & St. Lucie Counites, Inc.
LOW: $22,500--Misc.
GRANTS AWARDS: N/A
SERVICE AREA: Fl
COMMENTS: Scholarship reciepients are limited to those students who have graduated from a high school in Martin County, FL.
DEADLINES: Varies
OFFICERS: Calvasina, Corrine, TR; Danielson, Jan, TR; Wood, Steve, TR

CLEMENTS FAMILY CHARITABLE TRUST

C/O THOMAS CLEMENTS III
1025 FLEMING ST.
KEY WEST, FL 33040
305-292-1025

ID NUMBER: 341748724
FEDERAL REPORTING DATE: 05/02
AREAS OF INTEREST: Arts & Culture, Community, Education, Environment, Health, Medicine, Religion, Scholarships, Social Services
CURRENT ASSETS: $818,219 PRIOR ASSETS: $766,014
TOTAL AMOUNT AWARDED: $144,510
HIGH: $25,000--Cleveland Botanical Garden
MID: $5,000--Friends of Blue Hill Bay
LOW: $75--Harvard Magazine
GRANTS AWARDS: American Diabetes Association--$100, American Red Cross-Hancock Cty.--$200, Auburn Theological Seminary--$150, Bay School--$250, Blue Hill Fire Dept.--$400, Case Western Reserve University--$1,000, Central School of Practical Nursing--$20,000, Choate Rosemary Hall School--$2,000, Community Foundation of the Florida Keys--$5,000, Day School Foundation--$250, Film Forum--$150, First Congregation--$1,500, Florida Keys Discovery--$100, --$100
SERVICE AREA: National
COMMENTS: Gives to preselected organizations.
DEADLINES: None
OFFICERS: Clements, Helen T.,TR; Clements, Robert M., Jr., TR; Clements, Thomas III, TR; Key Bank, Agent for TR

COBB FAMILY FOUNDATION

255 ARAGON AVE.
STE. 333
CORAL GABLES, FL 33134
305-441-1700

ID NUMBER: 592477459
FEDERAL REPORTING DATE: 04/02
AREAS OF INTEREST: Arts & Culture, Community, Education, Environment, Health, Religion, Research, Scholarships, Social Services
CURRENT ASSETS: $7,956,726 PRIOR ASSETS: $8,089,629
TOTAL AMOUNT AWARDED: $529,345
HIGH: $125,000--Cobb Stadium
MID: $35,000--United Way of Dade County
LOW: $500--Courtelis Center for Research and Treatment in
GRANTS AWARDS: Dr Maxwell and Reva Daver Endowed Scholarship--$500, University of Miami's President's Fund--$25,000, Plymouth Church--$20,800, United Way of Dade County--$35,000, Stanford University--$25,000, Zoological Society of South Florida--$15,500

SERVICE AREA: FL, Dade County, National
COMMENTS: Write a request to any trustee / officer. Focus of foundation is on higher education and direct contribution to institutions of higher education. Requests for contributions should include a brief history of the organization, a current list of Members of the Board and senior executives, current annual budget, ratio of admin/grants, use of funds.
DEADLINES: None
OFFICERS: Cobb, Charles E. Jr., P; Cobb, Sue M., VP; Cobb, Tobin T., VP; Cobb, Christian M., VP

COCHRANE, WILLIAM H. EDUCATIONAL TRUST

C/O NORTHERN TRUST BANK
700 BRICKELL AVE.
MIAMI, FL 33131
561-231-2404

ID NUMBER: 596895373
FEDERAL REPORTING DATE: 02/01
AREAS OF INTEREST: Scholarships
CURRENT ASSETS: $108,866 PRIOR ASSETS: $65,612
TOTAL AMOUNT AWARDED: $2,300
HIGH: $400--Individual
MID: $400--Individual
LOW: $300--Individual
GRANTS AWARDS: N/A
SERVICE AREA: Vero Beach
COMMENTS: Send applications to Cochrane Educational Trust, Director of Human Resources at 1053 20th Street, Vero Beach, FL. 32960.
DEADLINES: None
OFFICERS: Northern Trust Bank of Vero Beach, TR; Reascos, Priscilla; Bursick, James; Maillet, Stephen J.

COHEN, NANCY Y. & MARTIN FAMILY CHARITABLE TRUST

3731 TOULOUSE DR.
PALM BEACH GARDENS, FL 33410-1463
561-626-6042

ID NUMBER: 526924875
FEDERAL REPORTING DATE: 04/02
AREAS OF INTEREST: Community, Education, Environment, Health, Medicine, Religion, Research, Scholarships, Social Services
CURRENT ASSETS: $2,724,671 PRIOR ASSETS: $2,760,472
TOTAL AMOUNT AWARDED: $148,350
HIGH: $25,000--Jobs Unlimited, Inc.
MID: $15,000--Housing Unlimited, Inc.
LOW: $50--Friends of MacArthur Beach State Park
GRANTS AWARDS: Arthritis Fdn.--$510, US Holocaust Memorial Museum--$2,500, United Negro College Fund--$1,000, Frenchman's Creek Fdn.--$1,515, Woodley House--$500, The Nature Conservancy--$5,250, Terri Lynne Lokoff Child Care Fdn.--$500, Planned Parenthood--$250, Together We Care--$800, Florida Stage--$2,500, Washington Hebrew Congregation--$400, Recording for Blind & Dyslectic--$500, Brown Univ.--$5,000, Childrens Hospital--$2,000, United Way--$2,000
SERVICE AREA: National
COMMENTS: Gives to preselected organizations.
DEADLINES: None
OFFICERS: Cohen, Nancy Y., TR; Cohen, Martin, TR

COHEN, WILLIAM & HANNAH FOUNDATION

11519 TIMBERLINE CIR.
FORT MYERS, FL 33912
941-768-775

ID NUMBER: 226085831
FEDERAL REPORTING DATE: 08/01
AREAS OF INTEREST: Community, Health, Religion, Scholarships
CURRENT ASSETS: $127,730 PRIOR ASSETS: $133,025
TOTAL AMOUNT AWARDED: $11,500
HIGH: $1,000--Individual
MID: $500--Cunac/Echo
LOW: $100--Simon Wiesenthal Center
GRANTS AWARDS: American Heart Association--$1,500, CJ Foundation--$200, Hadassah Children's Hospital--$200, United Jewish Foundation--$200
SERVICE AREA: National
DEADLINES: N/A
OFFICERS: Slotnick, Selma, D; Adler, Rochelle, D; Grimm, Dorothy, D

COKER, BRYANT L. SCHOLARSHIP LOAN FUND

P.O. BOX 545
WAUCHULA, FL 33873
813-773-6768

ID NUMBER: 592479238
FEDERAL REPORTING DATE: 01/02
AREAS OF INTEREST: Scholarships
CURRENT ASSETS: $484,577 PRIOR ASSETS: $456,995
TOTAL AMOUNT AWARDED: $0
GRANTS AWARDS: N/A
COMMENTS: Foundation makes loans to needy students. Submit narrative of need, references, application and grades.
DEADLINES: None
OFFICERS: Coker, Glakys, P; Archambault, Jean, S; Knight, Gerald, D; Shackelford, Marcus, D

COMMUNITY FOUNDATION FOR PALM BEACH & MARTIN COUNTIES

324 DATURA ST., STE. 340
WEST PALM BEACH, FL 33401-5431
561-659-6800

ID NUMBER: 237181875
FEDERAL REPORTING DATE: 06/99
AREAS OF INTEREST: Arts & Culture, Community, Education, Environment, Health, Religion, Scholarships, Social Services, Other
CURRENT ASSETS: $88,444,116 PRIOR ASSETS: $74,505,891
TOTAL AMOUNT AWARDED: $2,704,424
HIGH: $125,000--Glades Community Development Corp
LOW: $1,253--Miscellaneous
GRANTS AWARDS: N/A
SERVICE AREA: Palm Beach County, FL., Martin County, FL.
COMMENTS: An application form is required. Initial approach--telephone followed by a proposal. Must be a

501(c)(3) organization and not classified as a private foundation. Request guidelines for scholarship information, contact Email : info@cfpbmc.or Visit our Web Address: http://www. yourcommunity foundation.org
DEADLINES: 2/1, 10/1
OFFICERS: Sadler, Shannon G., P; sears, Beverly Pope, VP; Dodge, John B., C; Henry, Thornton M., VC

COMMUNITY FOUNDATION OF TAMPA BAY, INC.

4950 W. KENNEDY BLVD., STE. 250
TAMPA, FL 33609
813-282-1975

ID NUMBER: 593001853
FEDERAL REPORTING DATE: 06/01
AREAS OF INTEREST: Arts & Culture, Community, Education, Environment, Health, Medicine, Religion, Research, Scholarships, Social Services, Sports & Athletics, Other
CURRENT ASSETS: $75,562,861 PRIOR ASSETS: $71,007,591
TOTAL AMOUNT AWARDED: $7,036,232
HIGH: $1,075,000-West Virginia Univ. Fdn., Inc.
MID: $375,350--Metropolitan Ministries
LOW: $100,250--St. Mary's Episcopal Day School
GRANTS AWARDS: Tampa Bay Performing Arts Ctr. Fdn.--$287,427, Boys & Girls Clubs of Tampa Bay Fdn., Inc.--$236,424, Hyde Park United Methodist Church--$205,000, Beth-El Farmworkers Ministry--$190,600, Florida Orchestra, Inc.--$190,102, Tampa Bay Performing Arts Ctr.--$181,986, United Way of Hillsborough Co.--$153,175, Hillsborough Educ. Fdn.--$152,130, Univ. of So. Florida Fdn.--$130,000, Family First--$125,000, Lowry Park Zoological Society of Tampa, Inc.--$122,490, YMCA/YWCA of Tampa & Hillsborough Co.--$111,537
SERVICE AREA: Hillsborough Co., Pinellas Co., Pasco Co.
DEADLINES: None
OFFICERS: Baxter, George J., P; Romano, Barbara, C; Garcia, Joseph, VC; Murray, Raymond, S; Rief, Frank J., III, T

COMMUNITY SERVICE FOUNDATION OF BROWARD COUNTY

2131 HOLLYWOOD BLVD., STE. 101
HOLLYWOOD, FL 33020
954-922-3282

ID NUMBER: 650501497
FEDERAL REPORTING DATE: 06/01
AREAS OF INTEREST: Scholarships, Social Services
CURRENT ASSETS: $251,407 PRIOR ASSETS: $5,226
TOTAL AMOUNT AWARDED: $430
HIGH: $250--Greater Hollywood YMCA
LOW: $180--Kiwanis Scholarship Fdn.
GRANTS AWARDS: N/A
SERVICE AREA: Hollywood
COMMENTS: Submit in writing with exemption letter and organization background. Grants limited to children with disabilities.
DEADLINES: 9/1
OFFICERS: Giacin, Robert, TR

CONAWAY, FLOYD A. & BETTY H. SCHOLARSHIP FUND

C/O UNITED TRUST CO
333-3RD AVE. N. ,STE. 300
ST. PETERSBURG, FL 33701
727-824-8705

ID NUMBER: 596968103
FEDERAL REPORTING DATE: 04/02
AREAS OF INTEREST: Community, Education, Religion, Scholarships, Social Services
CURRENT ASSETS: $449,366 **PRIOR ASSETS:** $425,114
TOTAL AMOUNT AWARDED: $51,317
GRANTS AWARDS: N/A
SERVICE AREA: Pinellas County, MN
COMMENTS: Gives to preselected organizations. No unsolicited requests.
DEADLINES: None
OFFICERS: Stout, David L., T

CONN MEMORIAL FOUNDATION, INC.

2910 W. BAY TO BAY BLVD., STE. 200
TAMPA, FL 33629-8113
813-282-4922

ID NUMBER: 590978713
FEDERAL REPORTING DATE: 02/02
AREAS OF INTEREST: Arts & Culture, Community, Education, Religion, Scholarships, Social Services
CURRENT ASSETS: $23,287,532 **PRIOR ASSETS:** $23,407,789
TOTAL AMOUNT AWARDED: $884,026
HIGH: $50,000--YMCA - Tampa Metropolitan Area
MID: $10,000--St. Peter Claver School
LOW: $500--Individual
GRANTS AWARDS: All Sports--$25,000, Alpha House--$40,000, Ballet Society--$12,000, Bolesta Center, Inc.--$20,000, Brighter Community--$18,000, Center for Women--$25,000, Child Abuse Council--$40,000, Children' Home--$9,400, Christian Resource Center--$2,500, Computer Mentors--$20,000, Corporation to Develop Communities--$25,000, Healthy Start Coalition--$12,000
SERVICE AREA: Hillsborough County
COMMENTS: Submit a one-page letter outlining purpose of grant. An application form will be sent, if appropriate. Interests include disadvantaged and troubled youth. Scholarship programs are for high school graduates. Contact Fran Powers, Director of Services. 813-282-4922. Limited to Hillsborough County.
DEADLINES: 3/30, 11/30
OFFICERS: Crowder, Sheffield, P; Powers, Fran, D; Jenkins, Donna

CORNERSTONE FOUNDATION

C/O WALTER BRYS
1170 GULF BLVD., #1701
CLEARWATER, FL 33767
727-596-8350

ID NUMBER: 760407449
FEDERAL REPORTING DATE: 06/99
AREAS OF INTEREST: Community, Religion, Scholarships, Social Services
CURRENT ASSETS: $39,337 **PRIOR ASSETS:** $59,635

TOTAL AMOUNT AWARDED: $19,077
HIGH: $10,000--Elsa Wright - Rural Development
MID: $1,350--St. Cecilia Church
LOW: $10--Passionist Monastery
GRANTS AWARDS: St. Martha's Catholic Church--$50, International God Parenthood--$2,105, Toys for Toddlers--$65, Life in the Spirit--$200, St. Mary's Catholic Church--$100, Society of Little Flower--$20, Victory Campus Ministry--$400, The Marianist Mission--$10, Shrine Circus Fund--$27, St. Joseph Relig. Gift--$1,000, Sacred Heart Monastery--$20, Saint Barbara Parish--$75, Pilgrims Peace Center--$70, Paso--$30, James Keskeny, International M.S.--$100, Multiple Sclerosis Society--$2,650, Grace Ministries--$25, National Shrine - St. Jude--$20
SERVICE AREA: TX, FL, MT, IL, AL, OH
COMMENTS: Gives to the preselected organizations
DEADLINES: None
OFFICERS: Brys, Walter, P; Brys, Eileen, VP; Ramirez, Kathryn A., TR

COX, CHANDLER FOUNDATION (F/K/A MASHEK FOUNDATION)

125 WORTH AVE., STE. 204
PALM BEACH, FL 33480-4466
561-655-5118

ID NUMBER: 752080801
FEDERAL REPORTING DATE: 11/01
AREAS OF INTEREST: Arts & Culture, Community, Education, Environment, Health, Religion, Scholarships, Social Services
CURRENT ASSETS: $311,099 **PRIOR ASSETS:** $385,207
TOTAL AMOUNT AWARDED: $92,307
HIGH: $56,780--Memorial Sloan-Kettering
MID: $10,000--Southern Methodist Univ.
LOW: $16--March of Dimes
GRANTS AWARDS: American Red Cross--$2,100, Animal Rescue League of Palm Beach--$100, Central Park Conservancy--$10,800, Alan Davis Memorial Scholarship Fund--$1,000, Garden Club of Palm Beach--$60, Kravis Ctr. for the Performing Arts--$1,000, Long Island Univ.--$400, Middlesex School--$100, National Multiple Sclerosis Society--$26, New York Botanical Gardens--$2,500, South Hampton Fresh Air Home--$1,000, Special Olympics Florida--$1,300, Susan B. Komen Breast Cancer--$5,000, Trees New York--$125
SERVICE AREA: National
COMMENTS: Send applications to: Chandler C. Mashek, 125 Worth Ave., #204, Palm Beach, Fl. 33480-4466. (561)655-5118.
DEADLINES: None
OFFICERS: Mashek, Chandler C., TR; Mashek, Grant E., TR

CRISTINA FOUNDATION, INC.

P.O. BOX 2410
BRANDON, FL 33509-2410
813-685-4214

ID NUMBER: 592439694
FEDERAL REPORTING DATE: 04/02
AREAS OF INTEREST: Community, Education, Scholarsh
CURRENT ASSETS: $155,130 **PRIOR ASSETS:** $165,250
TOTAL AMOUNT AWARDED: $5,500
HIGH: $2,500--USF Latino Scholarship Fund

MID: $1,000--Delta Seta Scholarship
LOW: $1,000--Academy of Holy Names
GRANTS AWARDS: YMCA-Tampa Metro--$1,000
SERVICE AREA: Tampa
COMMENTS: Preference to Tampa Bay organizations
benefiting children. Submit written proposal which outlines
qualifications, budget and goals. Applications accepted at any
time. Notice of approval will be given within 60 days. Contact
Diane C. Ekonomou, 907 Hollow Oak Pl., Brandon, FL
33510 (813) 681-9989.
DEADLINES: None
OFFICERS: Campo, Ramon F., P; Ekonomou, Diane C.,
VP/M

CROSBY FAMILY FOUNDATION

C/O COX & NICI
3001 TAMIAMI TR. N., STE. 100
NAPLES, FL 34101
941-659-4495

ID NUMBER: 656236188
FEDERAL REPORTING DATE: 11/01
AREAS OF INTEREST: Education, Religion, Scholarships,
Sports & Athletics
CURRENT ASSETS: $1,270,737 PRIOR ASSETS:
$1,244,105
TOTAL AMOUNT AWARDED: $30,000
HIGH: $7,500--Linville Fdn.
MID: $5,000--Croquet Fdn. of America
LOW: $2,500--Emporia State Univ.
GRANTS AWARDS: St. Bartholomews Episcopal Church--
$5,000, Ahearn Scholarship Fund--$7,500
SERVICE AREA: National
COMMENTS: Gives to preselected organizations.
DEADLINES: N/A
OFFICERS: Crosby, Gordon E, Jr. , C; Crosby, Gordon E.,
III, P, T; Crosby, Douglas H., VP, S

DADDARIO CHARITABLE FOUNDATION

C/O FRANCIS E. DADDARIO
3200 N. OCEAN BLVD., STE. 2909
FORT LAUDERDALE, FL 33308
781-848-2396

ID NUMBER: 650969311
FEDERAL REPORTING DATE: 11/01
AREAS OF INTEREST: Scholarships
CURRENT ASSETS: $418,115 PRIOR ASSETS:
$270,968
TOTAL AMOUNT AWARDED: $10,000
HIGH: $10,000--Taft School
GRANTS AWARDS: N/A
COMMENTS: Gives to preselected organizations.
DEADLINES: None
OFFICERS: Daddario, Francis E., TR; Daddario, Lorena M.,
TR; Errico, V. Douglas, TR; Costello, Joseph P., TR; Richards,
Sidney C., TR

DALTON FOUNDATION

1100 FIFTH AVE., S., #301
NAPLES, FL 34102
941-261-3555

ID NUMBER: 223146570
FEDERAL REPORTING DATE: 05/99

AREAS OF INTEREST: Education, Scholarships
CURRENT ASSETS: $934,653 PRIOR ASSETS:
$752,719
TOTAL AMOUNT AWARDED: $22,900
HIGH: $11,900--The Comminity School of Naples
LOW: $11,000--The Immokalee Foundation
GRANTS AWARDS: N/A
SERVICE AREA: FL
COMMENTS: Gives to preselected organizations
DEADLINES: None
OFFICERS: Dalton, Timothy G. Jr., P; Dalton, Julie M., S/T;
Dalton, Alison M., T

DAVIS, FRED W. MEMORIAL FOUNDATION

C/O FIRST UNION NATIONAL BANK
200 SOUTH BISCAYNE BLVD
MIAMI, FL 33131
305-789-4615

ID NUMBER: 596717509
FEDERAL REPORTING DATE: 03/01
AREAS OF INTEREST: Religion, Scholarships
CURRENT ASSETS: $816,281 PRIOR ASSETS:
$801,170
TOTAL AMOUNT AWARDED: $15,000
HIGH: $5,000--Individual
MID: $5,000--Individual
LOW: $5,000--Individual
GRANTS AWARDS: N/A
COMMENTS: Scholarships are restricted to Episcopal
seminary students in their year of study.
DEADLINES: 30 Days Prior to Commencement
OFFICERS: First Union, TR

DEEB, JOS PATRICK MEMORIAL SCHOLARSHIP FUND, INC.

P. O. BOX 10193
TALLAHASSEE, FL 32302
850-575-5224

ID NUMBER: 237028231
FEDERAL REPORTING DATE: 08/01
AREAS OF INTEREST: Education, Scholarships
CURRENT ASSETS: $636,666 PRIOR ASSETS:
$602,683
TOTAL AMOUNT AWARDED: $51,893
HIGH: $51,893--Florida State Univ. Fdn.
GRANTS AWARDS: N/A
SERVICE AREA: FL
COMMENTS: Gvies to preselected organizations.
DEADLINES: None
OFFICERS: Marshall, J. Stanley, C; Ausley, Margaret B., S;
Long, J.R., T; Thornberry, Marcia D., D

DEELEY, THOMAS & ELSIE FOUNDATION

3274 W. PEBBLE BEACH CT.
LECANTO, FL 34461
352-527-3880

ID NUMBER: 541780341
FEDERAL REPORTING DATE: 11/01
AREAS OF INTEREST: Scholarships

CURRENT ASSETS: $670,899 PRIOR ASSETS: $698,223
TOTAL AMOUNT AWARDED: $40,000
HIGH: $40,000--Fairfield Univ.
GRANTS AWARDS: N/A
COMMENTS: Send applications to: Thomas E. Deeley Jr., The Thomas & Elsie Deeley Fdn., 3274 West Pebble Beach Ct., Lecanto, Fl. 34461. Write or telephone for application. Eligible individuals will belimited to the graduation senior of Sacred Heart High School in Waterbury, Ct.
DEADLINES: March 1 of the Graduating Year
OFFICERS: Deeley, Thomas E., Jr., D; Deeley, Gayle K., D

DEHAAN, JON HOLDEN FOUNDATION

975 SIXTH AVE., S., STE 103
NAPLES, FL 34102
941-435-9050

ID NUMBER: 346924212
FEDERAL REPORTING DATE: 05/01
AREAS OF INTEREST: Arts & Culture, Community, Education, Scholarships, Social Services
CURRENT ASSETS: $13,019,263 PRIOR ASSETS: $13,682,816
TOTAL AMOUNT AWARDED: $439,134
HIGH: $181,000--University of Denver
MID: $50,000--Park Tudor School
LOW: $65--WGCU TV
GRANTS AWARDS: St. Ann School Scholarship--$11,000, Friedman Foundation--$50,000, Professional Givers Anonymous--$15,000, Meadows School of Communications--$100,000, Collier County Fraternal Order of Police--$300, American Heart Associations--$5,269, Conservancy of SW Florida--$2,500, Judicial Watch--$10,000
SERVICE AREA: National
COMMENTS: Applicants should submit a written letter and include proof of 501(c)(3) tax-exempt status.
DEADLINES: None
OFFICERS: DeHaan, Jon H., TR; DeHaan, Thomas H., M

DETTMAN, LEROY E. FOUNDATION, INC.

1615 S. FEDERAL HWY., STE 300
BOCA RATON, FL 33432-7434
561-362-9104

ID NUMBER: 591784551
FEDERAL REPORTING DATE: 01/02
AREAS OF INTEREST: Arts & Culture, Community, Education, Medicine, Religion, Scholarships, Social Services, Sports & Athletics, Other
CURRENT ASSETS: $2,113,708 PRIOR ASSETS: $2,530,794
TOTAL AMOUNT AWARDED: $153,340
HIGH: $10,000--Open Door Education Foundation
MID: $7,500--Fort Lord Prep School
LOW: $50--Hospice by the Sea
GRANTS AWARDS: Individual--$1,000, Individual--$2,500, Covenant House--$1,500, United Way of Broward--$500, Handy--$250, Unis Family Scholarship Fund--$100, Kendrick English--$100, Coral Springs Divine Booster--$250, American Cancer Society--$250, US Lacrosse--$100, Broward Public Library Foundation--$1,000, JR Welfare--$1,000, St Lawrence Chapel--$650
SERVICE AREA: FL, National

COMMENTS: Primary support for scholarships for children of Interim Services of America employees. Write for application form.
DEADLINES: None
OFFICERS: Dettman, Gregory L., S/D; Dettman, Douglas R., P/D; Fleming, Barbara, VP/D; Rubin, Carolyn, T/D

DEUTSCH FAMILY FOUNDATION

6747 S.W. 122 DR.
MIAMI, FL 33156
305-358-6329

ID NUMBER: 656224006
FEDERAL REPORTING DATE: 08/01
AREAS OF INTEREST: Community, Education, Health, Medicine, Religion, Research, Scholarships, Social Services, Sports & Athletics
CURRENT ASSETS: $134,709 PRIOR ASSETS: $140,068
TOTAL AMOUNT AWARDED: $10,697
HIGH: $4,000--Bet Shira Congregation
MID: $2,000--UM Law School
LOW: $18--Pride Of Judea
GRANTS AWARDS: Bet Shira Sisterhood--$100, Rabbi's Descretionary Fund--$1,325, North Shore Hebrew Academy--$250, Ransom Everglades School--$250, Greater Miami Jewish Federation--$750, Miami Children's Hospital--$200, Habatit for Humanity--$100, Main Idea--$200
SERVICE AREA: Miami, FL, NY, ME
COMMENTS: Gives to selected organizations.
DEADLINES: None
OFFICERS: Deutsch, Steven K., T; Deutsch, Iane D., T

DEVOE, DICK BUICK CADILLAC SCHOLARSHIP FUND

2601 AIRPORT RD.
NAPLES, FL 34112
941-417-4106

ID NUMBER: 237296264
FEDERAL REPORTING DATE: 08/01
AREAS OF INTEREST: Scholarships
CURRENT ASSETS: $143,386 PRIOR ASSETS: $213,366
TOTAL AMOUNT AWARDED: $78,662
HIGH: $7,067--Individual
MID: $1,500--Individual
LOW: $500--Individual
GRANTS AWARDS: N/A
SERVICE AREA: Naples
COMMENTS: Students must be graduates of Naples High School and monies must be used for college education. Contact the Guidance Department, Naples High School, Naples, FL 3394. Phone: 941-261-3538. Submit written request stating name, address, extracurricular activities, honors/awards. State test score GPA, class rank, demonstrate need. FL Prepaid College Fdn.
DEADLINES: None
OFFICERS: Devoe, Barbara J., Advisory Committee; Devoe, Mark A., Advisory Committee; Halprin, Carol, Advisory Committee

DEYOUNG, MURRAY EDUCATIONAL FOUNDATION, INC.
P.O. BOX 522667
MARATHON SHORES, FL 33052-2667

ID NUMBER: 592758439
FEDERAL REPORTING DATE: 06/02
AREAS OF INTEREST: Education, Scholarships
CURRENT ASSETS: $927,745 PRIOR ASSETS:
$914,214
TOTAL AMOUNT AWARDED: $34,500
HIGH: $10,000--Exuma Educational Resource Ctr.
MID: $8,000--Individual
LOW: $2,000--Individual
GRANTS AWARDS: Individual--$7,000, Individual--$3,500,
Individual--$4,000
SERVICE AREA: National
COMMENTS: Submit a "Request for Financial Aid" form.
Awards based on income, obligations, net worth and
recommendations from teachers, counselors and welfare
agencies.
DEADLINES: None
OFFICERS: DeYoung, Murray, P; Matthews, Tom, VP;
Cody, Trinity, S/T

DIXON, ALTHEA M. EDUCATIONAL FUND
7605 MOKENA CT.
NEW PT. RICHEY, FL 34654-5659
727-849-8060

ID NUMBER: 596995341
FEDERAL REPORTING DATE: 04/99
AREAS OF INTEREST: Scholarships
CURRENT ASSETS: $65,374 PRIOR ASSETS: $63,453
TOTAL AMOUNT AWARDED: $1,500
HIGH: $1,500--Individual
GRANTS AWARDS: N/A
SERVICE AREA: MA
COMMENTS: Women, Senior or Graduate of Quaboag
Regional High School. Accepted to full time program at
accredited institution of higher learning.
DEADLINES: 05/15
OFFICERS: Golub, Marjorie M., T

DODWAY TUW, JOAN M. SCHOLARSHIP FUND
410 S. LINCOLN AVE.
CLEARWATER, FL 33756-5826
727-441-4516

ID NUMBER: 597120241
FEDERAL REPORTING DATE: 07/01
AREAS OF INTEREST: Scholarships
CURRENT ASSETS: $180,741 PRIOR ASSETS:
$179,077
TOTAL AMOUNT AWARDED: $5,538
HIGH: $5,214--Individual
GRANTS AWARDS: N/A
COMMENTS: Gives to preselected organizations.
DEADLINES: N/A

DRISCOLL FOUNDATION, INC.
12555 ORANGE DR., STE. 101
DAVIE, FL 33330-0716
954-862-1428

ID NUMBER: 591142501
FEDERAL REPORTING DATE: 05/02
AREAS OF INTEREST: Arts & Culture, Education,
Environment, Health, Religion, Scholarships
CURRENT ASSETS: $3,820,555 PRIOR ASSETS:
$4,152,398
TOTAL AMOUNT AWARDED: $189,000
HIGH: $109,673--Yale Univ.
MID: $50,000--United Way of St. Paul
LOW: $1,000--Chatham Hall
GRANTS AWARDS: Thomas Irvine Dodge Nature Ctr.--
$5,000, Ducks Unlimited--$1,000, Family Foundation of NA--
$1,000, Family Service of Greater St. Paul--$1,000, James J.
Hill Reference Library--$1,000, House of Hope Presbyterian
Church--$5,000, Macalester College--$1,000, Minneapolis
College of Art & Design--$1,000, Minneapolis Institute of
Arts--$826, Minnesota Museum of American Art--$1,000,
Minnesota Historical Society--$1,000, Ramsey County
Historical Society--$1,000, Science Museum of Minnesota--
$1,000, United Negro College Fund--$2,500, Vassar College--
$1,000
SERVICE AREA: National
COMMENTS: Written requests should be sent to W. John
Driscoll, President, Driscoll Foundation, Inc. 332 Minesota
Street, Suite 2100,. St. Paul, MN. 55101-1308. Include a
statement of the purpose of the project and a complete budget.
Include tax exemption issued by IRS, and private foundation
status.
DEADLINES: None
OFFICERS: Driscoll, W. John, P/D; Gardner, Frank C., VP;
Giefer, Michael J., S/T; Driscoll, Rudolph W., D; Driscoll,
John B., D

DUNBAR, HOWARD W. SCHOLARSHIP TRUST A
C/O SUNTRUST BANK
P. O. BOX 14728
FORT LAUDERDALE, FL 33302
954-759-7800

ID NUMBER: 656000044
FEDERAL REPORTING DATE: 10/01
AREAS OF INTEREST: Education, Scholarships
CURRENT ASSETS: $578,913 PRIOR ASSETS:
$537,928
TOTAL AMOUNT AWARDED: $24,200
HIGH: $3,000--Individual
MID: $2,600--Individual
LOW: $2,200--Individual
GRANTS AWARDS: N/A
SERVICE AREA: National
DEADLINES: None
OFFICERS: SunTrust Bank, South Florida, TR

DUNSPAUGH-DALTON FOUNDATION
1533 SUNSET DR., STE. 150
CORAL GABLES, FL 33143
305-668-4192

ID NUMBER: 591055300

FEDERAL REPORTING DATE: 11/01
AREAS OF INTEREST: Arts & Culture, Education,
Environment, Health, Medicine, Religion, Scholarships, Social
Services, Sports & Athletics
CURRENT ASSETS: $54,397,309 PRIOR ASSETS:
$68,346,567
TOTAL AMOUNT AWARDED: $2,059,700
HIGH: $312,000--Barry Univ.
MID: $105,000--Shake-A-Leg
LOW: $2,000--New Horizons for Community Bound
GRANTS AWARDS: 88.1 KLON--$6,000, Above the Line--
$10,000, American Cancer Society of Florida--$5,000,
American National Red Cross-Miami--$20,000, Baptist Health
Systems of South Florida--$35,000, Bayview Children's Ctr.--
$3,000, Beacon House--$10,000, Big Brothers Big Sisters of
Greater Miami, Inc.--$5,000, Big Brothers Big Sisters of
Monterey Co.--$3,000, Boy Scouts of America-South Florida--
$10,000, Boys & Girls Club of Miami, Inc.--$10,000, Boys &
Girls Club of Monterey Peninsula--$25,000, Camillus House,
Inc.--$15,000, Campolindo High School--$3,000, Carmel-By-
The-Sea Sunset Ctr.--$100,000
SERVICE AREA: Miami, FL, N.C., CA
COMMENTS: Gives mainly to USA, territories, religious,
educational, & or scientific purposes. Applications should
include name, address, project name, & IRS exeption number.
DEADLINES: None
OFFICERS: Lane, William A., P; Wakefield, Thomas H.,
S/T; Bonner, Sarah H., VP

DUPONT, ALFRED I. FOUNDATION

1650 PRUDENTIAL DR., STE 302
JACKSONVILLE, FL 32207
904-858-3123

ID NUMBER: 591297267
FEDERAL REPORTING DATE: 05/02
AREAS OF INTEREST: Arts & Culture, Community,
Education, Environment, Health, Medicine, Religion,
Research, Scholarships, Social Services, Sports & Athletics,
Other
CURRENT ASSETS: $33,537,890 PRIOR ASSETS:
$35,168,606
TOTAL AMOUNT AWARDED: $976,289
HIGH: $75,000--Macarthur School Family Assistance
MID: $35,000--Stetson Univ.
LOW: $150--Individual
GRANTS AWARDS: Alger Sullivan Historical Society--
$5,000, All Saints Catholic Nursing Home & Rehab Ctr--
$5,000, American Red Cross--$15,000, Anchroage Children's
Home--$10,000, BETA, Inc.--$20,000, Beaches Area
Historical Society--$3,000, Big Bend Hospice Fdn.--$10,000,
Cerebral Palsy of NE FL.--$5,000, Children's Hospital at
Strong Univ.--$7,500, Chipola Junior College--$50,000, Christ
the King School--$5,000, Delaware Symphony Assn.--$12,500,
Easter Seal Rehab Ctr., Inc.--$5,000, Dreams Come True--
$10,000, Flagler College--$30,000
SERVICE AREA: National
COMMENTS: After receiving request, forms will by mailed.
Individual grants are generally limited to elderly individuals
residing in the Southeastern United States who are in distressed
economic situations. Send applications to Rosemary C. WIllis
at 4600 Touchton Rd., Bldg 200, Ste. 120, Jacksonville, FL.
32246.
DEADLINES: None
OFFICERS: Nedley, R.E., P/T; Carlson, W.W., VP;
Brownlie, E.C., VP; Wills, Rosemary C., S

EBBA ALM EDUCATIONAL FUND

C/O SUNTRUST BANK OF TAMPA BAY
825 BROADWAY
DUNEDIN, FL 34698
727-736-7231

ID NUMBER: 510225186
FEDERAL REPORTING DATE: 03/02
AREAS OF INTEREST: Scholarships
CURRENT ASSETS: $342,553 PRIOR ASSETS:
$364,290
TOTAL AMOUNT AWARDED: $20,066
HIGH: $4,195--Individual
MID: $2,078--Individual
LOW: $800--Individual
GRANTS AWARDS: N/A
DEADLINES: None
OFFICERS: Suntrust Bank of Tampa Bay, TR

EDNEY, T.H. T/U/W SCHOLARSHIP

C/O BANK OF AMERICA
815 BEAL PKWY., N.W.
FT. WALTON BEACH, FL 32547
850-664-9585

ID NUMBER: 596217862
FEDERAL REPORTING DATE: 05/02
AREAS OF INTEREST: Scholarships
CURRENT ASSETS: $124,375 PRIOR ASSETS:
$125,748
TOTAL AMOUNT AWARDED: $5,430
HIGH: $500--Individual
MID: $250--Individual
LOW: $175--Individual
GRANTS AWARDS: Individual--$500, Individual--$450,
Individual--$250, Individual--$350, Individual--$350,
Individual--$260, Individual--$175, Individual--$250
SERVICE AREA: Okaloosa County, Walton County, FL, AK,
NC
COMMENTS: Apply by letter and interview. Contact Jerry
Parker, P.O. Box 1325, Crestview, FL 32536. Preferably
Okaloosa and Walton County residents persuant to trust
document.
DEADLINES: None
OFFICERS: Bank of America N.A., TR

EL-MAHDAWY, AHMED M. & FAWZIA A. FOUNDATION

P. O. BOX 141808
GAINESVILLE, FL 32614-1808
321-729-0116

ID NUMBER: 593412308
FEDERAL REPORTING DATE: 09/01
AREAS OF INTEREST: Community, Education,
Environment, Religion, Scholarships, Social Services
CURRENT ASSETS: $780,000 PRIOR ASSETS: $0
TOTAL AMOUNT AWARDED: $121,097
HIGH: $6,000--Al-Markazul Islami
MID: $1,000--Islamic American University
LOW: $45--Individual
GRANTS AWARDS: N/A
SERVICE AREA: National
DEADLINES: None
OFFICERS: El-Mahdawy, Ahmed M., P; El-Mahdawy,
Fawzia A., S; El-Mahdawy, Ahmed E., D

ENDICOTT, SAMUEL C. FUND

P. O. BOX 2242
PALM BEACH, FL 33480
561-802-4451

ID NUMBER: 46124121
FEDERAL REPORTING DATE: 05/02
AREAS OF INTEREST: Arts & Culture, Scholarships
CURRENT ASSETS: $377,920 **PRIOR ASSETS:**
$398,975
TOTAL AMOUNT AWARDED: $30,000
HIGH: $10,000--Boston Ballet
MID: $10,000--Indian Hill Music Center
LOW: $5,000--Boston Baroque
GRANTS AWARDS: Palm Beach Opera--$5,000
SERVICE AREA: National
COMMENTS: Applications should include a Grant Request
Form, Purpose of Request, History of the organization and
Tax-Exempt status. Application should be addressed to:
Norman Burwen, P.O. Box 2242, Palm Beach FL 33480 (561-
802-4451.
DEADLINES: None
OFFICERS: Burwen, Norman, TR; Endicott, Priscilla, TR;
Potter, Priscilla, TR

ENGLEWOOD BPO ELKS SCHOLARSHIP TRUST

401 N. INDIANA AVE.
ENGLEWOOD, FL 34223
941-474-1404

ID NUMBER: 596687568
FEDERAL REPORTING DATE: 10/01
AREAS OF INTEREST: Scholarships
CURRENT ASSETS: $221 **PRIOR ASSETS:** $215
TOTAL AMOUNT AWARDED: $13,500
HIGH: $1,500--Individual
MID: $1,500--Individual
LOW: $1,500--Individual
GRANTS AWARDS: N/A
DEADLINES: N/A
OFFICERS: Sun Trust Bank, Gulf Coast, TR

EPSTEIN, DONALD & LOUISE FOUNDATION, INC.

2800 PONCE DE LEON BLVD., STE. 1125
CORAL GABLES, FL 33134-6912
305-445-0707

ID NUMBER: 650175116
FEDERAL REPORTING DATE: 07/01
AREAS OF INTEREST: Education, Scholarships
CURRENT ASSETS: $109,893 **PRIOR ASSETS:** $96,187
TOTAL AMOUNT AWARDED: $5,000
HIGH: $3,000--Fruitland Primary School Salisbury
MID: $2,000--Kenyon College, OH
LOW: $100--Walters Art Galery
GRANTS AWARDS: Enoch Pratt Library--$500
SERVICE AREA: MD, OH
COMMENTS: Submit application to Robert Breier, C/O
Breier and Seif, P.A., 132 South Dixie Highway, Coral Gables,
FL 33146-2986
DEADLINES: None
OFFICERS: Epstein, Louise, T; Epstein, Daniel Mark, T

EXCHANGE CLUB OF VERO BEACH

SCHOLARSHIP FOUNDATION TRUST
P.O. BOX 1982
VERO BEACH, FL 32961
561-770-3649

ID NUMBER: 592967807
FEDERAL REPORTING DATE: 01/02
AREAS OF INTEREST: Scholarships
CURRENT ASSETS: $141,731 **PRIOR ASSETS:**
$118,357
TOTAL AMOUNT AWARDED: $10,000
HIGH: $2,000--Individual
MID: $1,500--Individual
LOW: $1,000--Individual
GRANTS AWARDS: N/A
SERVICE AREA: Indian River County, Vero Beach
COMMENTS: Limited to graduates of public high schools in
Indian River County, FL. Application form can be obtained
from Guidance Office at High Schools. Include personal
interests school activities, grades, honors, and financial need.
DEADLINES: August 1
OFFICERS: Foote, George, C; Stegenga, Stuart, T;
Wainwright, Andy, S

FALK FAMILY FOUNDATION

C/O H. FALK
316 EAGLE DR.
JUPITER, FL 33477-4066
561-575-9905

ID NUMBER: 133672704
FEDERAL REPORTING DATE: 09/01
AREAS OF INTEREST: Arts & Culture, Community,
Education, Religion, Scholarships, Social Services, Other
CURRENT ASSETS: $119,685 **PRIOR ASSETS:**
$132,181
TOTAL AMOUNT AWARDED: $17,425
HIGH: $5,000--Jewish Federation of Palm Beach
MID: $1,000--Temple Mt. Sinai
LOW: $25--Rally for the Cure
GRANTS AWARDS: Providence Alaska Fdn.--$1,000,
American Jewish Committee--$1,000, Florida Philharmonic--
$1,000, Jewish Guild for the Blind--$1,000, Reform Jewish
Appeal--$1,000, Memorial Sloan Kettering Cancer--$1,000,
Jupiter Medical Ctr.--$1,000, Norton Gallery--$1,000, Israel
Cancer Assn.--$500, Children's Charity--$300, Mayo Clinic--
$300, New York Univ.--$250, Marine Life Ctr. of Juno Beach-
-$250, Texas Hearing-Service Dogs--$200, WPBT--$200
SERVICE AREA: National
COMMENTS: Gives to preselected organizations.
DEADLINES: None
OFFICERS: Falk, Harvey, TR; Falk, Barbara, TR

FAMULARO, JOSEPH J. FOUNDATION, INC.

822 WASHINGTON ST.
KEY WEST, FL 33040-4735
212-297-4840

ID NUMBER: 650846581
FEDERAL REPORTING DATE: 08/01
AREAS OF INTEREST: Arts & Culture, Community,
Education, Health, Medicine, Religion, Scholarships, Social
Services

CURRENT ASSETS: $440,303 PRIOR ASSETS: $541,548
TOTAL AMOUNT AWARDED: $43,675
HIGH: $20,500--St. John's Roman Catholic Church
MID: $10,000--Take Stock in Children
LOW: $25--Heritage Foundation
GRANTS AWARDS: Catholic League--$100, American Lung Association of S. FL--$100, Culinary Institute of America--$500, National Legal and Policy Center--$50, Akin Hall Association--$2,600, Hartley House for Literacy--$1,200, John D. Calandra Italian-American Inst.--$500
SERVICE AREA: National
COMMENTS: Gives to preselected organizations.
DEADLINES: None
OFFICERS: Famularo, Joseph J., P/D; Abraham, Gerard S., T; Kinzer, Bernard, VP

FEICK FOUNDATION
235 CHILEAN AVE.
PALM BEACH, FL 33480

ID NUMBER: 237022609
FEDERAL REPORTING DATE: 05/99
AREAS OF INTEREST: Scholarships
CURRENT ASSETS: $30,646 PRIOR ASSETS: $33,940
TOTAL AMOUNT AWARDED: $17,601
HIGH: $17,601--The Amherst College
GRANTS AWARDS: N/A
SERVICE AREA: MA
COMMENTS: Gives to preselected organizations.
DEADLINES: None
OFFICERS: Feick, William Jr., C; Feick, Rosemary Chisholm, P; Feick, Alexander N., S

FELLOWS, J. HUGH & EARLE W. MEMORIAL FUND
P.O. BOX 12950
PENSACOLA, FL 32576
850-444-0533

ID NUMBER: 596132238
FEDERAL REPORTING DATE: 03/02
AREAS OF INTEREST: Scholarships
CURRENT ASSETS: $5,289,854 PRIOR ASSETS: $5,217,268
TOTAL AMOUNT AWARDED: $0
GRANTS AWARDS: N/A
SERVICE AREA: Escambia Cnty, FL, Okaloosa Cnty, FL, Santa Rosa Cnty, FL, Walton Cnty, FL
COMMENTS: Provides low-interest loans to students of medicine, nursing, medical technology, and theology who live in these four counties only. Submit letter of application to: Dr. Charles A. Atwell, President, Pensacola Junior College, 1000 College Blvd., Pensacola, FL 32504
DEADLINES: None
OFFICERS: Vinson, Judge Roger, Acting C; Rogers, Milton, S; Smith, H. Neal, VC; Pruit, Rev. Al, TR; Willis, Dr. Wayne, TR

FERGUSON, WALTER R. CHARITABLE FOUNDATION
2630 HILOLA ST.
MIAMI, FL 33133
305-856-4325

ID NUMBER: 656215023
FEDERAL REPORTING DATE: 03/02
AREAS OF INTEREST: Arts & Culture, Education, Religion, Scholarships
CURRENT ASSETS: $1,215,298 PRIOR ASSETS: $1,178,953
TOTAL AMOUNT AWARDED: $13,500
HIGH: $5,000--Christian Action Corporation
MID: $5,000--The Randy F. Numnicht Fund
LOW: $3,500--Friends of Steam
GRANTS AWARDS: N/A
SERVICE AREA: FL
COMMENTS: Send applications to: Walter R. Ferguson, 2630 Hilota St., Miami, Fl. 33133 (305)856-4235
DEADLINES: None
OFFICERS: Ferguson, Walter R., TR; Ferguson, Robert R., TR; Krater, Linda C., TR; Zerlin, Susan Faye, TR

FERTIC, ANNA FOUNDATION, INC.
P.O. BOX 621171
OVIEDO, FL 32762-1171
407-349-0078

ID NUMBER: 593096507
FEDERAL REPORTING DATE: 12/01
AREAS OF INTEREST: Scholarships
CURRENT ASSETS: $508,492 PRIOR ASSETS: $491,574
TOTAL AMOUNT AWARDED: $6,398
HIGH: $6,398--Valencia College
GRANTS AWARDS: N/A
SERVICE AREA: Orlando, FL
DEADLINES: None
OFFICERS: Pickford, Shirley R., P; Fertic, Volera; Asendorf, John

FINDLAY-CONSO EDUCATION FOUNDATION
5380 GULF OF MEXICO DR., BOX 407
LONGBOAT KEY, FL 34228
941-387-1258

ID NUMBER: 582315882
FEDERAL REPORTING DATE: 05/02
AREAS OF INTEREST: Education, Scholarships
CURRENT ASSETS: $437,668 PRIOR ASSETS: $494,693
TOTAL AMOUNT AWARDED: $19,457
HIGH: $8,000--Individual
MID: $4,000--Individual
LOW: $1,500--Individual
GRANTS AWARDS: N/A
SERVICE AREA: SC, MO
COMMENTS: Must be a full time employee of Conso International Corp., Meeting certain considerations or children or granchildren of that employee.
DEADLINES: Between Feb.1 & June 15 Annually
OFFICERS: Findlay, J. Cary, P/D; Findlay, Konstance J. K., VP/D; Hickman, Marcus T., S

FINLEY, ROSE MCFARLAND FOUNDATION

C/O FIRST UNION NATIONAL BANK
200 S. BISCAYNE BLVD., 14TH FL.
MIAMI, FL 33131
561-778-6104

ID NUMBER: 237414902
FEDERAL REPORTING DATE: 03/02
AREAS OF INTEREST: Scholarships
CURRENT ASSETS: $1,346,036 PRIOR ASSETS:
$1,374,674
TOTAL AMOUNT AWARDED: $153,340
HIGH: $2,000--Individual
MID: $1,000--Individual
LOW: $750--Individual
GRANTS AWARDS: N/A
SERVICE AREA: National
COMMENTS: Send applications to Rose McFarland Finley
Fdn. at 1053 Palmetto Avenue, Sebastian, FL. 32958 or call
561-589-4502.
DEADLINES: 4/1
OFFICERS: Smith, Charles, D; McComack, William Jr.,
MD, D; Waddell, Gene, D

FINO FAMILY FOUNDATION, INC.

8171 BAY COLONY DR.
NAPLES, FL 34108
941-513-1141

ID NUMBER: 223768929
FEDERAL REPORTING DATE: 05/02
AREAS OF INTEREST: Education, Health, Medicine,
Scholarships, Social Services
CURRENT ASSETS: $961,195 PRIOR ASSETS:
$1,033,050
TOTAL AMOUNT AWARDED: $48,840
HIGH: $12,000--ARC of Somerset
MID: $5,000--Hope Chest Scholarship Fund
LOW: $300--Rutgers Prep
GRANTS AWARDS: Bernardsville Time Dept.--$1,000,
College of Holy Cross--$1,000, Friends of the Shelter--$1,000,
American Cancer Society--$500, Women's Health & Counsel--
$1,000, United Way of Morris Cnty--$4,000, Revlon
Run/Walk--$600, Midland School Fdn.--$5,000, The Haines
Scholarship--$1,000, Bernardsville PBA--$500, NY Sept. 11
Neediest Cases--$1,000, Groove With Me--$500, Somerset
Medical Ctr.--$8,000, Douglas Project for Rutgers--$1,000,
Mercy Ctr.--$1,000
SERVICE AREA: National
COMMENTS: Send applications to Raymond Fino at 8171
Bay Colony Drive, Naples, FL.
DEADLINES: None
OFFICERS: Fino, Raymond, P; Fino, Sandra, VP; Fino,
Laura, D; Fino, Michelle, D

FISH, BERT FOUNDATION, INC.

P.O. BOX 46
DELAND, FL 32721
904-734-2124

ID NUMBER: 593020772
FEDERAL REPORTING DATE: 12/01
AREAS OF INTEREST: Education, Health, Medicine,
Scholarships, Social Services

CURRENT ASSETS: $7,491,751 PRIOR ASSETS:
$7,860,284
TOTAL AMOUNT AWARDED: $400,217
HIGH: $380,217--Fidelity Charitable Gift Foundation
LOW: $20,000--Florida Hospital
GRANTS AWARDS: N/A
SERVICE AREA: National
COMMENTS: Gives to preselected organizations. Scholarships
are in nursing and medical education only.
DEADLINES: None
OFFICERS: Schildecker, William, M.D., P; Renfroe, Lowell
E. TR; Master, Joseph J., VP/TR; Ward, Carl, TR; Ford,
Frank, TR; Keebler, William C., S

FISHER, FRANCENIA TRUST UNDER WILL

C/O BANK OF AMERICA
P.O. BOX 40200
JACKSONVILLE, FL 32203-0200
904-464-3664

ID NUMBER: 596884250
FEDERAL REPORTING DATE: 04/02
AREAS OF INTEREST: Education, Environment, Research,
Scholarships
CURRENT ASSETS: $200,751 PRIOR ASSETS:
$216,016
TOTAL AMOUNT AWARDED: $8,745
HIGH: $4,373--Michigan State University
MID: $2,186--International Society of Plant Pathology
LOW: $2,186--FL State University Foundation.
GRANTS AWARDS: N/A
SERVICE AREA: National
COMMENTS: Gives to preselected organizations.
DEADLINES: None
OFFICERS: Bank of America N.A., TR

FITZGERALD BROTHERS FOUNDATION, INC.

376 PIRATES BIGHT
NAPLES, FL 34103
941-434-7968

ID NUMBER: 362916459
FEDERAL REPORTING DATE: 05/02
AREAS OF INTEREST: Community, Environment,
Research, Scholarships, Sports & Athletics, Other
CURRENT ASSETS: $807,403 PRIOR ASSETS:
$823,376
TOTAL AMOUNT AWARDED: $47,000
HIGH: $7,500--Creche Holy Land
MID: $2,500--Easter Seal Society of Dade County
LOW: $1,000--The Cenacle
GRANTS AWARDS: Catholic Charities of Collier Co.--
$1,000, Habilitation Center for the Handicapped--$5,000,
Range Mental Health Ctr.--$3,500, The Joe Logsdon Fdn.--
$3,000, St. Jude Dominican Missions--$2,500, Sisters of
Mercy--$2,500, St. Mary of Providence School--$2,000, Good
Shepherd Manor--$2,000, Gabriel Home--$2,500, Casa
Jacinto y Francisco--$2,000
SERVICE AREA: National
COMMENTS: Letter should be submitted to John E.
Fitzgerald at 376 Pirates Bight, Naples, FL. 34103 (239) 434-
7968.
DEADLINES: None

OFFICERS: Fitzgerald, John E., P/D; Bogart, Mary K., S/T/D; Larish, Leslie, VP/D; Fitzgerald, Barbara, D; Fitzgerald, Brenda C., D

OFFICERS: McCulloch, Etta, C; Davison, Louise, M; Barnett, Jerry, T; Conlin, Judy, DOE Program D; Brisbin, Betty, HSE Supv.; Parcell, Rachel, State HOSA Adv.

FLORIDA AIR ACADEMY SCHOLARSHIP FUND, INC.

1950 S. ACADEMY DR.
MELBOURNE, FL 32901
321-723-3211

ID NUMBER: 591056104
FEDERAL REPORTING DATE: 11/01
AREAS OF INTEREST: Scholarships
CURRENT ASSETS: $33,977 PRIOR ASSETS: $55,465
TOTAL AMOUNT AWARDED: $10,745
HIGH: $5,000--Individual
MID: $1,000--Individual
LOW: $245--Individual
GRANTS AWARDS: N/A
SERVICE AREA: FL
COMMENTS: Send applications to: James Dwight, C/O Florida Air Academy, 1950 So. Academy Dr., Melbourne, Fl. 32901. (321)723-3211.
DEADLINES: None
OFFICERS: Dwight, James, TR; Dwight, J. Timothy, TR; Dwight, Deborah, TR

FLORIDA CARE FOUNDATION

P. O. BOX 330278
MIAMI, FL 33233
305-648-1883

ID NUMBER: 237197385
FEDERAL REPORTING DATE: 04/02
AREAS OF INTEREST: Community, Environment, Health, Religion, Scholarships, Social Services
CURRENT ASSETS: $16,764 PRIOR ASSETS: $56,155
TOTAL AMOUNT AWARDED: $90,610
HIGH: $21,195--Preservation Environment Rec. Comm. Inc.
MID: $1,000--Bahamas Mission Miami
LOW: $100--United Way, Miami
GRANTS AWARDS: One World Adoption--$9,000
SERVICE AREA: National
COMMENTS: Gives to preselected organizations.
DEADLINES: None
OFFICERS: Sochet, Ira, P/T; Karter, Harvey, M; Sochet, Laura, S

FLORIDA HEALTH OCCUPATIONS

C/O DEPARTMENT OF EDUCATION
325 W. GAINES ST., RM. 1102
TALLAHASSEE, FL 32399-6533
850-488-3473

ID NUMBER: 592638981
FEDERAL REPORTING DATE: 12/99
AREAS OF INTEREST: Scholarships
CURRENT ASSETS: $66,303 PRIOR ASSETS: $66,089
TOTAL AMOUNT AWARDED: $4,000
HIGH: $4,000--H.O.S.A. Student
GRANTS AWARDS: N/A
COMMENTS: Must be H.O.S.A. Member. Scholarship for education only. Application sent to Mr. Jerry Barnett, Room 730 325 West Gaines Street, Tallahassee, FL 32399-0400
DEADLINES: None

FLORIDA LAND SURVEYORS SCHOLARSHIP FOUNDATION, INC.

1689A MAHAN CTR. BLVD.
TALLAHASSEE, FL 32308
850-942-1900

ID NUMBER: 596209248
FEDERAL REPORTING DATE: 12/01
AREAS OF INTEREST: Scholarships
CURRENT ASSETS: $0 PRIOR ASSETS: $27,610
TOTAL AMOUNT AWARDED: $500
HIGH: $500--Individual
GRANTS AWARDS: N/A
COMMENTS: Application form should be requested from the fdn. Send applications to: Marilyn C. Evers, 1689A, Mahan Ctr. Blvd., Tallahassee, Fl. 32308.
DEADLINES: April 30
OFFICERS: Mastronicola, Arthur A., P; Bush, Louie G., VP; Reynolds, Joseph L., S; Nobles, Allen K., T

FOCARDI GREAT BAY FOUNDATION

2310 STARKEY RD.
LARGO, FL 33771

ID NUMBER: 592752893
FEDERAL REPORTING DATE: 05/02
AREAS OF INTEREST: Community, Education, Health, Religion, Scholarships, Social Services
CURRENT ASSETS: $492,889 PRIOR ASSETS: $590,859
TOTAL AMOUNT AWARDED: $112,150
HIGH: $30,000--YMCA of St. Petersburg
MID: $5,000--Eckerd College
LOW: $100--Friends of Florida Botanical Garden
GRANTS AWARDS: Abilities--$1,000, Academy Prep.--$500, Admiral Faragut--$3,000, All Children's Hospital--$5,000, Alpha House--$500, American Heart Assn.--$500, American Lung Assn.--$400, Arthritis Fdn.--$350, Art Ctr.--$400, Boy Scouts--$500, Boys & Girls Club--$3,000, Bravo--$250, Camp Endevor--$300, CASA--$600, Catholic Education--$1,000
SERVICE AREA: National
COMMENTS: Written application with explanation of Charitable function.
DEADLINES: None
OFFICERS: Focardi, Claude, TR; Focardi, Nina M., TR; Sokolowshi, Claudia, TR; Petrini, Ronald, TR

FORBES, MARY C. CHARITABLE FOUNDATION

101 PAAEDENA AVE., S., STE. 1
SOUTH PASADENA, FL 33701
727-892-3131

ID NUMBER: 597112797
FEDERAL REPORTING DATE: 11/01
AREAS OF INTEREST: Education, Religion, Scholarships

CURRENT ASSETS: $6,703,776 PRIOR ASSETS:
$7,014,649
TOTAL AMOUNT AWARDED: $427,669
HIGH: $65,145--Transfiguration Parish School
MID: $26,100--Pope John Paul School
LOW: $250--Individual
GRANTS AWARDS: Academy of Holy Names--$2,500,
Bishop Larkin Catholic School--$19,400, Blessed Sacrament
School--$4,450, Brendan Prendergast--$500, Catholic Univer
of Amer.--$5,000, Christian Brothers Univer.--$1,500,
Clearwater Brothers Univ.--$1,500, Collegio St. Isidoro--
$1,500, Franciscan Univ.--$5,000, Guardian Angels Catholic--
$4,275, Holy Family Catholic School--$11,400, Holy Name
School--$27,850, Incarnation Catholic School--$9,400, John
Carroll Univ.--$3,500, Mary Help of Christians--$500
SERVICE AREA: FL.
COMMENTS: Gives to preselected organizations.
DEADLINES: None
OFFICERS: Clarie, D'arcy R., TR

FORD, KATHLEEN DUROSS FUND
C/O CHOPIN & MILLER
505 S. FLAGLER DR., STE. 300
WEST PALM BEACH, FL 33401
561-655-9500

ID NUMBER: 650088771
FEDERAL REPORTING DATE: 05/01
AREAS OF INTEREST: Arts & Culture, Community,
Education, Medicine, Religion, Scholarships, Social Services,
Sports & Athletics
CURRENT ASSETS: $3,764,866 PRIOR ASSETS:
$3,324,843
TOTAL AMOUNT AWARDED: $128,630
HIGH: $100,000--Henry Ford II Scholarship
MID: $6,000--First Care
LOW: $20--The Tuesday Musicale
GRANTS AWARDS: Adopt-A-Family--$5,000, Preservation
Foundation--$500, WPBT2--$150, Neiman Marcus Charity
Gala--$1,200, Salvation Army--$100, Alzheimers Community
Care--$3,000, The Arc of Palm Beach County--$6,000
SERVICE AREA: West Palm Beach, National
COMMENTS: Submit written documents or letters indicating
purpose of charity and how funds will be used.
DEADLINES: None
OFFICERS: Ford, Kathleen DuRoss, P; Chopin, L. Frank, D

FOREMAN, MYRON JACOB U.S.
SCHOLARSHIP TRUST
560 VILLAGE BLVD., STE. 335
WEST PALM BEACH, FL 33409
561-686-1110

ID NUMBER: 656186928
FEDERAL REPORTING DATE: 11/01
AREAS OF INTEREST: Scholarships
CURRENT ASSETS: $1,009,346 PRIOR ASSETS:
$1,025,750
TOTAL AMOUNT AWARDED: $45,695
HIGH: $8,962--Individual
MID: $1,800--Individual
LOW: $500--Individual
GRANTS AWARDS: N/A
DEADLINES: N/A
OFFICERS: Boozer, Rufus Lee, TR; Sellari, Gary B., TR;
Cameron, Colin M., TR

FORREST, THOMAS W.
FOUNDATION
C/O JACK SHOEMAKE
6908 ARBOR OAKS CT.
BRADENTON, FL 34209
941-746-2887

ID NUMBER: 650039416
FEDERAL REPORTING DATE: 05/02
AREAS OF INTEREST: Scholarships
CURRENT ASSETS: $129,586 PRIOR ASSETS:
$125,890
TOTAL AMOUNT AWARDED: $2,700
HIGH: $2,700--Individual
GRANTS AWARDS: N/A
COMMENTS: Funds for educational assistance to qualified
candidates entering ministry or church vocations. Write to Jack
Shoemake for application.
DEADLINES: None
OFFICERS: Forrest, Jacquelyn, S/T; Forrest, Robert R., D;
Shoemake, Jack, P; Mills, Dr. Virgil, VP; Forrest, Doris, D

FOUNDATION FOR THE
ADVANCEMENT OF
MESOAMERICAN STUDIES, INC.
268 S. SUNCOAST BLVD.
CRYSTAL RIVER, FL 34429
352-795-5990

ID NUMBER: 593195520
FEDERAL REPORTING DATE: 11/01
AREAS OF INTEREST: Arts & Culture, Education, Research,
Scholarships, Social Services
CURRENT ASSETS: $235,659 PRIOR ASSETS:
$323,961
TOTAL AMOUNT AWARDED: $289,293
HIGH: $24,000--Individual
MID: $13,800--Individual
LOW: $467--Individual
GRANTS AWARDS: N/A
SERVICE AREA: National, International
COMMENTS: Grants awarded to projects concerning ancient
cultures of Belize, El Salvador, Guatemala, Honduras &
Mexico.
DEADLINES: September 15
OFFICERS: Ranieri, Lewis S., D/C/P; Ranieri, Margaret D.,
D/VP; Noble, Sandra, ED/S; Diehl, Richard, D; Reents-Budet,
Dorie, D; Barbera, Elizabeth, D/T

FROST, LINCOLN & ELIZABETH
C/O LINCOLN J. FROST, SR.
P.O. BOX 333
EVERGLADES CITY, FL 34139-0333
941-695-3333

ID NUMBER: 593510429
FEDERAL REPORTING DATE: 03/02
AREAS OF INTEREST: Education, Scholarships
CURRENT ASSETS: $30,143 PRIOR ASSETS: $27,450
TOTAL AMOUNT AWARDED: $2,500
HIGH: $1,000--Individual
MID: $1,000--Individual
LOW: $500--Individual
GRANTS AWARDS: N/A
COMMENTS: Gives to preselected organizations.

FRY FOUNDATION, INC.

4919 GARDENGATE LANE
ORLANDO, FL 32821-8251
407-345-1030

ID NUMBER: 593547265
FEDERAL REPORTING DATE: 06/02
AREAS OF INTEREST: Scholarships
CURRENT ASSETS: $325,055 PRIOR ASSETS:
$268,834
TOTAL AMOUNT AWARDED: $17,000
HIGH: $17,000--Pine Castle Christian Academy
GRANTS AWARDS: N/A
SERVICE AREA: Orlando, FL.
COMMENTS: Gives to preselected organizations.
DEADLINES: None
OFFICERS: Fry, William S., P; Fry, Alletha K., VP

FT. PIERCE MEMORIAL HOSPITAL SCHOLARSHIP FOUNDATION

1420 S.W. ST. LUCIE W. BLVD, STE. 105
PT. ST. LUCIE, FL 34986
561-461-4747

ID NUMBER: 590651084
FEDERAL REPORTING DATE: 07/01
AREAS OF INTEREST: Scholarships
CURRENT ASSETS: $6,243,162 PRIOR ASSETS:
$5,849,276
TOTAL AMOUNT AWARDED: $292,207
HIGH: $164,071--IRRC 2-yr Scholarships
MID: $10,000--Individual
LOW: $6,000--Individual
GRANTS AWARDS: N/A
SERVICE AREA: St. Lucie
COMMENTS: Scholarship program student must follow a
course of study leading to a career in the medical field. Must be
a Bona Fide resident of St. Lucie County, FL, unmarried
(unless a graduate student). Indigent Care Program only
available to qualifying indigent children.
DEADLINES: None
OFFICERS: King, Basil, CH; Cambron, C. Robert, M.D.,
CH; Johnson, Frederick T., S/T; Vogel, Bill, M; Gates, Philip
C., Sr., M; Fee, Frank H., III, M

FUNKHOUSER, FRED O. CHARITABLE FOUNDATION

2122 DEVONSHIRE WAY
PALM BEACH GARDENS, FL 33418
561-625-6692

ID NUMBER: 656243936
FEDERAL REPORTING DATE: 11/01
AREAS OF INTEREST: Education, Health, Scholarships
CURRENT ASSETS: $1,484,516 PRIOR ASSETS:
$1,713,852
TOTAL AMOUNT AWARDED: $260,000
HIGH: $250,000--Bridgewater College
MID: $10,000--Leukemia Society of America
GRANTS AWARDS: N/A
SERVICE AREA: VA, FL
COMMENTS: Gives to preselected organizations.

FUSST, JOHANN COMMUNITY LIBRARY

508 N. INDIANA AVE.
ENGLEWOOD, FL 34223-2704
941-964-2488

ID NUMBER: 590861994
FEDERAL REPORTING DATE: 05/01
AREAS OF INTEREST: Scholarships
CURRENT ASSETS: $2,891,701 PRIOR ASSETS:
$2,350,313
TOTAL AMOUNT AWARDED: $51,039
HIGH: $5,000--Individual
MID: $5,000--Individual
LOW: $41,039--Contributions less than $5000
GRANTS AWARDS: N/A
SERVICE AREA: Englewood, FL
COMMENTS: Funds available for graduating students of local
H.S. for tuition expenses. Applications must include a letter of
interview, the college to be attended and school transcripts
DEADLINES: None
OFFICERS: Burcham, Mr. Thomas, P; Hanley, Mrs. William,
VP; Cost, Mrs. Pansy P., S; Cutter, Mrs. Ladd, D; Csank, Mr.
Paul, D; Hooker, Mrs. Donald, D

FYFE FAMILY FOUNDATION, INC.

105 NEW YORK AVE.
LYNN HAVEN, FL 32444

ID NUMBER: 311579575
FEDERAL REPORTING DATE: 05/01
AREAS OF INTEREST: Education, Religion, Scholarships,
Social Services
CURRENT ASSETS: $162,483 PRIOR ASSETS:
$129,274
TOTAL AMOUNT AWARDED: $24,000
HIGH: $10,000--Life Management Center
MID: $5,000--Gulf Coast Children's Advocacy
LOW: $1,500--Widow Person's Services
GRANTS AWARDS: Gulf Yachting Association Fdn.--
$5,000, Lynn Haven Elementary School--$2,500
SERVICE AREA: FL
COMMENTS: Gives to preselected organizations.
DEADLINES: None
OFFICERS: Beck, Karen E., P; Freeman, Robin F., VP;
Dusseault, Brian, T

GAMMA ETA EDUCATIONAL FOUNDATION, INC.

2246 MONAGHAN DR.
TALLAHASSEE, FL 32308
850-222-9250

ID NUMBER: 593338740
FEDERAL REPORTING DATE: 11/01
AREAS OF INTEREST: Scholarships
CURRENT ASSETS: $42,828 PRIOR ASSETS: $41,834
TOTAL AMOUNT AWARDED: $1,500
HIGH: $500--Individual
MID: $500--Individual
LOW: $500--Individual
GRANTS AWARDS: N/A

COMMENTS: Submit a written, two page, application including type of degree, college transcript(s), letters of recomendation, extracurricular activities and jobs held.
DEADLINES: August 15th
OFFICERS: Yearty, John A., P; Ruff, P. Michael, VP; Murray, E. Edward, Jr., S; Clements, Merritt E., Jr., T

GARNER FOUNDATION
333 N.E. 23RD ST.
MIAMI, FL 33137
305-759-7800

ID NUMBER: 311471961
FEDERAL REPORTING DATE: 08/01
AREAS OF INTEREST: Arts & Culture, Community, Education, Environment, Medicine, Religion, Research, Scholarships
CURRENT ASSETS: $6,563,035 PRIOR ASSETS: $6,842,927
TOTAL AMOUNT AWARDED: $690,650
HIGH: $105,700--Barry University
MID: $50,000--Miami Country Day School
LOW: $500--Cummer Museum
GRANTS AWARDS: American Red Cross--$5,000, Bay Oaks Miami Soroptimist Home--$50,000, Betty Griffin House--$10,000, Carrolton School--$1,000, Community Partnership for Homeless, Inc.--$30,000, Cushman School--$50,000, Epilepsy Foundation of South Florida--$10,000, FIU--$5,000, Forman School--$1,000, Highlands-Cashiers Hospital, Inc.--$25,000, Jacksonville Symphony--$21,500
SERVICE AREA: FL, VA, NC, CT
COMMENTS: Since the above filing, additional gifts of $100,000 each have been given to Barry U. and Miami Country Day School.
DEADLINES: None
OFFICERS: Garner, Alberta W., P/D; Garner, John M., VP/D; Garner, Beverly G., VP/D; Moore, James W., S/D; Paulk, Kathryn A., T/D; Moore, Gerald W., D

GARRIDO FOUNDATION, INC.
8105 N.W. 77TH ST.
MIAMI, FL 33166
305-591-1111

ID NUMBER: 586057053
FEDERAL REPORTING DATE: 06/02
AREAS OF INTEREST: Education, Scholarships
CURRENT ASSETS: $18,729 PRIOR ASSETS: $9,904
TOTAL AMOUNT AWARDED: $71,250
HIGH: $44,890--Belen School
MID: $5,252--Epiphany School
LOW: $200--UNCT College Fund
GRANTS AWARDS: Killian Oaks--$4,350, St. Agatha Catholic Church--$4,358, ACU Church--$1,200, Lega Contra Cancer--$5,000, St. Agustin Church--$4,300, Obispado De Sta Clara--$1,000, Radio Paz--$250, Daughters of Charity--$200, Legionares of Christ--$250
COMMENTS: Applications should include information about the nature of the applicant's organization. Send applications to: Jose A. Garrido, 8105 N.W. 77 St., Miami, Fl. 33166 (305)591-1111.
DEADLINES: None
OFFICERS: Garrido, Jose A., P; Garrido, Jose A., Jr.; Morales, Manuel, Jr.; Garrido, Zady

GATEWOOD, MARILYN W. & ROBERT P. FOUNDATION
6 LOGGERHEAD LN.
MANALAPAN, FL 33462
561-582-9747

ID NUMBER: 521642251
FEDERAL REPORTING DATE: 02/02
AREAS OF INTEREST: Arts & Culture, Community, Education, Health, Medicine, Religion, Scholarships, Social Services
CURRENT ASSETS: $24,160 PRIOR ASSETS: $26,883
TOTAL AMOUNT AWARDED: $18,808
HIGH: $5,535--Roseaire Retreat, Inc.
MID: $2,450--St. Vincent Ferrer Catholic Church
LOW: $25--Delray Beach Historical Society
GRANTS AWARDS: Palm Trail, Inc.--$500, Raymond F. Kravis Center--$1,000, Sovereign Military Order of Malta--$850, Delray Beach Literary Society--$420, Old School Square, Inc.--$150, Kingsland Foundation--$500, Nortton Gallery and School of Art--$75,100, St Lucy Catholic Church--$2,300, Palm Beach Pops--$903, Archdiocese of Palm Beach--$2,000, Holy Spirit Catholic Church--$2,100
SERVICE AREA: FL, ML, DC, CA, NY
COMMENTS: Gives to preselected organizations.
DEADLINES: None
OFFICERS: Gatewood, Marilyn W., D/P/TR; Gatewood, Robert P., D/P/TR; Gatewood, John G., D/P/TR; Gatewood, Robert P., Jr., D/P/TR

GERRITS, MICHAEL FOUNDATION, INC.
3501 N.W. 2ND AVE.
MIAMI, FL 33137
305-573-2465

ID NUMBER: 650637340
FEDERAL REPORTING DATE: 05/02
AREAS OF INTEREST: Education, Health, Scholarships
CURRENT ASSETS: $335 PRIOR ASSETS: $2,311
TOTAL AMOUNT AWARDED: $11,900
HIGH: $10,000--Babson College
MID: $1,500--Individual
LOW: $100--American Cancer Society
GRANTS AWARDS: Indivudial--$300
SERVICE AREA: FL, National
COMMENTS: Send scholarship application to The Michael Gerrits Fdn. at 3501 N.W. 2nd Avenue, Miami, FL. 33137. Applications are completed and returned by mail with official transcript and one letyter of recomendation.
DEADLINES: March 31
OFFICERS: Gerrits, Michael, P; Broussard, Meredith, VP; Neiman, Jan S., S

GERSON, B. MILFRED TRUST
666 71ST ST.
MIAMI BEACH, FL 33141
305-868-3600

ID NUMBER: 596473286
FEDERAL REPORTING DATE: 03/02
AREAS OF INTEREST: Arts & Culture, Community, Education, Environment, Health, Medicine, Religion, Research, Scholarships, Social Services, Sports & Athletics
CURRENT ASSETS: $2,181,411 PRIOR ASSETS: $2,798,985

TOTAL AMOUNT AWARDED: $766,997
HIGH: $260,405--Greater Miami Jewish Federation
MID: $56,850--Temple Emanu-El
LOW: $20--Council of Indian Nations
GRANTS AWARDS: JCC Maccabi Games--$1,000, Beth David Congregation--$10,248, Alzheimer's Assn.--$20, Florida Grand Opera--$18,770, University of Florida Foundation, Inc.--$86,520, University of Miami Hurricanes Club--$500, American Cancer Society--$100, American Heart Assn.--$100, Miami City Ballet--$2,500, American Jewish Congress--$200, American Red Cross--$100, Kids Ecology Corps--$2,400, Anti-Defamation League--$3,500, Audubon of Florida--$100, Bar-Ilan Univ.--$1,250
SERVICE AREA: National
COMMENTS: Submit letter and description of charitable function if not self evident.
DEADLINES: None
OFFICERS: Gerson, Gary R.; Cypen, Irving

GEYER, MICHAEL E. EDUCATIONAL FOUNDATION

C/O BANK OF AMERICA,
P. O. BOX 40200, MC FL9-100-10-19
JACKSONVILLE, FL 32203-0200
877-446-1410

ID NUMBER: 596554900
FEDERAL REPORTING DATE: 11/01
AREAS OF INTEREST: Scholarships
CURRENT ASSETS: $89,273 **PRIOR ASSETS:** $93,187
TOTAL AMOUNT AWARDED: $3,500
HIGH: $3,500--Florida Atlantic Univ. (Individual)
GRANTS AWARDS: N/A
COMMENTS: Letter form detailing scholastic abilities. Send applications to: First Lutheran Church, Attn: Reverend Grimm, 441 NE 3rd Ave., Ft. Lauderdale, Fl. 33301-3233.
DEADLINES: None
OFFICERS: Bank of America, TR

GLAUBINGER FOUNDATION

437 GOLDEN ISLE DR.
HALLANDALE BEACH, FL 33009

ID NUMBER: 592862615
FEDERAL REPORTING DATE: 08/01
AREAS OF INTEREST: Education, Scholarships
CURRENT ASSETS: $3,819,297 **PRIOR ASSETS:** $3,597,718
TOTAL AMOUNT AWARDED: $230,299
HIGH: $105,500--Indiana Univ. Scholarship Fnd
MID: $87,504--Trustees of Columbia University
LOW: $1,363--University Laval
GRANTS AWARDS: College of Staten Island--$1,477, Jemicy School--$13,750, McGill Univeristy--$3,028, Suny Albany--$9,952
SERVICE AREA: IN, NY
COMMENTS: Gives to preselected organizations.
DEADLINES: None
OFFICERS: Glaubinger, Lawrence D., TR; Jordan, James E., TR; Glaubinger, Jane, TR; Glaubinger, Lucienne M., TR

GLIMPSE, HELEN P. CHARITABLE FOUNDATION

C/O BANK OF AMERICA
P.O. BOX 40200, MC FL9100-10-19
JACKSONVILLE, FL 32203-0200
877-446-1410

ID NUMBER: 593340126
FEDERAL REPORTING DATE: 04/02
AREAS OF INTEREST: Education, Environment, Health, Medicine, Research, Scholarships, Social Services
CURRENT ASSETS: $3,257,414 **PRIOR ASSETS:** $1,068,432
TOTAL AMOUNT AWARDED: $119,378
HIGH: $35,000--HIllsborough Cnty Education Fdn.
MID: $8,500--Univ. of Florida
LOW: $500--Twilight Mini Maniacs
GRANTS AWARDS: Lukemia & Lymphoma Society--$4,000, Clearwater Manne Aquarium--$2,700, Muscular Dystrophy Fdn--$1,000, Individual scholarship--$1,478, Univ. of South FL.--$4,000, Univ. of Tampa--$5,000, Univ. of Miami--$3,000, Florida State University--$4,200, St. Mary's Elementary School--$25,000, Hillsborough Cnty Child Abuse Council--$25,000
SERVICE AREA: National
COMMENTS: Submit applications in letter form to Helen P Glimpse Charitable Foundation, C/O Billie Cox-Glimpse at 5303 N. Branch Avenue, Tampa, FL. 33603. 501 (c) (3) organizations.
DEADLINES: None
OFFICERS: Cox-Glimpse, Billie, D

GOLDSMITH, A. PHILLIP & FRIEDA FOUNDATION, INC.

2780 S. OCEAN BLVD, APT. 802
PALM BEACH, FL 33480-5569
212-730-9595

ID NUMBER: 650613640
FEDERAL REPORTING DATE: 05/02
AREAS OF INTEREST: Community, Education, Religion, Scholarships
CURRENT ASSETS: $814,327 **PRIOR ASSETS:** $848,325
TOTAL AMOUNT AWARDED: $93,500
HIGH: $90,000--Ranaz School
MID: $2,500--Congregation Kehilate
LOW: $1,000--Dix Hills Jewish Center
GRANTS AWARDS: N/A
SERVICE AREA: National
COMMENTS: The foundation does not accept unsolicited applications.
DEADLINES: None
OFFICERS: Goldsmith, Frieda, VP/D; Zeidman, Betty, T/D

GOLDSMITH-GREENFIELD FOUNDATION, INC.

1800 2ND ST., STE. 750
SARASOTA, FL 34236
941-957-0442

ID NUMBER: 650301946
FEDERAL REPORTING DATE: 10/01
AREAS OF INTEREST: Arts & Culture, Community, Education, Health, Religion, Research, Scholarships, Social Services, Other

CURRENT ASSETS: $12,889,359 PRIOR ASSETS: $13,088,624
TOTAL AMOUNT AWARDED: $599,849
HIGH: $218,000--Harvard Univ.
MID: $35,000--Cascade Policy Institute
LOW: $3,000--Nursing Mothers
GRANTS AWARDS: Also for Gay Youth, Inc.--$11,050, Burns Recovered Support Group--$10,000, Campbell Montessori School--$5,000, Champions of Caring--$10,000, Colorado Therapeutic Riding Ctr.--$10,000, Education Fdn. of Sarasota Co.--$20,000, Florida Studio Theatre Inc.--$20,000, Kelly Anne Dolan Memorial Fund--$10,000, Le Leche League of Missouri--$3,695, Longmont Humane Society--$10,000, Outreach United Resources--$10,000, Philadelphia Citizens for Children & Youth--$20,000, Planned Parenthood--$12,000, Project HOME--$12,000, Sarasota Co. Arts Council--$5,000
SERVICE AREA: National
COMMENTS: Fdn. provides grants to schools & organizations for scientific, literary, & educational purposes.
DEADLINES: None
OFFICERS: Greenfield, Robert K., TR; Greenfield, Louise, TR; Greenfield, James R., TR; Davenport, Mary G., TR; Greenfield, Lauren, TR; Clark, Emily, TR

GOODWIN, LEO FOUNDATION, INC.

800 CORPORATE DR., STE. 510
FORT LAUDERDALE, FL 33334
954-772-6863

ID NUMBER: 526054098
FEDERAL REPORTING DATE: 03/02
AREAS OF INTEREST: Arts & Culture, Community, Education, Environment, Health, Religion, Research, Scholarships, Social Services
CURRENT ASSETS: $16,857,829 PRIOR ASSETS: $18,244,273
TOTAL AMOUNT AWARDED: $611,000
HIGH: $121,000--Kids In Distress, Inc.
MID: $77,000--Nova Southeastern University Law School
LOW: $1,000--Bonnet House Florida
GRANTS AWARDS: American Cancer Society--$5,000, Ann Strock Center, Inc.--$10,000, Boys & Girls Clubs of Broward Cnty, Inc.--$27,500, Broward's Children's Center--$5,000, Church-By-The-Sea--$10,000, Covenant House of FL, Inc.--$10,000, Cystic Fibrosis of FL.--$7,500, East Side House Settlement--$9,000, Family Central, Inc.--$5,000, Ft. Lauderedale Children's Theatre--$5,000, Gilda's Club--$10,000, Henderson Mental Health Clinic--$1,000, Holy Cross Hospital Auxiliary--$5,000, Humane Society of Broward Cnty.--$2,500, Make-A-Wish Fdn, Inc.--$2,000
SERVICE AREA: South Florida
COMMENTS: Submit request to Helen Furia. Must be charitable 501(c)(3) organization. Describe purpose of program, amount requested, objectives, number of persons to be reached, budget, and names of board members, strategic partners or alliances.
DEADLINES: None
OFFICERS: Goodwin, Frances B., P; Borkson, Elliot P., VP; Furia, Helen M., S/T; Goldberg, Alan J., TR

GORE FAMILY MEMORIAL FOUNDATION

C/O SUNTRUST BANK
P.O. BOX 14728
FORT LAUDERDALE, FL 33302
954-781-8634

ID NUMBER: 596497544
FEDERAL REPORTING DATE: 06/01
AREAS OF INTEREST: Arts & Culture, Community, Education, Environment, Health, Medicine, Religion, Research, Scholarships, Social Services, Sports & Athletics, Other
CURRENT ASSETS: $19,078,319 PRIOR ASSETS: $18,097,306
TOTAL AMOUNT AWARDED: $1,226,202
HIGH: $80,000--Salvation Army
MID: $25,000--American Red Cross
LOW: $165--Silver Impact, Inc.
GRANTS AWARDS: ITT Technical Institute--$1,000, Georgia Instituteof Technology--$1,000, Miami-Dade Community College--$732, In Focus Optical--$285, Foroham Univ.--$1,000, St. Coleman Church--$43,200, Freedom Fighters--$2,574, DMR--$5,449, Univ. of Florida--$572, Univ. of Notre Dame--$1,000, St. Laurence Chapel--$1,100, Texas A&M Univ.--$667, Greenville College--$851, Univ. of Michigan--$1,000, Bank Atlantic--$1,333
SERVICE AREA: National
COMMENTS: Applications should include a letter.
DEADLINES: None
OFFICERS: SunTrust Bank, TR; Gore, Joseph, TR; Gore, George, TR; Gore, Theodore T., TR

GOULD, WILLIAM & HARRIET FOUNDATION

520 N. COUNTRY CLUB DR.
LAKE WORTH, FL 33462-1006
561-967-4860

ID NUMBER: 366067474
FEDERAL REPORTING DATE: 06/02
AREAS OF INTEREST: Arts & Culture, Community, Education, Medicine, Research, Scholarships, Social Services
CURRENT ASSETS: $344,273 PRIOR ASSETS: $347,341
TOTAL AMOUNT AWARDED: $37,000
HIGH: $6,000--Kewanee Public Library
MID: $2,500--Nephenthic Society
LOW: $500--American Field Services
GRANTS AWARDS: Fine Arts Museum of San Francisco--$1,000, Brain Research Foundation--$6,000, Brookings Food Pantry--$500, Bowdoin College--$500, Ecumenical Ministry in the Haight Ashbury--$1,000, Gould Scholarship Fund--$1,000, Gow School--$1,000, Hamilton Family Center--$1,000, Thomas College--$1,500, Haight Ashbury Free Medical Center--$500, Kewanee Food Pantry--$500, Mount Holyoke College--$1,500, Healdsburg Museum and Historical Society--$1,000, So. Dakota Agricultural Heritage Museum--$2,000
SERVICE AREA: National
COMMENTS: Gives to preselected organizations.
DEADLINES: None
OFFICERS: Grant, Eleanor, VP; Waller, Barodel, P

GRADO, JOHN FAMILY FOUNDATION

1137 BLUE HILL CREEK DR.
CAPTAIN HORR'S ISLAND
MARCO ISLAND, FL 34145
941-394-7959

ID NUMBER: 61518391
FEDERAL REPORTING DATE: 05/02
AREAS OF INTEREST: Arts & Culture, Community,
Education, Medicine, Research, Scholarships, Social Services,
Other
CURRENT ASSETS: $22,901 PRIOR ASSETS: $170,643
TOTAL AMOUNT AWARDED: $246,809
HIGH: $100,209--Marco Health Care Ctr.
MID: $19,250--American Cancer Society
LOW: $20--Veterans of Foreign Wars
GRANTS AWARDS: Virginia Tech Fdn.--$100,000,
Wishing Well Fdn.--$2,000, Ara Parseghian Medical Research-
-$5,000, Alumnae Club of Marco--$50, Alzheimer's Fdn.--$50,
Arthritis Fdn.--$100, Cathy Fiala Cancer Treatment Fund--
$1,000, Guadaloupe Tution Fund--$1,000, Island Coutry
Club Fdn.--$4,000, Kiwani's Club "Care & Share" Fund--$30,
Marco Island Charter Middle School--$10,000, Naples
Equestrian Challenge--$2,000, Naples Illusion--$2,000,
Shriner's Hospital for Children--$100
SERVICE AREA: National
COMMENTS: Gives to preselected organizations.
DEADLINES: None
OFFICERS: Grado, John, TR

GREEN, HERSCHEL V. & NANCY FOUNDATION

9155 S. DADELAND BLVD.
MIAMI, FL 33156
305-670-1000

ID NUMBER: 586425960
FEDERAL REPORTING DATE: 05/02
AREAS OF INTEREST: Community, Environment, Health,
Medicine, Research, Scholarships, Social Services
CURRENT ASSETS: $32,561 PRIOR ASSETS: $146,354
TOTAL AMOUNT AWARDED: $52,700
HIGH: $20,000--Performing Arts Center Fdn.
MID: $10,000--Coconut Grove Playhouse
LOW: $700--Health Foundation of South Florida
GRANTS AWARDS: Jewish Community Services of S.
Florida--$1,000, Greater Miami JewishFederation--$10,000,
Temple Israel--$10,000, Manimum Dance Company--$1,000
SERVICE AREA: FL
COMMENTS: Gives to preselected organizations.
DEADLINES: None
OFFICERS: Green, H.V., TR; Green Nancy, TR; Green,
Elizabeth, TR

GREENBURG-MAY FOUNDATION, INC.

P.O. BOX 54-5816
MIAMI BEACH, FL 33154
305-864-8639

ID NUMBER: 136162935
FEDERAL REPORTING DATE: 05/01
AREAS OF INTEREST: Arts & Culture, Community,
Education, Health, Medicine, Religion, Research, Scholarships,
Social Services

CURRENT ASSETS: $6,333,897 PRIOR ASSETS:
$6,008,231
TOTAL AMOUNT AWARDED: $357,860
HIGH: $101,625--Miami Jewish Home for Aged
MID: $27,030--Temple Beth Sholom
LOW: $50--Fund for the Poor
GRANTS AWARDS: National Parkinson Fdn.--$70,500, Mr.
Sinai Medical Center--$57,500, Diabetes Research--$15,150,
Temple Israel--$12,750, Miami Jewish Federation--$12,060,
FL. Grand Opera--$11,000, Laura Rosenberg Fdn.--$10,000,
Coconut Grove Playhouse--$3,500, Anti-Defamation League--
$3,000, Sloan Kettering Cancer Research--$2,000, Community
Chest--$2,000, Children's Home Society--$2,000, National
Council Jewish Women--$1,250, Cushman School--$1,000,
Greater Women's Auxilary--$1,030
SERVICE AREA: Miami, FL, National
COMMENTS: Submit by simple letter. Should be for medical
research, aid to aging, artistic or religious purposes and
primarily in South Florida. Send applications to 9999 Collins
Avenue #15A, Bal Harbour, FL. 33154.
DEADLINES: None
OFFICERS: May, Isabel, P; May, Peter W., VP; Sklar,
Linda,

GRIBETZ, ESTELLE FAMILY FOUNDATION, INC.

1900 N. ATLANTIC BLVD, STE. V-3
FORT LAUDERDALE, FL 33305
954-476-6700

ID NUMBER: 650759086
FEDERAL REPORTING DATE: 05/02
AREAS OF INTEREST: Scholarships
CURRENT ASSETS: $402,615 PRIOR ASSETS:
$503,610
TOTAL AMOUNT AWARDED: $104,188
HIGH: $104,188--Students at American Heritage School
GRANTS AWARDS: N/A
SERVICE AREA: FL
COMMENTS: Scholarship grants for half of the cost of tuition
and all costs of books and uniforms for students of American
Heritage and/or American Academy. Gives to preselected
organizations.
DEADLINES: N/A
OFFICERS: Gribetz, Michael, D/P/S/T; Hogan, Myra, D;
Hodor, Sheryl, D

GROSSMAN, ALEXANDER J. SCHOLARSHIP FOUNDATION

C/O AMSOUTH BANK OF FLORIDA
P.O. BOX 2918
CLEARWATER, FL 33757-2918
727-592-6907

ID NUMBER: 596782085
FEDERAL REPORTING DATE: 06/01
AREAS OF INTEREST: Scholarships
CURRENT ASSETS: $1,902,423 PRIOR ASSETS:
$1,815,794
TOTAL AMOUNT AWARDED: $78,457
HIGH: $6,500--Individual
MID: $3,000--Individual
LOW: $457--Individual
GRANTS AWARDS: N/A
SERVICE AREA: Dunedin
COMMENTS: Must be a graduate of Dunedin
Comprehensive High School with high academic rank,

pursuing an engineering or science program. Unsolicited
applications not accepted.
DEADLINES: None
OFFICERS: AmSouth Bank of Florida, T; Superintendent,
Pinellas County Schools; Principal and Registrar Dunedin High
School

GULDEN, SANDRA & LEON GOLDBERGER PRIVATE FOUNDATION

C/O ANTON ABRAMS, P.A.
P.O. BOX 229010
HOLLYWOOD, FL 33020
954-921-5500

ID NUMBER: 316630464
FEDERAL REPORTING DATE: 05/02
AREAS OF INTEREST: Arts & Culture, Health, Religion,
Scholarships, Social Services
CURRENT ASSETS: $2,126,640 PRIOR ASSETS:
$1,181,758
TOTAL AMOUNT AWARDED: $117,500
HIGH: $35,000--American Fund For Charities
MID: $10,000--JAFFCO
LOW: $1,250--Board of the Globe Theaters
GRANTS AWARDS: Memorial Hospital Foundation--
$10,000, Jewish Federation of Broward County--$5,000,
Hollywood Scholarship Fdn.--$10,000, Temple Solel--$2,500,
WPBT Channel 2--$2,500, C.A.R.E.--$2,500, Miami Rescue
Mission--$2,500, The Salvation Army--$2,500, Miami Jewish
Home and Hospital--$10,000
SERVICE AREA: FL, National
COMMENTS: Gives to preselected organizations.
DEADLINES: None
OFFICERS: Glasser, Gene K., TR; Bryant, Jeanne, TR

HAGENS, ANNETTE J. MEMORIAL FOUNDATION TRUST

800 SOUTH OSPREY AVE.
SARASOTA, FL 34236
941-366-3600

ID NUMBER: 656248208
FEDERAL REPORTING DATE: 06/01
AREAS OF INTEREST: Community, Education, Health,
Religion, Scholarships, Social Services, Sports & Athletics
CURRENT ASSETS: $4,339,631 PRIOR ASSETS:
$4,203,995
TOTAL AMOUNT AWARDED: $319,798
HIGH: $45,000--Boys & Girls Clubs of Sarasota
MID: $20,000--St. Wilfred's Episcopal
LOW: $3,000--Sarasota Riptite Quad Rugby
GRANTS AWARDS: Gulf Coast Marine Institute--$8,948,
McClellan Park School--$15,000, Oak Park school--$5,000,
Police Athletic League--$15,000, Sarasota Family YMCA--
$25,000, Second Chance Last--$7,500, Women's Resource
Center--$10,000, Girls, Inc.--$10,000
SERVICE AREA: Sarasota, FL
COMMENTS: Gives to preselected organizations.
DEADLINES: None
OFFICERS: Shea, Norman J., TR; Sperling, Matt A., TR;
Northern Turst Bank of Florida, TR

HAHN, ROBERT L. FOUNDATION, INC.

2800 CASEY KEY RD.
NOKOMIS, FL 34275
941-966-6645

ID NUMBER: 593100586
FEDERAL REPORTING DATE: 06/02
AREAS OF INTEREST: Scholarships
CURRENT ASSETS: $561,801 PRIOR ASSETS:
$567,875
TOTAL AMOUNT AWARDED: $43,500
HIGH: $2,500--Individual
MID: $2,000--Individual
LOW: $1,500--Individual
GRANTS AWARDS: N/A
SERVICE AREA: Sarasota, Gainesville
COMMENTS: Gives to preselected organizations.
DEADLINES: None
OFFICERS: Hahn, Robert L., P; Bienkowski, Kenneth, D;
Lieberman, Erik R., D

HALL, ELIZABETH EDGAR CORPORATION

4427 HERSCHEL ST.
JACKSONVILLE, FL 32210
904-387-1740

ID NUMBER: 592396975
FEDERAL REPORTING DATE: 11/01
AREAS OF INTEREST: Education, Scholarships
CURRENT ASSETS: $264,715 PRIOR ASSETS:
$250,457
TOTAL AMOUNT AWARDED: $14,375
HIGH: $5,000--Univ. of North Florida
MID: $4,875--Florida Community College
LOW: $250--ITT Technical Institute
GRANTS AWARDS: Jacksonville Univ.--$4,250
COMMENTS: Forms provided at schools. Focus is on women
and education-related issues. Grants and scholarships are given
to women who need financial assistance for post-secondary
education. Send applications to: Scholarship Committee,
Elizabeth E. Hall Corp., 4427 Herschel St., Jacksonville, Fl.
32207
DEADLINES: 4/15

HALMOS, STEVEN J. FAMILY FOUNDATION, INC.

21 W. LAS OLAS BLVD.
FORT LAUDERDALE, FL 33301
954-760-4979

ID NUMBER: 830305837
FEDERAL REPORTING DATE: 05/02
AREAS OF INTEREST: Arts & Culture, Education, Health,
Religion, Scholarships, Social Services
CURRENT ASSETS: $1,841,140 PRIOR ASSETS:
$1,906,659
TOTAL AMOUNT AWARDED: $191,565
HIGH: $110,000--United way of Broward County
MID: $2,500--Junior Welfare Society
LOW: $50--Far East Help Foundation
GRANTS AWARDS: Children's Harbor--$250, Community
Fdn. of Broward--$100, Pine Crest School--$1,000, Humane
Society of Broward County--$650, Museum of Discovery &
Science--$1,000, Jack & Jill Children's Center--$100,

Cleveland Clinic Florida--$100, Covenant House--$300, Children's Aid Club--$250
SERVICE AREA: National
COMMENTS: Gives to preselected organizations.
DEADLINES: None
OFFICERS: Halmos, Steven J., P; Halmos, Jeffry, D; Halmos, Madelaine G., D; Halmos, Stephanie, D

HAMILTON BANK FOUNDATION

13601 S.W. 103RD AVE.
MIAMI, FL 33176
305-551-6126

ID NUMBER: 650240306
FEDERAL REPORTING DATE: 05/02
AREAS OF INTEREST: Arts & Culture, Community, Education, Health, Medicine, Research, Scholarships
CURRENT ASSETS: $77,607 **PRIOR ASSETS:** $65,253
TOTAL AMOUNT AWARDED: $101,420
HIGH: $15,000--Comite Prociegos y Sordos de Guatemala
MID: $6,995--Sunrise Community
LOW: $100--St. Catholic Church
GRANTS AWARDS: Florida International University--$11,000, Jackson Memorial Foundation--$11,000, Leukemia & Lymphoma Society--$1,500, The Learning Experience--$400, UNICEF--$1,000, League Against Cancer--$2,000, Centro Mater--$10,000, City of South Florida--$1,000
SERVICE AREA: Miami, FL
COMMENTS: Submit written request. Include documentation, if needed.
DEADLINES: None
OFFICERS: Masferrer, Eduardo A., C; Alexander, William, VC; Rosell, Santiago J., Esq., S; Acosta, Maura A., T; Diaz-Oliver, Mrs. Remedios, D; Jorge, Dr. Antonio, D

HAMMER FAMILY FUND

560 HARBOR POINT RD.
LONGBOAT KEY, FL 34228-3504
941-356-5026

ID NUMBER: 112585895
FEDERAL REPORTING DATE: 05/02
AREAS OF INTEREST: Arts & Culture, Community, Education, Environment, Medicine, Religion, Scholarships, Social Services
CURRENT ASSETS: $1,005,113 **PRIOR ASSETS:** $1,064,298
TOTAL AMOUNT AWARDED: $42,500
HIGH: $10,000--National Multiple Sclerosis
MID: $5,000--Sarasota Manatee Jewish Federation
LOW: $500--United Way
GRANTS AWARDS: Animal Rescue--$5,000, US Holocaust Memorial Museum--$500, Helen Payne Day Care--$500, Florida Studio Theatre--$10,000, Van Wezel Foundation--$1,400, Asolo Theatre--$2,500, Community Mobile Meals--$600, Interdenominal Worship Center--$1,000, Sarasota Memorial--$3,000, Kobernick House--$2,500
SERVICE AREA: National
COMMENTS: Gives to preselected organizations.
DEADLINES: None
OFFICERS: Hammer, Marjorie, TR; Hammer, Mark, TR

HAND FOUNDATION

1499 FOREST HILL BLVD., STE 116
WEST PALM BEACH, FL 33406
561-439-0171

ID NUMBER: 650118848
FEDERAL REPORTING DATE: 08/01
AREAS OF INTEREST: Scholarships
CURRENT ASSETS: $35,497 **PRIOR ASSETS:** $8,142
TOTAL AMOUNT AWARDED: $145,951
HIGH: $20,250--Individual
MID: $10,000--Individual
LOW: $384--Individual
GRANTS AWARDS: N/A
COMMENTS: Apply by specific letter request to be reviewed by selection committee. Should include information about personal history, education, economic situation, educational goals, etc. Inactive in 1994 and 1995.
DEADLINES: None
OFFICERS: Ledesma, Ruben Jr., D; Altman, Thomas L., D; Orsenigo, Paul, D; Hand, Homer J., D

HARLLEE-WHISENANT SCHOLARSHIP TRUST

C/O BANK OF AMERICA
P. O. BOX 40200, MC FL9-100-10-19
JACKSONVILLE, FL 32203-0200
877-446-1410

ID NUMBER: 596713037
FEDERAL REPORTING DATE: 10/01
AREAS OF INTEREST: Scholarships
CURRENT ASSETS: $62,708 **PRIOR ASSETS:** $63,204
TOTAL AMOUNT AWARDED: $1,050
HIGH: $300--Individual
MID: $150--Individual
LOW: $150--Individual
GRANTS AWARDS: N/A
COMMENTS: Call for application form. Agricultural scholarships to residents of Manatee county, Fl.
DEADLINES: 4/15
OFFICERS: Bank of America, TR

HARRIS, MEL & FRAN FAMILY FOUNDATION

10800 BISCAYNE BLVD.
MIAMI, FL 33161
305-899-0404

ID NUMBER: 651063032
FEDERAL REPORTING DATE: 03/02
AREAS OF INTEREST: Community, Education, Health, Medicine, Religion, Research, Scholarships
CURRENT ASSETS: $932,074 **PRIOR ASSETS:** $100,139
TOTAL AMOUNT AWARDED: $166,753
HIGH: $100,000--Hebrew Home for Aged at Rivered
MID: $20,000--Aventurer Turnberry Temple
LOW: $2,500--Mount Sinai Medical Foundation
GRANTS AWARDS: UM Sylvester Cancer Center--$10,000, Bar-ilan University--$5,000, Diabetec Research Institute--$15,000, Miami Jewish Home and Hospital--$4,253, Young Audiences--$10,000
SERVICE AREA: National
COMMENTS: Initial contact thru written concept letter.
DEADLINES: None

OFFICERS: Harris, Mel, P; Harris, Fran, S/T

HARTLESS FOUNDATION
112 GRAND PALM WAY
PALM BEACH GARDENS, FL 33418
561-799-0911

ID NUMBER: 366084263
FEDERAL REPORTING DATE: 09/01
AREAS OF INTEREST: Education, Environment, Religion,
Scholarships, Other
CURRENT ASSETS: $2,978,464 PRIOR ASSETS:
$2,738,913
TOTAL AMOUNT AWARDED: $90,280
HIGH: $26,390--Misc. Organizations
MID: $15,450--Disadvantaged Youth
LOW: $8,740--Wildlife & Enviroment
GRANTS AWARDS: Christian Science Organizations--
$21,100, Education & Scholarships--$18,600
COMMENTS: Gives to preselected organizations.
DEADLINES: None
OFFICERS: Hartless, Robert B. II, P; Hartless, Carole J., S;
Rilighed, Ron, D; McManus, James, D; Darling, Patrick E., D

HARTZ FOUNDATION
13773 WM DAVIS PKWY., W.
JACKSONVILLE, FL 32224-6603
904-992-7113

ID NUMBER: 416041638
FEDERAL REPORTING DATE: 10/01
AREAS OF INTEREST: Arts & Culture, Community,
Education, Environment, Health, Religion, Scholarships, Other
CURRENT ASSETS: $4,807,503 PRIOR ASSETS:
$4,807,120
TOTAL AMOUNT AWARDED: $221,550
HIGH: $25,000--Thief River Falls
MID: $10,000--Mayo Fdn.
LOW: $200--Pennington Co. Extension
GRANTS AWARDS: Falls DAC--$5,000, Fergus Falls
YMCA--$20,000, ISD #564--$13,000, Kittson Co. Sheriff--
$13,500, Northern Pines, Park Rapids--$10,000, Northland
Community College--$15,000, Our Savior's Lutheran Church-
-$10,000, Viking--$5,000, Warroad--$12,500, Augustana
College--$3,500, Bemidji State Univ.--$1,000, Boy Scouts--
$4,000, Falls Delivered Meals--$3,000, Gallaudet Univ.--
$3,500, Girl Scouts--$3,000
SERVICE AREA: MN
COMMENTS: Send applications to: Onealee Hartz, P. O. Box
642, Theif River Falls, MN., 56701. Purpose on use of funds
applied for / copy of exemption / project budget. Primary
consideration given to Minnesota & N. Dakota.
DEADLINES: None
OFFICERS: Hartz, Onealee, S/T; Sjoberg, Richard, P;
Tangquist, Dwight, VP

HASTINGS, ROBERT F. & MARY P. FOUNDATION, INC.
429 WALLS WAY
OSPREY, FL 34229
716-318-9207

ID NUMBER: 61600836
FEDERAL REPORTING DATE: 04/02
AREAS OF INTEREST: Community, Scholarships, Other

CURRENT ASSETS: $511,945 PRIOR ASSETS:
$426,265
TOTAL AMOUNT AWARDED: $13,500
HIGH: $11,000--Aquinas Institute
MID: $1,000--Moose Lodge
LOW: $500--Seneca Park Zoo Society
GRANTS AWARDS: Class of 53 Scholarship Fund--$1,000
SERVICE AREA: National
COMMENTS: Gives to preselected organizations.
DEADLINES: None
OFFICERS: Hastings, Robert F., P; Hastings, Mary P., VP;
Edmiston, Marcy M., D

HAVEN, NINA CHARITABLE FOUNDATION
555 COLORADO AVE.
STUART, FL 34994
772-288-6090

ID NUMBER: 136099012
FEDERAL REPORTING DATE: 03/02
AREAS OF INTEREST: Community, Education, Scholarships
CURRENT ASSETS: $167,109 PRIOR ASSETS:
$1,631,214
TOTAL AMOUNT AWARDED: $189,807
HIGH: $73,058--YMCA of the Treasure Coast
MID: $2,000--Individual
LOW: $250--Individual
GRANTS AWARDS: N/A
SERVICE AREA: Martin County
COMMENTS: Educational scholarships. Write foundation to
obtain forms. Students should show need, scholastic
achievement and meet other intangible criteria. Awards are
usually given to graduates of the Martin County, Florida,
school system and local community colleges. Send forms to
Guidance Office, Martin County H.S., 281 S. Kanner Hwy.,
Stuart, FL 34994.
DEADLINES: None
OFFICERS: Webber, Judy, P; Gaster, Gordon D., T; Crary,
Lawrence E. III, S; Anderson, Charles, D

HEALTH EDUCATIONAL FUND
C/O BANK OF AMERICA
P. O. BOX 15507
ST. PETERSBURG, FL 33733-5507
727-298-5925

ID NUMBER: 596218458
FEDERAL REPORTING DATE: 01/02
AREAS OF INTEREST: Scholarships
CURRENT ASSETS: $137,577 PRIOR ASSETS:
$151,514
TOTAL AMOUNT AWARDED: $9,450
HIGH: $630--Individual
MID: $630--Individual
LOW: $630--Individual
GRANTS AWARDS: N/A
SERVICE AREA: SE United States
COMMENTS: Restricted to male high school graduates from
schools within the Southeastern United States who wish to
study for the ministry, missionary activities or social work. Send
applications to: Bank of America, P.O. Box 15507 St.
Petersburg, FL. 33733.
DEADLINES: None
OFFICERS: Bank of America, TR

HEALTHY NUTRITIONAL FOODS FOUNDATION

777 S. FLAGLER DR., EAST TOWER
STE. 1000
WEST PALM BEACH, FL 33401
561-820-1320

ID NUMBER: 133665450
FEDERAL REPORTING DATE: 11/01
AREAS OF INTEREST: Arts & Culture, Education, Health, Medicine, Religion, Research, Scholarships, Social Services, Sports & Athletics, Other
CURRENT ASSETS: $1,388,715   PRIOR ASSETS: $1,339,430
TOTAL AMOUNT AWARDED: $1,637,938
HIGH: $333,333--Shefa Fund
MID: $162,000--Bar Ilan Univ.
LOW: $150--Veterans of Foreign Wars
GRANTS AWARDS: Adopt A Classroom--$5,000, Alan Brown Fdn.--$25,000, American Friends of Aish Hatorah--$25,000, American Friends of Eretz Hemdah--$500, Amer.Friends of Koryat Sans Laniado Hospital--$1,000, American Friends of Zefal--$360, Avon Breast Cancer--$500, Chabad House Lubavitch--$18,000, Chal Life Line--$25,000, Chamah--$5,000, Council for a Beautiful Israel--$30,000, Cystic Fibrosis--$25,000, Friends of Yachaven Daat--$50,000, Hillel Day School--$5,000, Hineni, Inc.--$36,000
SERVICE AREA: National
COMMENTS: Gives to preselected organizations.
DEADLINES: None
OFFICERS: Abraham, S. Daniel , D/P; Steinberg, Dr. Edward L., D/VP; Lauer, Eliot, D

HELLER, DIANE STAR CHARITABLE FOUNDATION, INC.

50 WEST DI LIDO DR.
MIAMI BEACH, FL 33139
305-358-5544

ID NUMBER: 650504389
FEDERAL REPORTING DATE: 04/02
AREAS OF INTEREST: Arts & Culture, Education, Health, Religion, Scholarships, Social Services
CURRENT ASSETS: $525,059   PRIOR ASSETS: $556,132
TOTAL AMOUNT AWARDED: $39,120
HIGH: $10,000--University of Miami Lowe Art Museum
MID: $3,200--Florida Grand Opera
LOW: $100--American Civil Liberties Foundation of Florida
GRANTS AWARDS: New World Symphony--$500, Beth Torah Synagogue--$1,000, Friends of Art - Lowe Art Museum--$1,000, Concert Association of Florida--$10,000, Jewish Museum of Florida Mosaic--$500, Mt. Sinai Medical Center--$5,000, Maximum Dance Co.--$1,000, Miami Beach Arts Trust--$1,000, FIU Scholarship Fund--$500
SERVICE AREA: National
DEADLINES: None
OFFICERS: Heller, Diane Star, P/T; Heller, Daniel Neal, VP/S

HENDERSON, A. D. FOUNDATION

P. O. BOX 14096
FORT LAUDERDALE, FL 33302
954-764-2819

ID NUMBER: 237047045
FEDERAL REPORTING DATE: 07/01
AREAS OF INTEREST: Arts & Culture, Community, Education, Environment, Health, Medicine, Research, Scholarships, Social Services, Sports & Athletics, Other
CURRENT ASSETS: $53,211,861   PRIOR ASSETS: $52,739,931
TOTAL AMOUNT AWARDED: $3,664,681
HIGH: $107,000--Marlboro College
MID: $45,000--Mount Independence Coalition
LOW: $500--Adm. Wm. Nelson Foundation, Inc,
GRANTS AWARDS: N/A
SERVICE AREA: SE FL, VT
COMMENTS: Limited to projects or programs of charitable organizations involving education of children, day care for children, population control, preservation of society history, protection of abandoned animals and furthering family, children and parent relations. The projects should be in South Florida or Vermont. No grants to individuals.
DEADLINES: None
OFFICERS: Henderson, Allen Douglas, P/T; Henderson, Barbara, VP/T; Lyon, Jim, VP/T; Henderson, Lucia, VP/T; Oberfest, Bruce D., S/T

HENNESSY, EDWARD L. & RUTH S. FOUNDATION, INC.

500 ISLAND DR.
PALM BEACH, FL 33864
973-455-4811

ID NUMBER: 223140476
FEDERAL REPORTING DATE: 05/02
AREAS OF INTEREST: Arts & Culture, Community, Education, Health, Medicine, Religion, Scholarships, Social Services
CURRENT ASSETS: $422,924   PRIOR ASSETS: $627,419
TOTAL AMOUNT AWARDED: $320,500
HIGH: $200,000--Palm Beach United Way
MID: $50,000--Gregoian University Foundation
LOW: $1,000--New Vernon First Aid Squad
GRANTS AWARDS: American Cancer Society--$1,500, American Heart Association--$12,500, Bascom Palmer Eye Institutechildren and Adults--$5,000, Tri County Scholarship Fund--$12,500, Project Acron--$2,500, Morristown Memorial Hospital--$5,000, March of Dimes--$5,000
SERVICE AREA: Palm Beach, FL., Morristown, NJ
COMMENTS: Gives to preselected organizations. Does not accept unsolicited requests.
DEADLINES: None
OFFICERS: Hennessy, Edward L. Jr., P; Hennessy, Ruth S., T; Hennessy, Michael E., VP; Hennessy, Elizabeth R., S

HERTZ, ARTHUR H. FOUNDATION

610 FLUVIA AVE.
CORAL GABLES, FL 33134
305-529-1400

ID NUMBER: 592496218
FEDERAL REPORTING DATE: 10/01
AREAS OF INTEREST: Community, Education, Scholarships
CURRENT ASSETS: $101,587   PRIOR ASSETS: $121,764
TOTAL AMOUNT AWARDED: $33,000
HIGH: $10,000--United Way of Miami
MID: $10,000--Univ. of Miami
LOW: $3,000--Pulse

GRANTS AWARDS: Univ. of Miami (Elizabeth Dee Scholarship Fund)--$10,000
SERVICE AREA: FL.
COMMENTS: Gives to preselected organizations.
DEADLINES: None
OFFICERS: Hertz, Arthur, TR; Brown, Michael, TR

HIRSCHHORN FOUNDATION, INC.

2600 DOUGLAS RD., PH. #1
CORAL GABLES, FL 33134
305-445-5320

ID NUMBER: 592159670
FEDERAL REPORTING DATE: 09/01
AREAS OF INTEREST: Education, Scholarships
CURRENT ASSETS: $36,624 PRIOR ASSETS: $39,223
TOTAL AMOUNT AWARDED: $2,450
HIGH: $1,000--Univ. of Connecticut
LOW: $450--Hope Ctr.
GRANTS AWARDS: Univ. of Wisconsin--$1,000
COMMENTS: Send applications to: Joel Hirschhorn, Esq. C/O Hirschhorn Fdn., Inc., 2600 Douglas Rd.-Ph.#1, Coral Gables, Fl. 33134-6125.
DEADLINES: None
OFFICERS: Hirschhorn, Joel, P; Hirschhorn, Evelyn, T; Hirschhorn, Douglas, VP - Finance; Hirschhorn, bennett, VP - Scholarship

HOAGLIN, GEORGE F. CHARITABLE FOUNDATION

4308 HANOVER PARK DR.
JACKSONVILLE, FL 32224-8602
904-633-6000

ID NUMBER: 650857785
FEDERAL REPORTING DATE: 06/01
AREAS OF INTEREST: Scholarships
CURRENT ASSETS: $13,418 PRIOR ASSETS: $13,500
TOTAL AMOUNT AWARDED: $3,000
HIGH: $3,000--East Palestine High School
GRANTS AWARDS: N/A
COMMENTS: Gives to preselected organizations.
DEADLINES: N/A
OFFICERS: Hoaglin, George F. Jr.; Bonis, Judith A.; Clark, Nancy

HOETING, JOHN F. SCHOLARSHIP TRUST UNDER WILL

C/O BANK OF AMERICA, TRUSTEE
P. O. BOX 40200
JACKSONVILLE, FL 32203-0200
877-446-1410

ID NUMBER: 597102513
FEDERAL REPORTING DATE: 11/01
AREAS OF INTEREST: Scholarships
CURRENT ASSETS: $478,918 PRIOR ASSETS: $474,516
TOTAL AMOUNT AWARDED: $19,375
HIGH: $1,562--Individual
MID: $1,250--Individual
LOW: $1,250--Individual
GRANTS AWARDS: N/A
SERVICE AREA: Pasco County, Fl.

COMMENTS: Students must be graduating seniors of Hudson High School in Pasco Co., Fl. Send applications to: Sally Herny, John Hoeting Scholarship Fund, Private Bank 3rd Fl., 600 Cleveland St., Clearwater, Fl. 33755-4151.
DEADLINES: None
OFFICERS: Bank of America, TR

HOLCOMBE, HERBERT D. SR. & JR. MEMORIAL SCHOLARSHIPS

4523 CLEARWATER HARBOR DR.
LARGO, FL 33770
727-585-2296

ID NUMBER: 222792227
FEDERAL REPORTING DATE: 05/02
AREAS OF INTEREST: Scholarships, Other
CURRENT ASSETS: $85,543 PRIOR ASSETS: $86,291
TOTAL AMOUNT AWARDED: $4,500
HIGH: $1,500--David Clink
MID: $1,500--Joshua Geisler
LOW: $1,500--Racheal Ziegler
GRANTS AWARDS: N/A
SERVICE AREA: National
COMMENTS: Gives only to students of Troy Senior High School who are interested in pursuing a business curriculum or business degree or career. Applications should be addressed to Grace M. Holcombe, 4523 Clarwater Harbor Drive, Largo, FL. 33770.
DEADLINES: None
OFFICERS: Holcombe, Grace M., TR

HOLES FOUNDATION, INC.

3111 CARDINAL DR., STE. B
VERO BEACH, FL 32963
772-231-6900

ID NUMBER: 131946867
FEDERAL REPORTING DATE: 11/01
AREAS OF INTEREST: Arts & Culture, Community, Education, Scholarships, Other
CURRENT ASSETS: $2,357,527 PRIOR ASSETS: $2,519,880
TOTAL AMOUNT AWARDED: $165,500
HIGH: $60,000--Ctr. for the Arts
MID: $10,000--VNA Hospice House
LOW: $1,000--Indian River Co. Habitat
GRANTS AWARDS: Better Chance of Wilton--$4,000, Centaurus High School Scholarship Fund--$3,000, Children's Law Ctr.--$18,000, Community Child Care Resources--$2,000, Cultural Council of Indian River Co.--$3,000, Cumberland College--$5,000, Equal Justice Initiative of Alabama--$4,000, Fairfield Prepartory School--$2,500, John W. Nick Fdn., Inc.--$7,000, Mercy Learning Ctr.--$7,000, Monarch High School Scholarship--$5,000, Mt. Alvernia Sisters of St. Francis--$8,000, Pratt Institute--$5,000, Riverside Children's Theatre--$8,000, Southern Scholarship Fdn.--$6,000
COMMENTS: Gives to preselected organizations.
DEADLINES: None
OFFICERS: Holmes, Jay Tyler, P; O'Haire, Michael , S; Monahan, Tom, T; Holmes, Claudette, VP; Christ, Alexandria Negin, D

HOLT, LOIS FOUNDATION OF CENTRAL FLORIDA

530 E. CENTRAL AVE., STE. 1201
ORLANDO, FL 32801
407-841-6938

ID NUMBER: 593143622
FEDERAL REPORTING DATE: 02/03
AREAS OF INTEREST: Education, Medicine, Scholarships, Social Services
CURRENT ASSETS: $1,052,259 PRIOR ASSETS: $982,780
TOTAL AMOUNT AWARDED: $56,100
HIGH: $12,000--University of Central Florida Fdn.
MID: $3,000--Individual
LOW: $500--Holocaust Memorial
GRANTS AWARDS: Individual--$1,500, Individual--$1,000, Individual--$1,500, Rollins College--$2,500, Valencia Community College--$7,500, Individual--$1,000, Individual--$1,000, University of South Florida--$3,000, Junior Achievement--$500, Individual--$2,500, Individual--$1,500, Individual--$1,500, Individual--$2,000, Individual--$1,500, Individual--$1,500
SERVICE AREA: FL, ME, NJ, MN
COMMENTS: Applicants should call the office (407-841-6938) to receive a forms packet.
DEADLINES: None
OFFICERS: Sunshine, Herbert, VP; Morrison, Steve, S; Stilwell, John P. II, Admin; Buckner, Bob, D; Hofma, Edward, P; Hunt, Bonny Morrison, D

HOLTZ CHARITABLE FOUNDATION, INC.

C/O BETH B. HOLTZ
9209 CROMWELL PARK PL.
ORLANDO, FL 32827
407-240-8403

ID NUMBER: 352042978
FEDERAL REPORTING DATE: 11/01
AREAS OF INTEREST: Education, Health, Religion, Research, Scholarships
CURRENT ASSETS: $1,910,595 PRIOR ASSETS: $311,697
TOTAL AMOUNT AWARDED: $47,363
HIGH: $25,500--Lou Holtz Upper Ohio Valley Hall of Fame
MID: $15,000--Catholic Youth Organization
LOW: $125--Health Research Institute
GRANTS AWARDS: Univ. of Notre Dame--$5,000
COMMENTS: Gives to preselected organizations.
DEADLINES: None
OFFICERS: Holtz, Louis L., C; Holtz, Beth B., P/D; Mackay, Harvey, D; Altenbaumer, Luanne E., D; Holtz, Louis L., Jr., D; Holtz, Kevin R., S/T

HORTON, DONALD D. & MARGARET B. MEMORIAL FUND

900 W. MEMORIAL HWY. 50
CLERMONT, FL 34711
352-394-4008

ID NUMBER: 596584043
FEDERAL REPORTING DATE: 01/02
AREAS OF INTEREST: Scholarships
CURRENT ASSETS: $45,879 PRIOR ASSETS: $47,223
TOTAL AMOUNT AWARDED: $2,750

HIGH: $1,000--Individual
MID: $1,000--Individual
LOW: $7,500--Individual
GRANTS AWARDS: N/A
SERVICE AREA: Clermont
COMMENTS: Restricted to Clermont, Florida area residents. Contact the Kiwanis Club of Clermont by letter.
DEADLINES: None
OFFICERS: Horton, Dennis L., TR

HOUSE OF HUSTON FOUNDATION, INC.

1001 MANAT AVE.
CORAL GABLES, FL 33146
305-661-0557

ID NUMBER: 596152540
FEDERAL REPORTING DATE: 02/02
AREAS OF INTEREST: Arts & Culture, Environment, Health, Religion, Research, Scholarships, Social Services
CURRENT ASSETS: $407,312 PRIOR ASSETS: $480,568
TOTAL AMOUNT AWARDED: $29,707
GRANTS AWARDS: N/A
SERVICE AREA: FL
COMMENTS: Gives to preselected organizations. Send applications to Tom Huston, Sr. at 1001 Manati Avenue, Coral Gables, FL. 33146.
DEADLINES: None
OFFICERS: Huston, Tom, P

HUIZENGA, JOYCE M. FOUNDATION

450 E. LAS OLAS BLVD., STE. 1500
FORT LAUDERDALE, FL 33301
954-627-5000

ID NUMBER: 656380105
FEDERAL REPORTING DATE: 05/02
AREAS OF INTEREST: Scholarships
CURRENT ASSETS: $12,451 PRIOR ASSETS: $0
TOTAL AMOUNT AWARDED: $0
GRANTS AWARDS: N/A
COMMENTS: Applications should be sent to H. Wayne Huizenga Jr. 450 E. Las Olas Blvd. Suite 1500 Ft. Lauderdale, Fl 33301.
DEADLINES: Not yet determined
OFFICERS: Huizenga, H. Wayne Jr., TR

HUNGERFORD, ROBERT CHAPEL TRUST

P.O. BOX 2822
WINTER PARK, FL 32790

ID NUMBER: 592350325
FEDERAL REPORTING DATE: 03/02
AREAS OF INTEREST: Education, Scholarships
CURRENT ASSETS: $578,484 PRIOR ASSETS: $725,218
TOTAL AMOUNT AWARDED: $35,300
HIGH: $3,000--Individual
MID: $2,000--Individual
LOW: $1,000--Individual
GRANTS AWARDS: N/A
SERVICE AREA: FL

COMMENTS: Send applications to Frank Otay, Leroy Brown, P O BOX 2822, Winter Park, Fl. 32790
DEADLINES: May 31
OFFICERS: Hall, Richard T. Jr., TR; Morrison, Ms., TR; Ray, Annie, S; Henry, Sandra, T

HURST, LONNIE BOB SCHOLARSHIP TRUST

C/O DONNA C. LONG.
11465 75TH DR.
LIVE OAK, FL 32060-7118
386-362-3862

ID NUMBER: 597011644
FEDERAL REPORTING DATE: 11/01
AREAS OF INTEREST: Scholarships
CURRENT ASSETS: $105,205 PRIOR ASSETS: $104,889
TOTAL AMOUNT AWARDED: $9,915
HIGH: $2,500--Individual
MID: $1,500--Individual
LOW: $400--Individual
GRANTS AWARDS: N/A
SERVICE AREA: FL
COMMENTS: Send applications to: Donna C. Long, 11465 75 Dr., Live Oak, Fl. 32060 (904)364-5210
DEADLINES: None
OFFICERS: Long, Donna C., TR

HUSSEY, HERBERT E. SCHOLARSHIP FUND

P.O. BOX 40200
MC FL9-100-10-19
JACKSONVILLE, FL 32203-0200
800-832-9071

ID NUMBER: 596126197
FEDERAL REPORTING DATE: 05/02
AREAS OF INTEREST: Scholarships
CURRENT ASSETS: $531,246 PRIOR ASSETS: $560,394
TOTAL AMOUNT AWARDED: $26,000
HIGH: $5,000--Individual
MID: $5,000--Individual
LOW: $5,000--Individual
GRANTS AWARDS: Individual--$5,000, Individual--$5,000, Individual--$5,000, Individual--$5,000
SERVICE AREA: National
COMMENTS: Forms are provided by Trustee. Only children of GTE employees are eligivle.
DEADLINES: June 30
OFFICERS: Bank of America, TR

IMAMI FAMILY FOUNDATION, INC.

2118 AARON ST.
PT. CHARLOTTE, FL 33952
941-629-4000

ID NUMBER: 656249234
FEDERAL REPORTING DATE: 08/01
AREAS OF INTEREST: Education, Health, Religion, Research, Scholarships, Social Services
CURRENT ASSETS: $405,418 PRIOR ASSETS: $291,103

TOTAL AMOUNT AWARDED: $1,656
HIGH: $250--Individual
MID: $100--American Eritrean Relief Organization
LOW: $25--American Institute for Cancer Research
GRANTS AWARDS: Disabled American Veterans--$40, ISNA Development Foundation--$250, Islamic American Relief Agency--$100, American Red Cross--$100
SERVICE AREA: National
DEADLINES: None
OFFICERS: Imami, Riazul H., D; Imami, Azra R., D; Imami, Ifran R., D

ISENBERG FAMILY CHARITABLE TRUST

C/O PRICE, WATERHOUSE, COOPERS LLP, ATTN: W. FONG
515 N. FLAGLER DR., STE. 400
WEST PALM BEACH, FL 33401

ID NUMBER: 596874814
FEDERAL REPORTING DATE: 11/01
AREAS OF INTEREST: Arts & Culture, Education, Environment, Health, Scholarships
CURRENT ASSETS: $12,572,067 PRIOR ASSETS: $12,681,337
TOTAL AMOUNT AWARDED: $480,592
HIGH: $100,000--Massachusetts General Hospital
MID: $53,635--Metropolitan Opera Assn.
LOW: $47--Massachusetts Outdoor Scholarship
GRANTS AWARDS: American Diabetes Assn.--$264, American Friends of the Philharmonic--$5,000, American Institute of Cancer--$100, Anti-Defamation League--$1,800, Atlantic Salmon Federation--$100, Alzheimer's Disease Fdn.--$100, Avon Breast Cancer Fdn.--$1,000, Ballet Florida--$800, Brigham Medical Ctr.--$300, Congregation B'Nai Jeshurun--$1,000, Cystic Fibrosis Fdn.--$50, Sophie Davis School of Biomedical Education--$500, Duke Co. Patrolman Assn.--$100, EWAM--$10,000, Friends of Sengekontocket--$350
COMMENTS: Gives to preselected organizations.
DEADLINES: None
OFFICERS: Papouras, Christopher, TR; Isenberg, Diane S., TR

JACOBS, HYMAN S. & SADYE FOUNDATION

THREE LA JOLLA CT.
ORMOND BEACH, FL 32174
770-425-8199

ID NUMBER: 586042913
FEDERAL REPORTING DATE: 03/02
AREAS OF INTEREST: Arts & Culture, Community, Education, Health, Medicine, Religion, Scholarships, Social Services, Sports & Athletics
CURRENT ASSETS: $436,203 PRIOR ASSETS: $455,771
TOTAL AMOUNT AWARDED: $51,733
HIGH: $7,162--Temple Beth El
MID: $3,800--Campus Sea Gull
LOW: $20--American Lung Association
GRANTS AWARDS: AA Synagogue--$500, American Cancer Society--$200, Bet Safer Heritage School--$2,688, Blue Star Camp--$750, Camp Coleman--$2,125, Daytona Beach Comm. College--$100, Disabled Veterans--$60, Easter Seals--$25, Floyd Chapel Baptist Church--$100, Gate City Caretakers--$1,350, Hadassah--$120, Jewish Federal Chronicle--$2,370

SERVICE AREA: Volusia County, National
COMMENTS: Submit written request. Give name, address, telephone number and state amount requested. Briefly describe the person or organization. No post-graduate and no capital grants. Scholarships limited to $1000 per year based on need and high school record. Applications available on request and scholarship budget set in August for following year.
DEADLINES: None
OFFICERS: Bagen, S.J., P; Dempsey, R.B., S

JAFFE, FRANCES & RONALD FOUNDATION

69 CACHE CAY DR.
VERO BEACH, FL 32963
561-231-1440

ID NUMBER: 656319680
FEDERAL REPORTING DATE: 04/02
AREAS OF INTEREST: Scholarships
CURRENT ASSETS: $186,586   PRIOR ASSETS:
$140,748
TOTAL AMOUNT AWARDED: $7,000
HIGH: $7,000--Dollars for Scholars
GRANTS AWARDS: N/A
COMMENTS: Gives to preselected organizations.
DEADLINES: None
OFFICERS: Jaffe, Ronald J., TR; Jaffe, Frances P., TR; Jaffe, David A, TR; Jaffe, Fraulein F., TR; Alexander, Rebecca J., TR; Kornicks, Margot, TR

JAHARIS FAMILY FOUNDATION

1001 BRICKELL BAY DR., 25TH FL.
MIAMI, FL 33131
305-523-3637

ID NUMBER: 592751110
FEDERAL REPORTING DATE: 05/02
AREAS OF INTEREST: Arts & Culture, Education, Medicine, Religion, Scholarships, Social Services, Sports & Athletics
CURRENT ASSETS: $26,434,243   PRIOR ASSETS:
$26,503,018
TOTAL AMOUNT AWARDED: $1,607,500
HIGH: $808,000--Greek Orthodox Archdiocese
MID: $150,000--St. Michaels Home for the Elderly
LOW: $2,000--ENH Evanston & Galenbrook Hospital
GRANTS AWARDS: Cycladic Art Foundation--$10,000, U.H.A.C.--$2,500, Cathedral Philoptpchos Society--$5,000, Florida Grand Opera--$2,000, Kyrenia Cardiovascular Centre--$25,000, Holy Trinity Cathedral--$18,000, Helenic College--$35,000, St Andrews Church--$40,000, Metropolitan Museum of Art--$32,000, Little Orchestra Society, Inc.--$15,000, Ball State University--$15,000, Partnership for Kids--$1,000, Indian University Southeast--$5,000, St. Michaels Home for the Elderly--$150,000, Order of St. andrew--$10,000
SERVICE AREA: National
COMMENTS: Applications should be sent to Kathryn Jaharis at 1001 Brickell Bay Drive, 25th Floor, Miami, FL. 33131. (305) 523-3637.
DEADLINES: None
OFFICERS: Jaharis, Kathryn, D/P/TR/S; Jaharis, Michael, D; Aronoff, Steven K., D; Jaharis, Steven, D

JALBERT CHARITABLE TRUST

C/O SALEEBY
359 S. COUNTY RD.
PALM BEACH, FL 33480
561-655-5766

ID NUMBER: 656179327
FEDERAL REPORTING DATE: 05/01
AREAS OF INTEREST: Education, Religion, Scholarships
CURRENT ASSETS: $570,966   PRIOR ASSETS:
$582,318
TOTAL AMOUNT AWARDED: $11,000
HIGH: $2,000--Sacred Heart
MID: $2,000--Cardinal Newman High School
LOW: $1,000--St. John Baptist Catholic Church
GRANTS AWARDS: Hope Rural School--$2,000, Holy Spirit Catholic Church--$2,000, St. Nicolas Building Fund--$2,000
SERVICE AREA: National
COMMENTS: Gives to preselected organizations.
DEADLINES: None
OFFICERS: Saleeby, Richard E., TR; Kelly, Rita J., TR; Macgabhann, Rev. Kevin P., TR

JAYNE FOUNDATION

3399N PGA BLVD., SUITE 450
PALM BEACH GARDENS, FL 33410
561-630-6110

ID NUMBER: 650709380
FEDERAL REPORTING DATE: 08/01
AREAS OF INTEREST: Education, Scholarships
CURRENT ASSETS: $108,261   PRIOR ASSETS:
$163,143
TOTAL AMOUNT AWARDED: $9,000
HIGH: $9,000--St. Michaels Independant
GRANTS AWARDS: N/A
SERVICE AREA: FL
COMMENTS: Gives to preselected organizations.
DEADLINES: N/A
OFFICERS: Cummings, Keith L., P/T; Rrabnovitch, Flora R., D; Reitman, Howard J., S

JOY FOUNDATION, INC.

P.O. BOX 895007
LEESBURG, FL 34789-5007
352-343-4000

ID NUMBER: 592825965
FEDERAL REPORTING DATE: 02/02
AREAS OF INTEREST: Scholarships
CURRENT ASSETS: $149,973   PRIOR ASSETS: $71,279
TOTAL AMOUNT AWARDED: $23,205
HIGH: $21,205--Friendship C.M.E. Church
LOW: $1,000--Individual
GRANTS AWARDS: Individual--$1,000
SERVICE AREA: FL
COMMENTS: Send applications to: John D. McLeod, P.O.Box 895007, Leesburg, Fl. 34789-5007 904-787-4000
DEADLINES: None
OFFICERS: McLeod, John D., P/D; McLeod, Sherry S., S/D; Taylor, Patrick J.,T/D

KAGAN, LEE PERELSTINE CHARITABLE TRUST

C/O ELLIOT HARRIS, ESQ.
111 S.W. 3RD ST., 6TH FL.
MIAMI, FL 33130-1926
305-358-0146

ID NUMBER: 656319038
FEDERAL REPORTING DATE: 03/02
AREAS OF INTEREST: Education, Medicine, Religion, Scholarships
CURRENT ASSETS: $3,860,496 PRIOR ASSETS: $3,929,330
TOTAL AMOUNT AWARDED: $104,541
HIGH: $50,000--Brandeis University, MA
MID: $18,300--Conquer Fragile X Foundation
LOW: $18,000--Foundation of Jewish Phil. of Greater Miami
GRANTS AWARDS: American Friends of Beitissie Shapiro--$18,241
SERVICE AREA: FL, MA
COMMENTS: Gives to preselected organizations.
DEADLINES: None
OFFICERS: Harris, Elliot, Esq., TR

KAHLER, ANNE & CARL SCHOLARSHIP TRUST

C/O BANK OF AMERICA
P.O. BOX 40200
JACKSONVILLE, FL 32203-0200
904-464-3664

ID NUMBER: 596872008
FEDERAL REPORTING DATE: 04/02
AREAS OF INTEREST: Education, Scholarships
CURRENT ASSETS: $126,767 PRIOR ASSETS: $151,968
TOTAL AMOUNT AWARDED: $5,000
HIGH: $1,000--University of Florida
MID: $1,000--University of West Florida
LOW: $1,000--Auburn University
GRANTS AWARDS: Manatee Community College--$1,000, Florida State University--$1,000
SERVICE AREA: FL
COMMENTS: Provides scholarships to needy graduates of Venice H.S. in Venice, FL - considering academic performance, financial need, motivation and potential. Applications are sent to the Nominating-Advisory Committee and should be addressed to Richard Hazen, Esq., 227 Pensacola Road, Venice, FL 34285-2327
DEADLINES: End of May each year.
OFFICERS: Bank of America N.A., TR

KANDERS FOUNDATION, INC.

2100 S. OCEAN BLVD., STE. 302N
PALM BEACH, FL 33480
561-585-4726

ID NUMBER: 650124714
FEDERAL REPORTING DATE: 03/02
AREAS OF INTEREST: Arts & Culture, Education, Health, Scholarships
CURRENT ASSETS: $2,174,631 PRIOR ASSETS: $2,323,995
TOTAL AMOUNT AWARDED: $154,973
HIGH: $68,000--Cornell U.
MID: $25,000--Norton Museum of Art
LOW: $100--Palm Beach Fellowship
GRANTS AWARDS: Temple Sinai--$750, Westminstrer School--$5,000, Atlanta Speech School--$1,000, The High Museum of Art--$1,500, WNYC Radio--$180, Morristown & Morris Townsh--$100, Palm Beach Fellowship--$100, Anti-Defamation Leage--$1,000, Jewish Federation of Palm Beach--$360, Flagler Museum--$150, Palm Beach Opera--$5,650, NPR Foundation--$1,000, Flagler Museum--$150
SERVICE AREA: Palm Beach, NE United States
COMMENTS: Gives to preselected organizations. No unsolicited requests.
DEADLINES: None
OFFICERS: Kanders, Dr. Ralph, D; Kanders, Jeanne, D; Kanders, Warren, D

KASPER EDUCATIONAL TRUST

C/O GARY D. SCHROEDER
4016 TERIWOOD AVE.
ORLANDO, FL 32812
407-855-7688

ID NUMBER: 237273517
FEDERAL REPORTING DATE: 03/02
AREAS OF INTEREST: Education, Religion, Scholarships
CURRENT ASSETS: $0 PRIOR ASSETS: $116,671
TOTAL AMOUNT AWARDED: $119,137
HIGH: $119,137--Trinity Lutheran School
GRANTS AWARDS: N/A
SERVICE AREA: Orlando, FL
COMMENTS: Send applications to Gary D. Schroeder at 4016 Teriwood Avenue, Orlando, FL. 32812
DEADLINES: N/A
OFFICERS: Penberthy, Helen, TR; Vorpagel, David, TR; Schroeder, Gary D., TR

KATCHER FAMILY FOUNDATION, INC.

1399 S.W. 1ST AVE.
MIAMI, FL 33130
305-358-4222

ID NUMBER: 650715498
FEDERAL REPORTING DATE: 01/02
AREAS OF INTEREST: Arts & Culture, Community, Education, Scholarships
CURRENT ASSETS: $4,015,422 PRIOR ASSETS: $3,992,677
TOTAL AMOUNT AWARDED: $778,967
HIGH: $376,255--The Early Childhood Institute
MID: $186,450--Museum for African Art
LOW: $100--Juvenile Diabetes Foundation
GRANTS AWARDS: Ransom Everglades School--$10,000, Close Encounters With Music--$2,000, Temple Beth Am--$4,018, The Apen Institute--$1,550, Brooklyn College Fund--$100, Studio In A School--$2,000, St. Louis Humanities Program--$250, Hope School of Fine Arts--$500, Facing History and Ourselves--$500, The Melissa Institute--$100, Museum for Modern Art--$2,500, Miami City Ballet--$2,500, MADD--$150, Midori & Friends--$500, Lowe Art Museum--$500, Greater Miami Jewish Federation--$25,000
SERVICE AREA: FL, NY, CT, CO
COMMENTS: Send applications to Gerald Katcher, 1399 SW 1ST AVE., 4TH FL, Miami, Fl 33130 305-358-4222
DEADLINES: None
OFFICERS: Katcher, Gerald, D; Katcher, Jane, D; Heller, Lesley, D

KATES FOUNDATION, INC.

P.O. BOX 4153
SARASOTA, FL 34230-4153
941-365-2922

ID NUMBER: 650401513
FEDERAL REPORTING DATE: 04/02
AREAS OF INTEREST: Arts & Culture, Community,
Education, Medicine, Religion, Scholarships, Social Services,
Sports & Athletics
CURRENT ASSETS: $2,306,254 PRIOR ASSETS:
$2,305,286
TOTAL AMOUNT AWARDED: $118,728
HIGH: $18,823--The Education Foundation of Sarasota
MID: $5,000--Florida Sheriffs Youth Ranch
LOW: $150--Hadassah
GRANTS AWARDS: American Jewish Committee--$1,000,
Big Brothers, Big Sisters--$5,000, Art League of Manatee--
$1,000, First Step--$4,200, Adopt A Family--$1,000, Women's
Legal Fund--$2,500, Forty Carrots--$7,500, Florida Studio
Theater--$10,000, Meals on Wheels--$500, Jewish Community
Ctr.--$1,000, Suncoast Basketball Corp--$500, Planned
Parenthood--$10,000, Flanzer Jewish Community Center--
$325, Sarasota-Manatee Jewish Fdn.--$10,600
SERVICE AREA: FL
COMMENTS: Primary focus is the state of Florida but other
areas may be considered. there are no other restrictions. Send
applications to: Lisa Kates, P.O. Box 4153, Sarasota, FL 34230
DEADLINES: 2/28, 5/31, 8/31, 11/30
OFFICERS: Kates, Beatrice H., P; Kates, Mena Lisa, S/T;
Kates, Alan J., VP

KATZEN FAMILY FOUNDATION, INC.

P.O. BOX 5r1073
PUNTA GORDA, FL 33951-1073
941-639-8363

ID NUMBER: 650452246
FEDERAL REPORTING DATE: 05/02
AREAS OF INTEREST: Arts & Culture, Community,
Education, Environment, Medicine, Religion, Research,
Scholarships, Social Services
CURRENT ASSETS: $33,038 PRIOR ASSETS: $49,022
TOTAL AMOUNT AWARDED: $16,300
HIGH: $5,000--Charlotte County Family YMCA
MID: $1,000--University of Miami
LOW: $100--American Cancer Society
GRANTS AWARDS: Richard David Kann--$100, American
Heart Association--$125, Marta Hernandez Burchers--$1,000,
C.A.R.E.--$100, Florida Gulf Coast University--$5,000,
Bernice A. Russel Center--$2,000, New Operation Cooper
Street, Inc.--$650
SERVICE AREA: National
COMMENTS: Gives to preselected otganizations. Application
should be addressed to Melvin J. Katzen at PO BOX 1073
Punta Gorda, FL. 33951.
DEADLINES: None
OFFICERS: Katzen, Melvyn J. MD, D; Katzen, Jullian A., D;
Katzen, Tanya, D

KAYLOR, JAMES REEVES MEMORIAL FOUNDATION, INC.

2766 DOUGLAS RD.
MIAMI, FL 33133
703-547-3141

ID NUMBER: 592359415
FEDERAL REPORTING DATE: 12/01
AREAS OF INTEREST: Community, Scholarships
CURRENT ASSETS: $127,118 PRIOR ASSETS:
$114,667
TOTAL AMOUNT AWARDED: $7,150
HIGH: $7,150--Beaver Creek Arts Foundation
GRANTS AWARDS: N/A
SERVICE AREA: , CO
COMMENTS: No required form. Submit requests to: R.
James Kaylor, P.O. Box 4179, Avon, CO 81620
DEADLINES: None
OFFICERS: Kaylor, R. James, P/D; Kaylor, Diana, S/T;
Hirschhorn, Joel, D

KEARNS FAMILY FOUNDATION

1919 WINSLOE DR.
NEW PORT RICHEY, FL 34655-5635

ID NUMBER: 66476254
FEDERAL REPORTING DATE: 06/02
AREAS OF INTEREST: Arts & Culture, Community,
Education, Environment, Religion, Research, Scholarships,
Sports & Athletics
CURRENT ASSETS: $700,416 PRIOR ASSETS:
$807,580
TOTAL AMOUNT AWARDED: $48,000
HIGH: $5,000--Loyola High School, Baltimore
MID: $2,000--Lifewater International
LOW: $500--School of Visual Arts
GRANTS AWARDS: St. James Academyt--$1,000, Harley
School--$2,500, Montezuma Land Conservation--$1,000,
Rochester Area Community--$1,000, ACA/George N Sudduth
Endowment--$1,000, ACA/Winona Campership Fund--
$1,000, ACF/George N Sudduth Endowment--$500,
ACF/Sudduth Endowment - Wyonego--$500, American
Camping Association - Wyonego--$500
SERVICE AREA: National
COMMENTS: Gives to preselected organizations.
DEADLINES: None
OFFICERS: Kearns, David T., TR; Kearns, Shirley C., TR;
Clark, Lucy, TR

KEENAN, PEGGY FOUNDATION

C/O BANK OF AMERICA
P. O. BOX 40200 MC FL9-100-10-19
JACKSONVILLE, FL 32203-0200
877-446-1410

ID NUMBER: 597025773
FEDERAL REPORTING DATE: 06/02
AREAS OF INTEREST: Education, Scholarships
CURRENT ASSETS: $226,289 PRIOR ASSETS:
$227,397
TOTAL AMOUNT AWARDED: $10,624
HIGH: $5,312--University of Sourthern California
LOW: $5,312--New School Univ.
GRANTS AWARDS: N/A
SERVICE AREA: NY, CA
COMMENTS: Gives to preselected organizations.
DEADLINES: None

OFFICERS: Bank of America, TR

KELCO FOUNDATION
4595 BAYVIEW DR.
FORT LAUDERDALE, FL 33308

ID NUMBER: 650019085
FEDERAL REPORTING DATE: 02/02
AREAS OF INTEREST: Education, Religion, Scholarships
CURRENT ASSETS: $1,338,559 PRIOR ASSETS:
$1,271,821
TOTAL AMOUNT AWARDED: $380,000
HIGH: $355,000--St. Thomas Aquinas Catholic High School
LOW: $25,000--St. Senan's Scholarship
GRANTS AWARDS: Clare Scholarship Fund--$10,000, St.
Senan's Scholarship--$25,000
SERVICE AREA: FL, TX, Ireland
COMMENTS: No requests are invited. Promoting Catholic
education and evangelization.
DEADLINES: None
OFFICERS: Kelly, Vincent, D; Shaheen, Susan, D; Molchan,
Janet, D

KELLY FOUNDATION, INC.
801 E. SUGARLAND HWY.
CLEWISTON, FL 33440
800-232-2282

ID NUMBER: 596153269
FEDERAL REPORTING DATE: 04/02
AREAS OF INTEREST: Community, Education,
Environment, Health, Medicine, Religion, Research,
Scholarships, Social Services
CURRENT ASSETS: $9,894,701 PRIOR ASSETS:
$9,414,827
TOTAL AMOUNT AWARDED: $228,788
HIGH: $124,787--Misc. Organizations
LOW: $104,000--Educational Grants awarded to Individuals
GRANTS AWARDS: N/A
SERVICE AREA: National
COMMENTS: Send applications to: Robert W. Kelly, 801 E.
Sugarland Hwy., Clewiston, Fl. 33440. Submit copy of
application with original.
DEADLINES: None
OFFICERS: Kelly, R. W., P; Kelly, Marjorie, D; Wyse, Alden
M., S/T; Kelly, Robert W., Jr, D; Kelly, Eileen, D; Kelly, L.G.,
VP

KEY WEST ROTARY FOUNDATION, INC.
C/O JOHN G. PARKS, JR. CPA, P.A.
815 PEACOCK PLAZA
KEY WEST, FL 33040

ID NUMBER: 592826669
FEDERAL REPORTING DATE: 11/01
AREAS OF INTEREST: Scholarships
CURRENT ASSETS: $203,609 PRIOR ASSETS:
$185,617
TOTAL AMOUNT AWARDED: $21,975
HIGH: $9,000--Individual
MID: $3,000--Individual
LOW: $500--Individual
GRANTS AWARDS: N/A
DEADLINES: N/A

OFFICERS: Labrada, Pat, C; Gage, Walter, S; Soos, Robert
L., Jr., VC; Parks, John G., Jr., TR; Martin, Jack, TR;
Carraway, Robert, TR

KIRBO, SUC TUA THOMAS M.
C/O BANK OF AMERICA
P.O. BOX 40200
JACKSONVILLE, FL 32203-0200
877-446-1410

ID NUMBER: 596472588
FEDERAL REPORTING DATE: 05/02
AREAS OF INTEREST: Education, Scholarships
CURRENT ASSETS: $975,003 PRIOR ASSETS:
$1,008,752
TOTAL AMOUNT AWARDED: $60,015
HIGH: $13,515--Univ. of Florida
MID: $13,500--Florida State Univ.
LOW: $11,000--Jacksonville Univ.
GRANTS AWARDS: Florida Community College--$11,000,
Univ. of North Florida--$11,000
SERVICE AREA: FL
COMMENTS: Gives to preselected organizations.
DEADLINES: None
OFFICERS: Bank of America, TR

KIRSCH, HYMAN FOUNDATION
C/O LEE KIRSCH
630 MASTERS WAY
PALM BEACH GARDENS, FL 33418-8493

ID NUMBER: 116025681
FEDERAL REPORTING DATE: 04/02
AREAS OF INTEREST: Arts & Culture, Community,
Education, Environment, Health, Medicine, Religion,
Research, Scholarships, Social Services, Sports & Athletics,
Other
CURRENT ASSETS: $436,180 PRIOR ASSETS:
$423,047
TOTAL AMOUNT AWARDED: $39,650
HIGH: $4,000--American Red Cross
MID: $2,500--NYS World Trade Ctr. Relief Fund
LOW: $250--One Art, Inc.
GRANTS AWARDS: Alliance for Aging--$500, Alpert Jewish
Family & Children's Services--$250, American Technion
Society--$500, Anti-Defamation League--$250, AVON Breast
Cancer--$250, Branders Univ. NWC--$1,000, Charlee Homes
for Children--$1,500, CJ Fdn. for Sudden Infant Death
Syndrome (SIDS)--$1,000, Diabetes Research Inst. Fdn.--
$500, FIU Fdn.--$250, Florida Sheriff's Youth Ranches--
$1,000, Friends of Abused Children--$250, Greater Miami
Jewish Federation--$400, Greg Chan Scholarship Fund--$500,
Hadassah Miami Region--$500
SERVICE AREA: National
DEADLINES: None
OFFICERS: Kirsch, Bertha, P/D; Kirsch, David, VP/D;
Lampert, Sara K., S/D; Kirsch, Leon, T/D

KIRSNER, HYMAN A. & IDA FAMILY FOUNDATION
C/O MARVIN KIRSNER
2255 GLADES RD., STE. 419A
BOCA RATON, FL 33431
561-912-3230

ID NUMBER: 650711872

FEDERAL REPORTING DATE: 10/01
AREAS OF INTEREST: Education, Religion, Research, Scholarships, Social Services
CURRENT ASSETS: $402,149 PRIOR ASSETS: $385,915
TOTAL AMOUNT AWARDED: $29,300
HIGH: $10,000--Chabad of Space Coast
MID: $4,200--Temple Beth Am
LOW: $400--Jewish Federation of Breva
GRANTS AWARDS: Beth El of the Beaches Syn.--$4,400, Beth Shira Congregation--$2,400, Dade Comm. Fdn.--$2,400, Sanford L. Jiff Jewish Mus.--$500, Wuesthoff Brevard College--$2,000, Ramah Darom, Inc.--$3,000
SERVICE AREA: FL, GA
COMMENTS: Gives to preselected organizations.
DEADLINES: None
OFFICERS: Kirsner, Hyman, M; Kirsner, Ida, M; Kirsner, Harry, D; Goldberg, Diane A., D; Kirsner, Marvin A., D; Kirsner, Steven, D

KIWANIS OF LITTLE HAVANA FOUNDATION

701 S.W. 27TH AVE., STE. 900
MIAMI, FL 33135
305-664-8888

ID NUMBER: 650093807
FEDERAL REPORTING DATE: 12/01
AREAS OF INTEREST: Education, Scholarships
CURRENT ASSETS: $354,935 PRIOR ASSETS: $294,457
TOTAL AMOUNT AWARDED: $81,547
HIGH: $12,292--Riverside Elementary School
MID: $5,000--Coral Gables Elementary School
LOW: $130--Individual
GRANTS AWARDS: Orange Bowl Committee--$750, Individual--$1,394, Individual--$138, Individual--$472, Individual--$3,619
COMMENTS: Gives to preselected organizations.
DEADLINES: N/A
OFFICERS: Cuervo, Manuel A., CH; Halley, Carlos, VCH; Gonzales, Manuel A., VCH; Perez, Rual A., S; Bolano, Andres, Jr., T

KNIGHT, JOHN S. & JAMES L. FOUNDATION

2 S. BISCAYNE BLVD.
1 BISCAYNE TOWER, STE. 3800
MIAMI, FL 33131-1803
305-908-2600

ID NUMBER: 650464177
FEDERAL REPORTING DATE: 12/01
AREAS OF INTEREST: Arts & Culture, Community, Education, Environment, Health, Medicine, Religion, Research, Scholarships, Social Services, Sports & Athletics, Other
CURRENT ASSETS: $2,124,460,152 PRIOR ASSETS: $1,838,992,265
TOTAL AMOUNT AWARDED: $70,746,766
HIGH: $5,000,000-Cornell Univ.
MID: $1,000,000-American Battle Monuments Commission
LOW: $10,000--Tallahassee Symphony Orchestra
GRANTS AWARDS: Alternate ROOTS--$150,000, Alvin Ailey Dance Theater Fdn.--$100,000, American Assn. of Museums--$100,000, American Composers Forum--$200,000, American Dance Festival--$100,000, American Library Assn.--

$250,000, American Symphony Orchestra League--$700,000, American Wind Symphony--$25,000, Appalshop--$125,000, Arena Stage--$150,000, Arts Midwest--$50,000, Bay Chamber Concerts--$100,000, College of Santa Fe--$155,000, Dance/USA--$200,000, Ensemble Studio Theatre--$100,000
SERVICE AREA: National
DEADLINES: None
OFFICERS: Hodding, Carter III, P/CEO; McPhee, Penelope, VP; Crowe, Timothy, VP; Clossick, Beatriz, VP/T

KOHNKEN FAMILY FOUNDATION, INC.

C/O DONALD H. KOHNKEN
1799 SABAL PALM DR.
BOCA RATON, FL 33432
561-394-3721

ID NUMBER: 650799146
FEDERAL REPORTING DATE: 05/02
AREAS OF INTEREST: Arts & Culture, Community, Education, Health, Medicine, Scholarships, Sports & Athletics
CURRENT ASSETS: $2,342,961 PRIOR ASSETS: $2,357,736
TOTAL AMOUNT AWARDED: $104,000
HIGH: $50,000--Monkami Fdn.
MID: $13,000--Boca Raton Comm. Hospital
LOW: $250--National Outdoor Leadership School
GRANTS AWARDS: Monkami, Inc.--$3,250, Boca Raton Museum of Art--$1,000, Atlantis Children's Hospital--$250, Rutgers Univ.--$2,000, Averett College--$1,500, Harvard Business School--$2,000, Lynn Univ.--$1,000, Monkami, Inc.--$12,750, American Heart Assn.--$3,000, Palm Beach Cultural Council--$1,000, Baltimore Christian School--$3,000, Maryland Hall for Creative Arts--$1,000, Greenville SC Zoo--$500, Camperdown Academy--$1,000, Key School Capital Fund--$2,500
SERVICE AREA: National
COMMENTS: Gives to preselected organizations.
DEADLINES: None
OFFICERS: Kohnken, Donald H., P/T; Kohnken, Beverlee M., VP/S; Hoffacker, Lynda, TR; Cole, Dana, TR; Lewis, Tenley, TR; Wiseman, Melissa, TR

KRAUSMAN, ESSIE SCHOLARSHIP TRUST

C/O BANK OF AMERICA
P.O. BOX 40200
JACKSONVILLE, FL 32203-0200
877-446-1410

ID NUMBER: 596161774
FEDERAL REPORTING DATE: 01/02
AREAS OF INTEREST: Scholarships
CURRENT ASSETS: $832,060 PRIOR ASSETS: $924,676
TOTAL AMOUNT AWARDED: $46,750
HIGH: $1,000--Individual
MID: $600--Individual
LOW: $250--Individual
GRANTS AWARDS: N/A
SERVICE AREA: Pinellas County
COMMENTS: Contact NationsBank N.A., P.O. Box 11388, St. Petersburg, FL 33733, for standard application form. Include personal characteristics, educational background, financial data and references. Factors considered are scholastic standing, need and moral and religious attributes. Request deadline information. Undergrads only.

DEADLINES: End of each academic year.
OFFICERS: Bank of America N.A., TR

KUGELMAN FOUNDATION

4300 BAYOU BLVD., STE. 21
PENSACOLA, FL 32503
850-478-3995

ID NUMBER: 596177695
FEDERAL REPORTING DATE: 05/01
AREAS OF INTEREST: Arts & Culture, Community,
Education, Health, Medicine, Religion, Scholarships, Social
Services, Other
CURRENT ASSETS: $4,103,109 PRIOR ASSETS:
$4,035,253
TOTAL AMOUNT AWARDED: $260,653
HIGH: $50,000--Gulf Coast Kids House
MID: $15,000--Pace Center
LOW: $300--Mental Health
GRANTS AWARDS: Ronald McDonald House--$250, PJC
Fdn.--$1,250, Fiesta Five Flags--$2,549, Pensacola Jr. College--
$10,000, American Red Cross--$1,000, Art Council--$2,500,
Alzheimer's Family Services--$500, Baptist Healthcare--
$50,000, Favor House--$5,000, Loaves & Fishes--$2,290,
Hospice of NW FL.--$12,000, Interfaith Jail Ministries--$500,
Learn to Read--$500, Lups Fdn.--$500, New Beginning--
$1,000
SERVICE AREA: NW FL, Pensacola
COMMENTS: Send appliations to D. Jack Kugelman at P.O.
Box 30130 Pensacola, FL. 32503.
DEADLINES: None
OFFICERS: Kugelman, D. Jack, C

LAKE TOWERS GOOD SAMARITAN FUND

101 TRINITY LAKES DR.
SUN CITY CENTER, FL 33573
813-634-6039

ID NUMBER: 596777442
FEDERAL REPORTING DATE: 04/02
AREAS OF INTEREST: Education, Scholarships
CURRENT ASSETS: $141,982 PRIOR ASSETS:
$133,855
TOTAL AMOUNT AWARDED: $120
HIGH: $120--Individual
GRANTS AWARDS: N/A
SERVICE AREA: National
DEADLINES: None
OFFICERS: Hedgecock, Durwood J., C; Busbee, Ruth, T;
Herron, Berneice, S

LAMB, KIRKLAND S. AND RENA B. FOUNDATION

1312 ECKLES DRIVE
TAMPA, FL 33612
813-932-9830

ID NUMBER: 566062394
FEDERAL REPORTING DATE: 05/02
AREAS OF INTEREST: Education, Religion, Scholarships
CURRENT ASSETS: $4,756,309 PRIOR ASSETS:
$5,345,926
TOTAL AMOUNT AWARDED: $469,674
HIGH: $85,000--Dallas Theological Seminary

MID: $23,000--Christ Community Church Tampa
LOW: $500--Child Evangelism Fellowship of Greater Dallas
GRANTS AWARDS: Cam International--$2,640, Josh
MacDowell's Ministries--$25,000, Peter Deyneka Russian
Ministries--$10,000, Mission Discovery--$20,000, June
Shelton School & Evaluation Ctr.--$10,000, Advancing
Churches Missions Commitment--$20,000, Dallas Theological
Seminary--$80,771, Wycliffe Bible Translators--$10,000,
Leighton Ford Ministries--$15,000, Chrysalis Ministries--
$5,000, Jerusalem Univ. College--$8,760
SERVICE AREA: National
COMMENTS: Gives to preselected organizations.
DEADLINES: None
OFFICERS: Johnston, Wendell G., P; Williams, Lillian L.,
VP; Johnston, Martha L., S; Williams, Richard A., T

LAMBERT FAMILY FOUNDATION, INC.

C/O HARRY W. LAMBERT
437 GARDENIA ST.
BELLEAIR, FL 33756
727-584-6384

ID NUMBER: 593293497
FEDERAL REPORTING DATE: 06/01
AREAS OF INTEREST: Arts & Culture, Community,
Education, Health, Medicine, Religion, Scholarships, Social
Services
CURRENT ASSETS: $323,004 PRIOR ASSETS:
$324,131
TOTAL AMOUNT AWARDED: $20,420
HIGH: $5,500--Haywood Regional Medical
MID: $3,600--Holy Trinity St. Nicholas
LOW: $100--Mountian Center
GRANTS AWARDS: Haywood County Arts Council--$320,
Morton Plant Meese Foundation--$1,050, Salvation Army--
$1,000, United Way of Haywood County--$2,500, University
of Cincinnati Foundation--$4,000, Haywood Christian
Ministry--$150, Florida Blood Bank--$1,000, M.J. Fory
Foundation--$1,000
SERVICE AREA: National
COMMENTS: Applications should be addressed to Harry W.
Lambert, 437 Ga Belleair, FL. 33756, (727) 584-6384. Form
in which applications should be submitted is by letter decribing
the purpose and needs of the organization.
DEADLINES: None
OFFICERS: Lambert, Harry W., D; Lambert, Susanne R.,
D; Lambert, William A., D; Lambert, Laurie., D; Rilling,
Pamela L., D

LAMBERT FOUNDATION

1025 FLAMEVINE LN., STE 3
VERO BEACH, FL 32963
561-231-4446

ID NUMBER: 650749367
FEDERAL REPORTING DATE: 08/01
AREAS OF INTEREST: Community, Education, Health,
Religion, Scholarships, Social Services
CURRENT ASSETS: $1,763,268 PRIOR ASSETS:
$1,598,004
TOTAL AMOUNT AWARDED: $72,512
HIGH: $25,537--IRCC Foundation
MID: $5,000--National Apt. Assoc. Edu. Fdn.
LOW: $100--Indian River Memorial
GRANTS AWARDS: Oslo Middle School--$575, Progressive
Civic League of Gifford--$1,000, St. Edward's School Bldg.

Capital Campaign--$20,000, The Salvation Army--$1,000, U of Illinois Foundation--$5,000, Visiting Nurse Assoc & Hospice Fdn.--$1,000, Dollars for Scholars Foundation--$1,000, Community Child Care Resources--$4,500
SERVICE AREA: FL, IL, National
COMMENTS: Gives to preselected organizations.
DEADLINES: None
OFFICERS: Lambert, Roy H., P/D; Lambert, Patsy J., VP/D; Davis, Donna G., D; Lambert, Roy H. JR., D; Lambert, Philip A., D; Lambert, Ronald S., D

LARKIN, LENORE AND HAROLD PHILANTHROPIC
1400 S. OCEAN BLVD. N., STE. 1405
BOCA RATON, FL 33432

ID NUMBER: 650310975
FEDERAL REPORTING DATE: 05/01
AREAS OF INTEREST: Arts & Culture, Community, Education, Medicine, Religion, Scholarships, Sports & Athletics
CURRENT ASSETS: $1,030,665 **PRIOR ASSETS:** $611,521
TOTAL AMOUNT AWARDED: $420,354
HIGH: $100,000--Boston University Medical School, MA
MID: $42,054--Temple Beth El, MA
LOW: $100--American Cancer Society
GRANTS AWARDS: Temple Sinai--$15,000, Hebrew Rehabilitation--$2,500, Boston Aid to the Blind--$5,000, Boca Raton Community Hopsital--$5,000, Secret Santa Foundation--$5,000, Bnai Brith Sports Lodge--$16,000, Covenant Senior Center--$5,000, LEAH--$600, American Jewish Committee--$25,000, JCC Cultural Arts--$5,000, The Haven--$500, Jewish Community Foundation--$87,500, Jewish Braille America--$1,000, Simon Weisenthal Center--$2,500
SERVICE AREA: MA, FL
COMMENTS: Gives to preselected organizations.
DEADLINES: None
OFFICERS: Larkin, Harold., P; Larkin, Lenore., VP; Spector, Andrew R., S; Larkin, Susan., T; Larkin, A.J., T

LASH, HILDEGARD FOUNDATION
C/O B. PAUL KATZ
ONE FLORIDA PARK DR. S., ATRIUM STE.
PALM COAST, FL 32137
904-446-4469

ID NUMBER: 593379072
FEDERAL REPORTING DATE: 05/02
AREAS OF INTEREST: Scholarships, Social Services
CURRENT ASSETS: $940,796 **PRIOR ASSETS:** $768,910
TOTAL AMOUNT AWARDED: $64,000
HIGH: $64,000--Orphan Foundation of America
GRANTS AWARDS: N/A
SERVICE AREA: National
COMMENTS: Gives to preselected organizations.
DEADLINES: None
OFFICERS: Katz, B. Paul, P; Taber, Stuart., D; Lipner, Seth E., D

LAUFFER, CHARLES A. TRUST
C/O BANK OF AMERICA
P.O. BOX 40200
JACKSONVILLE, FL 32203-0200
877-446-1410

ID NUMBER: 596121126
FEDERAL REPORTING DATE: 01/01
AREAS OF INTEREST: Medicine, Scholarships, Other
CURRENT ASSETS: $3,421,553 **PRIOR ASSETS:** $3,426,228
TOTAL AMOUNT AWARDED: $187,906
HIGH: $94,640--Scholarships - $3,640 Each
MID: $11,372--Young Men's Christian Association
LOW: $2,275--Salvation Army
GRANTS AWARDS: Young Woman's Christian Association--$11,372, Brookwood--$11,372, University of South Florida--$2,275, United Way of Pinellas County--$2,275, American Red Cross--$2,275, West Central Florida Council BSA--$2,275, Suncoast Girl Scouts--$2,275, University of Pennsylvania--$2,275, Hood College--$2,275, Big Brothers Big Sisters--$2,275, Florida Blood Services--$2,275
SERVICE AREA: Pinellas County, National
COMMENTS: Send application to Bank of America, 3839 Fourth St. N., St. Petersburg, FL 33703-6198, Attn: Elizabeth Knowles FL2-210-01-01; Letter of application, documentation of school attendance, major course of study, GPA and financial; Priority for: 1) medical students 2)agriculture 3) eng.
DEADLINES: None
OFFICERS: Bank of America NA, TR

LEESBURG POLICE DEPARTMENT SCHOLARSHIP FOUNDATION
P.O. BOX 3838
ORLANDO, FL 32802

ID NUMBER: 586976025
FEDERAL REPORTING DATE: 05/02
AREAS OF INTEREST: Scholarships
CURRENT ASSETS: $141,535 **PRIOR ASSETS:** $140,212
TOTAL AMOUNT AWARDED: $5,288
GRANTS AWARDS: N/A
COMMENTS: Gives to preselected organizations.
DEADLINES: None

LEGORE, IVAN F. & INA C. SCHOLARSHIP FUND
C/O BANK OF AMERICA
P.O. BOX 40200
JACKSONVILLE, FL 33203-0200
904-464-3664

ID NUMBER: 656008408
FEDERAL REPORTING DATE: 07/01
AREAS OF INTEREST: Scholarships, Social Services
CURRENT ASSETS: $496,230 **PRIOR ASSETS:** $523,779
TOTAL AMOUNT AWARDED: $22,000
HIGH: $7,000--Individual
MID: $4,000--Individual
LOW: $2,000--Individual
GRANTS AWARDS: N/A
SERVICE AREA: Sarasota
COMMENTS: Scholarships are for student participants of Sailor Circus sponsored by Sarasota High School. Write Barnett

Banks Trust Company at the above address for application and guidelines. Contact Elizabeth Clarke at Barnett Bank.
DEADLINES: 4/15
OFFICERS: Bank of America, TR

LENNAR FOUNDATION
700 N.W. 107TH AVE.
MIAMI, FL 33172
305-229-6400

ID NUMBER: 650171539
FEDERAL REPORTING DATE: 07/01
AREAS OF INTEREST: Education, Environment, Scholarships, Social Services
CURRENT ASSETS: $5,255,198 PRIOR ASSETS: $3,936,292
TOTAL AMOUNT AWARDED: $668,000
HIGH: $210,000--The United Way of Dade County
MID: $125,000--The South Fla Annenberg Challenge, Inc
LOW: $3,000--National Conference for Comm. & Justice
GRANTS AWARDS: Miami Dade Alliance for Ethical Gov.--$10,000, I Have A Dream Foundation--$5,000, The Nat Moore Foundation--$5,000, Fla. Atlantic University--$2,000, PAVE--$60,000, Zoological Society of So. Fla.--$50,000
SERVICE AREA: Miami
COMMENTS: Submit letter along with copy of IRS Determination Letter regarding exempt status, type of organization, i.e. education, charitable, scientific, medical to Allan J. Pekor at the above address.
DEADLINES: None
OFFICERS: Miller, Leonard, P/TR; Miller, Stuart A., VP/TR; Pekor, Allan J., VP/TR

LEVIN & PAPANTONIO FAMILY FOUNDATION, INC.
316 S. BAYLEN ST., STE. 600
PENSACOLA, FL 32501
850-435-7157

ID NUMBER: 593107428
FEDERAL REPORTING DATE: 05/02
AREAS OF INTEREST: Community, Education, Health, Medicine, Religion, Scholarships, Social Services, Sports & Athletics
CURRENT ASSETS: $1,663,916 PRIOR ASSETS: $2,284,554
TOTAL AMOUNT AWARDED: $534,772
HIGH: $73,000--Loaves & Fishes
MID: $24,000--United Way of Escambia County, Inc.
LOW: $38--B'nai Israel Men's Club
GRANTS AWARDS: N/A
SERVICE AREA: FL
COMMENTS: Primary objective is to assist children in Northwest Florida.
DEADLINES: None
OFFICERS: Levin, Martin H., P; Logan, Flack, S/T; Papantonio, Michael, D

LEVINE FAMILY FOUNDATION, INC.
2608 N. DIXIE HWY., STE. 100
WEST PALM BEACH, FL 33407
207-871-0036

ID NUMBER: 650834879

FEDERAL REPORTING DATE: 10/01
AREAS OF INTEREST: Community, Education, Health, Religion, Research, Scholarships, Social Services, Other
CURRENT ASSETS: $767 PRIOR ASSETS: $0
TOTAL AMOUNT AWARDED: $106,300
HIGH: $25,000--Beth Isreal Synagogue
MID: $10,000--Mid-Maine Homeless
LOW: $1,000--Arthritis Fdn.
GRANTS AWARDS: Maine Pre-Trial Services--$3,000, Temple Beth El--$1,500, Serenity House--$5,500, Bath Family Crisis Ctr.--$1,000, Univ. of Maine Law School--$2,500, Mt. Sinai Cemetary Assn.--$1,000, Seacoast Health Net--$2,500, Habitat for Humanity Portland--$1,500, Immigrant Legal Advocacy Project--$5,000, Milestone Fdn.--$2,500, Catholic Charities--$5,000, YMCA--$5,000, Muscular Dystrophy--$1,800
SERVICE AREA: ME, NH
COMMENTS: Gives to preselected organizations.
DEADLINES: None
OFFICERS: Levine, Robert A., P; Taggersell, Vilean, S; Taggersell, Lance, VP

LEVINE, ABNER & MILDRED FAMILY FOUNDATION
16858 RIVER BIRCH CIR.
DELRAY BEACH, FL 33445
561-498-1500

ID NUMBER: 136172502
FEDERAL REPORTING DATE: 05/01
AREAS OF INTEREST: Arts & Culture, Community, Education, Environment, Health, Religion, Research, Scholarships, Social Services
CURRENT ASSETS: $1,328,522 PRIOR ASSETS: $1,220,997
TOTAL AMOUNT AWARDED: $386,365
HIGH: $26,500--Waxman Cancer Research
MID: $5,000--FL. Atlantic Univ.
LOW: $25--Spiritual Ins.
GRANTS AWARDS: Yeshiva High School--$100, Philharmonic Orchestra--$4,000, Miami Ballet--$180, Temple Beth El NY--$300, Jewish Theory--$1,500, NY Board of Rabbi's--$108, B'Nai Torah--$24,340, Alzheimer's Disease--$36, BRCH Fdn.--$500, American Cancer Society--$108, American Red Cross--$108, Institute for Music--$1,000, Brotherhood Mishki--$180, Soup Kitchen--$500, Diabetes Institute--$180
SERVICE AREA: National
COMMENTS: Gives to preselected organizations. No solicitations accept
DEADLINES: None
OFFICERS: Levine, Abner, D; Levine, Mildred, D; Miller, Ellen K., D; Levine, Lawrence, D; Levine, Michael F., D

LEWIS, CLARA TRUST UNDER WILL
3471 THOMASVILLE RD.
TALLAHASSEE, FL 32309
850-205-5160

ID NUMBER: 596554188
FEDERAL REPORTING DATE: 05/02
AREAS OF INTEREST: Education, Religion, Scholarships
CURRENT ASSETS: $236,142 PRIOR ASSETS: $267,727
TOTAL AMOUNT AWARDED: $14,683
HIGH: $11,120--First Church of Christ

LOW: $3,563--Florida State University
GRANTS AWARDS: N/A
SERVICE AREA: Tallahassee
COMMENTS: Gives to preselected organizations.
DEADLINES: None
OFFICERS: Bank of America N.A., TR; Synovus Trust Company, TR

LEWIS, MACK & ELEANOR FAMILY FOUNDATION

P. O. BOX 2523
PANAMA CITY, FL 32402
850-785-7174

ID NUMBER: 592604288
FEDERAL REPORTING DATE: 10/01
AREAS OF INTEREST: Arts & Culture, Education, Health, Religion, Scholarships, Social Services
CURRENT ASSETS: $231,777   PRIOR ASSETS: $243,404
TOTAL AMOUNT AWARDED: $23,045
HIGH: $5,000--First United Methodis Church
MID: $2,200--Bay Medical Ctr.
LOW: $70--Shaddai Shrine Temple
GRANTS AWARDS: Visual Arts Ctr.--$1,000, Kiwanis Club--$75, Jr. Museum of Bay Co.--$1,000, Salvation Army--$1,000, Martin Theatre Building--$5,000, Tom Hancy Education Fdn.--$1,000, Panama City Music Assn.--$1,000, Friends of St. Andrews State Park--$200, F. S. U.--$1,000, Kaleidoscope Theatre--$1,000, Red Cross--$1,000, Early Childhood Services--$500, Panama City Rescue Mission--$500, GCCL Scholarship--$1,000
SERVICE AREA: FL
COMMENTS: Gives to preselected organizations.
DEADLINES: None
OFFICERS: Lewis, Eleanor, P; Moore, Nancy, S/T; Moore, Joe, VP

LIBERTY, ELIZABETH J. CHARITABLE TRUST

3899 N.W. 23 CT.
BOCA RATON, FL 333431
561-852-9754

ID NUMBER: 656226498
FEDERAL REPORTING DATE: 04/02
AREAS OF INTEREST: Arts & Culture, Community, Education, Health, Religion, Scholarships, Social Services
CURRENT ASSETS: $81,666   PRIOR ASSETS: $72,508
TOTAL AMOUNT AWARDED: $6,700
HIGH: $2,200--George Snow Scholarship
MID: $700--Sheridan House
LOW: $200--Kids in Distress
GRANTS AWARDS: Childrens Home Society of Fl.--$500, Ministry of Good Shepherd--$600, Nazareth Friends--$500, Little Palm Family Theater--$300, Boca Raton Community Hospital--$200, Global Outreach--$600
SERVICE AREA: FL
COMMENTS: Gives to preselected organizations.
DEADLINES: None
OFFICERS: Liberty, Elizabeth J., TR; Liberty, Philip A., TR; Castillo, Frann J., TR; Liberty-Wayne, Anita, TR

LINCOLN FOUNDATION

P.O. BOX 163
WINDERMERE, FL 34786

ID NUMBER: 383014819
FEDERAL REPORTING DATE: 05/02
AREAS OF INTEREST: Scholarships
CURRENT ASSETS: $84,275   PRIOR ASSETS: $818,981
TOTAL AMOUNT AWARDED: $5,097
HIGH: $3,345--Individual
MID: $1,000--Individual
LOW: $752--individual
GRANTS AWARDS: N/A
SERVICE AREA: National
COMMENTS: Submit on organization letterhead. State cirriculum, activities, goals, ambitions. Show financial need.
DEADLINES: November 30
OFFICERS: Lincoln, P. M., P; Lincoln, Timothy, S/T

LIVINGSTON, GRACIA B. FOUNDATION

C/O FIRST UNION
CMG/FL2840, P.O. BOX 1000
ORLANDO, FL 32802-1000
407-649-5571

ID NUMBER: 593615446
FEDERAL REPORTING DATE: 05/02
AREAS OF INTEREST: Scholarships
CURRENT ASSETS: $539,250   PRIOR ASSETS: $554,132
TOTAL AMOUNT AWARDED: $0
GRANTS AWARDS: N/A
COMMENTS: Gives to preselected organizations.
DEADLINES: None
OFFICERS: Livingston, Gracia B., CH; Wilder, Charles D., P; David, C. Christine, VP; Waugh, M. Faye, T

LOCKHART FAMILY FOUNDATION

2307 CASTILLA ISLE
FORT LAUDERDALE, FL 33301
954-527-0890

ID NUMBER: 943347363
FEDERAL REPORTING DATE: 11/01
AREAS OF INTEREST: Health, Scholarships, Other
CURRENT ASSETS: $417,780   PRIOR ASSETS: $601,616
TOTAL AMOUNT AWARDED: $21,000
HIGH: $10,000--Boule Fdn.
MID: $5,500--ICAM
LOW: $2,000--Individual
GRANTS AWARDS: Bay Area Urban League--$2,500, Martha's Vineyard--$1,000
COMMENTS: Gives to preselected organizations.
DEADLINES: None
OFFICERS: Lockhart, James B., P/T; Lockhart, Ruth D., VP/S; Lockhart, Marc B., AVP; Williams, Diallo H., AVP

LYDEN FOUNDATION, INC.

P.O. BOX 700
WINTER PARK, FL 32790-0700
407-679-8181

ID NUMBER: 593469366

FEDERAL REPORTING DATE: 10/01
AREAS OF INTEREST: Scholarships
CURRENT ASSETS: $376,280 PRIOR ASSETS:
$335,914
TOTAL AMOUNT AWARDED: $13,000
HIGH: $4,000--Individual
MID: $3,000--Individual
LOW: $2,000--Individual
GRANTS AWARDS: N/A
COMMENTS: Gives to preselected organizations.
DEADLINES: None
OFFICERS: Lyden, James P., P/T; Lyden, Scott A., VP;
Lyden, Kristin M., S

MAGIC ACTION TEAM
COMMUNITY FUND
8701 MAITLAND SUMMIT BLVD.
ORLANDO, FL 32810

ID NUMBER: 593287579
FEDERAL REPORTING DATE: 02/02
AREAS OF INTEREST: Scholarships
CURRENT ASSETS: $21,329 PRIOR ASSETS: $0
TOTAL AMOUNT AWARDED: $26,000
HIGH: $5,000--Individual
MID: $1,000--Individual
LOW: $1,000--Individual
GRANTS AWARDS: N/A
COMMENTS: Call for applications.
DEADLINES: January 7th
OFFICERS: Bowman, Scott, D; Conley, Kan, S; Fritz, Jim, T

MAKE A DIFFERENCE
FOUNDATION, INC.
3205 ST. JAMES DR.
BOCA RATON, FL 33434
561-541-0942

ID NUMBER: 650843714
FEDERAL REPORTING DATE: 03/02
AREAS OF INTEREST: Arts & Culture, Community,
Education, Medicine, Religion, Scholarships, Social Services,
Sports & Athletics
CURRENT ASSETS: $925,014 PRIOR ASSETS:
$630,657
TOTAL AMOUNT AWARDED: $59,100
HIGH: $10,000--Spina Bifida Assoc
MID: $5,000--University of Texas
LOW: $150--M. Stoleresky Memorial Fund
GRANTS AWARDS: Daily Bread Food Bank--$500, Tri
County Meals on Wheels--$500, Congregation Emanu-El
Israel--$1,000, Washington University--$1,000, The Children's
Place--$1,000, Mae Volen Senior Center--$1,000, Mihal
Stolarevsky Memorial--$500, Ruth Rales Jewish Family Service-
-$2,000, Greenburg Public Library--$500, Friends of Abused
Children--$1,000
SERVICE AREA: National
COMMENTS: Letter describing charitable needs and
confirmation of charitable status with Federal ID number. Send
applications to: S.Firestone, 3205 St. James Dr., Boca Raton,
Fl. 33434
DEADLINES: None
OFFICERS: Firstone, Susan, ED; Glasser, Stuart, S/D

MARCO ISLAND WOMEN'S CLUB
FOUNDATION
P. O. BOX 604
MARCO ISLAND, FL 34146
941-659-2175

ID NUMBER: 650144269
FEDERAL REPORTING DATE: 10/01
AREAS OF INTEREST: Scholarships
CURRENT ASSETS: $159,771 PRIOR ASSETS:
$147,796
TOTAL AMOUNT AWARDED: $20,100
HIGH: $12,800--Individual
MID: $600--Individual
LOW: $500--Individual
GRANTS AWARDS: N/A
COMMENTS: Send applications to: June McGannon, 1857
Honduras Ct., Marco Island, Fl. 34145. (941)394-8683.
Applicaitons are accepted anytime. Notice of approval,
rejections, or requests for additional information are usually
sent within 2 months.
DEADLINES: None
OFFICERS: Rodgers, Lorraine, P; Schroll, Joan, VP;
Burkhart, Nancy, S; Martindell, Joyce, S; Ferraro, Catherine,
T; Peterson, Eunice, AT

MARCO, SEYMOUR R. FAMILY
FOUNDATION, INC.
8265 BAYBERRY RD.
JACKSONVILLE, FL 32256

ID NUMBER: 592197357
FEDERAL REPORTING DATE: 10/01
AREAS OF INTEREST: Education, Health, Research,
Scholarships
CURRENT ASSETS: $2,955,760 PRIOR ASSETS:
$2,964,972
TOTAL AMOUNT AWARDED: $179,000
HIGH: $20,000--So. Coll. of Optometry
MID: $10,000--Univ. of Calif., Berkeley
LOW: $4,000--Pace Ctr. for Girls, Inc.
GRANTS AWARDS: Optometric Ctr. of N.Y.--$10,000, S.
Calif. Coll. of Optometry--$10,000, Univ. of Houston--
$10,000, New England Medical Ctr.--$15,000, Emory Eye
Ctr.--$10,000, New Engld Coll. of Opt.--$10,000, Univ. of
MO-St. Louis--$10,000, Univ. of Alabama--$10,000, Mich.
College of Opt.--$20,000, Northeastern State Univ.--$10,000,
Penn College of Opt.--$10,000, USF Eye Inst.--$10,000, Ill
College of Opt.--$10,000
SERVICE AREA: National
COMMENTS: Gives to preselected organizations.
DEADLINES: None
OFFICERS: Marco, David A., P/TR; Marco, Carolyn C.,
VP/TR; Ansbacher, Lewis, S/TR; Shorstein, Jack F., T/TR;
Dyer, Charon M., TR; Shorstein, Samuel R., TR

MARDEN, BERNARD A. & CHRIS
FOUNDATION
1290 S. OCEAN BLVD.
PALM BEACH, FL 33480
561-833-2001

ID NUMBER: 650409920
FEDERAL REPORTING DATE: 11/01
AREAS OF INTEREST: Arts & Culture, Community,
Education, Medicine, Religion, Scholarships, Social Services

CURRENT ASSETS: $2,061,723 PRIOR ASSETS:
$2,367,530
TOTAL AMOUNT AWARDED: $176,666
HIGH: $50,000--Jewish Federation of Palm Beach County
MID: $25,650--Palm Beach Opera
LOW: $100--Memorial Sloan-Kettering
GRANTS AWARDS: American Jewish Commtree--$5,000,
United States Holocaust Memorial Museum--$16,666,
American Cancer Society--$100, Patrons of the Arts in the
Vatican Museums--$1,000
SERVICE AREA: National
COMMENTS: Gives to preselected organizations.
DEADLINES: None
OFFICERS: Marden, Bernard A., P; Marden, Chris, VP;
Marden, James, D; Marden, Patrice A., D

MAROONE FAMILY FOUNDATION
2494 S. OCEAN BLVD.
BOCA RATON, FL 33432
561-447-0002

ID NUMBER: 166466934
FEDERAL REPORTING DATE: 03/02
AREAS OF INTEREST: Education, Environment, Health,
Medicine, Research, Scholarships, Social Services, Sports &
Athletics
CURRENT ASSETS: $420,755 PRIOR ASSETS:
$445,600
TOTAL AMOUNT AWARDED: $574,050
HIGH: $204,800--Children's Cancer Caring Center
MID: $100,000--Our Lady of Victory
LOW: $100--Special Olympics
GRANTS AWARDS: Alzheimer's Assn.--$1,000, American
Lung Assn.--$500, American Red Cross--$1,000, Caravan
Research--$1,000, Cleveland Clinic--$200,000, Covenant
House--$3,000, Cystic Fiberosis Fdn.--$5,000, Sheridan House
Family Fdn.--$25,000, Univ. at BFBO Fdn.--$15,000, Hospice
& Homecare by the Sea--$1,000, Kendall Speech & Language-
-$10,000, Lighthouse for the Blind--$500, Make A Wish Fdn.-
-$2,500, National Multiple Sclerosis Society--$500, The
Salvation Army--$2,000
SERVICE AREA: FL
COMMENTS: Gives to preselected organizations.
DEADLINES: None
OFFICERS: Maroone, Albert, TR; Maroone, Katherine, TR;
Maroone, Michael, TR; Reese. Donald J., TR

MARTIN COUNTY II COMMUNITY FOUNDATION, INC.
C/O T. MICHAEL CROOK
33 FLAGLER AVE.
STUART, FL 34994
561-283-2356

ID NUMBER: 650024030
FEDERAL REPORTING DATE: 11/01
AREAS OF INTEREST: Community, Education, Religion,
Scholarships, Social Services
CURRENT ASSETS: $1,691,604 PRIOR ASSETS:
$1,647,288
TOTAL AMOUNT AWARDED: $62,077
HIGH: $18,604--Sylvan Learning Ctr.
MID: $7,858--All Saints Episcopal
LOW: $500--United States International Univ.
GRANTS AWARDS: All Saints Episcopal--$7,858, Duke
Univ.--$1,250, Florida State Univ.--$3,000, Marshall Univ.--
$2,500, New College of the Univ. of So. Fl.--$2,500, New

York Univ.--$2,500, Stanford Univ.--$1,250, Univ. of Fl.--
$3,000, Women's Ctr. of Martin Co.--$8,615, Embry Riddle
Aero Univ.--$500, Lagrange College--$1,000, Stetson Univ.--
$1,000, Univ. of Central Fl.--$1,000, Boston College--$2,500,
Georgia Institute of Tech.--$2,500
COMMENTS: Send applications to Martin County II
Community Fdn., P.O. Box 251, Stuart, FL 34995.
Application deadlines are set by high school guidance
counselor's office. Awards are given to graduates of Martin
County High Schools, in compliance with donor restrictions.
Contribution schedule not available.
DEADLINES: None
OFFICERS: Jordan, Floyd D., P; Fowler, William C., T;
Weber, Thomas E., Jr., S; Crook, T. Michael, D

MARTIN, G. ROY & ELIZABETH C. CHARITABLE TRUST
C/O SUNTRUST BANK
P.O. BOX 3838
ORLANDO, FL 32802

ID NUMBER: 596920693
FEDERAL REPORTING DATE: 04/02
AREAS OF INTEREST: Education, Religion, Scholarships
CURRENT ASSETS: $2,929,569 PRIOR ASSETS:
$3,152,505
TOTAL AMOUNT AWARDED: $215,813
HIGH: $25,000--Stetson University
MID: $5,000--Joining Hands Inc. of Florida
LOW: $250--Lake-Sumter Community College
GRANTS AWARDS: University of Notre Dame--$2,500,
University of Central Florida--$4,000, Baptist Bible College--
$1,000, Palm Beach Atlantic College--$1,500, Emory
University--$1,250, Pennsylvania State University--$1,000,
Junior Achievement of Central Florida--$6,000, Harding
University--$1,000, Florida A&M University--$500, Golden
Triangle YMCA--$5,000
SERVICE AREA: National
COMMENTS: Applications should be in letter form and
include a description of the nature and purpose of the request.
Applications should be sent to: Suntrust Bank c/o Teresa
Borcheck, P.O. Box 49008, Leesburg, FL 34749
DEADLINES: None
OFFICERS: SunTrust Bank, TR; Pullum, J. Stephen;
Haliday, Alfred C. Jr.; Weiss, David

MARTIN, RAY & ANNA SCHOLARSHIP TRUST
C/O BANK OF AMERICA,
P.O. BOX 40200
JACKSONVILLE, FL 32203-0200
877-466-1410

ID NUMBER: 596794285
FEDERAL REPORTING DATE: 12/01
AREAS OF INTEREST: Scholarships
CURRENT ASSETS: $271,053 PRIOR ASSETS:
$293,087
TOTAL AMOUNT AWARDED: $25,243
HIGH: $6,000--Individual
MID: $2,000--Individual
LOW: $39--Individual
GRANTS AWARDS: N/A
SERVICE AREA: FL
COMMENTS: Send applications to Shari Sawyers, Bank of
America 331 S.FL Ave, Lakeland FL. No standard form.

Applicants must be persons who are morally and mentally worthy and competent.
DEADLINES: None
OFFICERS: Bank of America, TR

MATTHEW 28:18-20 CHARITABLE TRUST

C/O STEPHEN F. SAINT
3708 S.E. 4TH ST.
OCALA, FL 34471
352-694-3175

ID NUMBER: 593091298
FEDERAL REPORTING DATE: 12/01
AREAS OF INTEREST: Education, Health, Religion, Scholarships, Other
CURRENT ASSETS: $970,980 PRIOR ASSETS: $750,241
TOTAL AMOUNT AWARDED: $65,771
HIGH: $29,646--Wao Projects
MID: $10,000--World Radio Network
LOW: $500--Gospel Missionary Union
GRANTS AWARDS: I-Tec--$23,625, Kornel Gerstner--$1,000, Ozark Christian College--$1,000
COMMENTS: Send applications to: Stephen F. Saint, 3708 S.E. 4th St., Ocala, Fl. 34471. (352)694-3175. Generally for religious missionary activities.
DEADLINES: None
OFFICERS: Van Der Puy, Abraham C. & Marjorie, TR; Saint, Stephen F. & Jennie, P; Drown, Ross S., TR

MAY, THERESA GAIL SCHOLARSHIP FOUNDATION

P.O. BOX 1162
PENSACOLA, FL 32595-1162
850-433-1064

ID NUMBER: 597127677
FEDERAL REPORTING DATE: 05/02
AREAS OF INTEREST: Education, Scholarships
CURRENT ASSETS: $1,137,278 PRIOR ASSETS: $1,176,190
TOTAL AMOUNT AWARDED: $28,000
HIGH: $24,000--Pensacola Junior College
LOW: $4,000--University of West Florida
GRANTS AWARDS: N/A
SERVICE AREA: FL
COMMENTS: Gives to preselected organizations.
DEADLINES: None
OFFICERS: Smith, Ricky, TR; Williams, Albert, TR; Jones, J. R., TR; Hopkins E. W., TR

MCARTHUR, CHARLES FOUNDATION, INC.

P.O. BOX 1603
OKEECHOBEE, FL 34973
863763-2835

ID NUMBER: 596194396
FEDERAL REPORTING DATE: 01/02
AREAS OF INTEREST: Education, Scholarships
CURRENT ASSETS: $383,443 PRIOR ASSETS: $376,980
TOTAL AMOUNT AWARDED: $15,000
HIGH: $10,000--Indian River Community College

MID: $2,000--Okeechobee County Farm Bureau
LOW: $1,000--Florida State University
GRANTS AWARDS: Take Stock in Children--$1,500
COMMENTS: Submit a letter of request.
DEADLINES: None
OFFICERS: Conely, Thomas W., III, D; Larson, Grace, D; Underhill, Cynthia C., D

MCCLURE, D. P. FAMILY CHARITABLE FOUNDATION

P. O. BOX 936
PALMETTO, FL 34220
941-722-4545

ID NUMBER: 650759915
FEDERAL REPORTING DATE: 10/01
AREAS OF INTEREST: Education, Religion, Scholarships, Other
CURRENT ASSETS: $900,815 PRIOR ASSETS: $832,354
TOTAL AMOUNT AWARDED: $52,261
HIGH: $40,000--Bradenton Christian School
MID: $10,000--United Way of Manatee
LOW: $2,261--Manatee Co. Youth for Christ
GRANTS AWARDS: N/A
COMMENTS: Gives to preselected organizations.
DEADLINES: None
OFFICERS: McClure, Daniel P., TR; McClure, Corrine A., TR

MCCRACKEN FAMILY FOUNDATION, INC.

1010 HWY. 98 E., STE. 202
DESTIN, FL 32541

ID NUMBER: 710673809
FEDERAL REPORTING DATE: 05/01
AREAS OF INTEREST: Education, Religion, Scholarships, Other
CURRENT ASSETS: $31,513 PRIOR ASSETS: $37,384
TOTAL AMOUNT AWARDED: $8,566
HIGH: $4,550--St. Mark's Episcopal Church
MID: $2,991--Univ. of Alabama
LOW: $25--Misc.
GRANTS AWARDS: In Touch Ministries--$500, American Cancer Society--$100, Little Rock Central High--$200, Catholic High Fdn.--$200
SERVICE AREA: National
DEADLINES: None
OFFICERS: McCraken, John D., P; Burnett, Dana, S; McCraken, Martha S., TR

MCCREADY, STEPHEN F. SCHOLARSHIP FUND

P. O. BOX 2080-FL-0135
JACKSONVILLE, FL 32231-0010
352-620-7132

ID NUMBER: 596577844
FEDERAL REPORTING DATE: 05/02
AREAS OF INTEREST: Religion, Scholarships
CURRENT ASSETS: $575,127 PRIOR ASSETS: $596,921
TOTAL AMOUNT AWARDED: $36,514
HIGH: $36,514--First United Methodist Church, Ocala

GRANTS AWARDS: N/A
SERVICE AREA: Fl.
COMMENTS: Gives to preselected organizations. Submit to First United Methodist Church, 1126 East Silver Springs Blvd., Ocala, FL 34470. Students attending any accredited inst. of higher learning, including junior colleges. Special consideration is given to Marion County, FL residents who are attending theological seminaries or who have indicated that intention
DEADLINES: 6/1, 12/1
OFFICERS: First Union National Bank, TR

MCCUNE, C.N. FOUNDATION, TA
C/O SUNTRUST BANK
P. O. BOX 14728
FORT LAUDERDALE, FL 33302

ID NUMBER: 592000849
FEDERAL REPORTING DATE: 12/01
AREAS OF INTEREST: Scholarships
CURRENT ASSETS: $381,998 PRIOR ASSETS: $319,314
TOTAL AMOUNT AWARDED: $14,000
HIGH: $750--Individual
MID: $500--Individual
LOW: $250--Individual
GRANTS AWARDS: N/A
COMMENTS: Recipients must be graduates of Broward County high schools
DEADLINES: N/A
OFFICERS: Suntrust Bank, TR

MCCUNE, C.N. SCHOLARSHIP FOUNDATION FUND
C/O SUNTRUST BANK
P.O. BOX 14728
FORT LAUDERDALE, FL 33302
954-765-7400

ID NUMBER: 596667689
FEDERAL REPORTING DATE: 01/02
AREAS OF INTEREST: Scholarships
CURRENT ASSETS: $299,144 PRIOR ASSETS: $310,480
TOTAL AMOUNT AWARDED: $24,412
HIGH: $500--Individual
MID: $375--Individual
LOW: $152--Individual
GRANTS AWARDS: N/A
SERVICE AREA: Florida
DEADLINES: None
OFFICERS: Suntrust Bank, TR

MCCURRY FOUNDATION, INC.
3161-4 ST. JOHN'S BLUFF RD. S.
JACKSONVILLE, FL 32246
904-645-6555

ID NUMBER: 593287752
FEDERAL REPORTING DATE: 07/01
AREAS OF INTEREST: Scholarships
CURRENT ASSETS: $236,277 PRIOR ASSETS: $231,720
TOTAL AMOUNT AWARDED: $22,000
HIGH: $1,500--Individual
MID: $1,000--Individual
LOW: $500--Individual

GRANTS AWARDS: N/A
DEADLINES: N/A
OFFICERS: McCurry, Edgar W., Jr., M

MCDOUGALL, I. FOUNDATION
C/O SUNTRUST BANK, TAMPA BAY
P.O. BOX 1498
TAMPA, FL 33601-1498
813-224-2458

ID NUMBER: 596981356
FEDERAL REPORTING DATE: 05/02
AREAS OF INTEREST: Education, Scholarships
CURRENT ASSETS: $720,781 PRIOR ASSETS: $950,727
TOTAL AMOUNT AWARDED: $50,001
HIGH: $11,166--Individual
MID: $2,356--Individual
LOW: $931--Individual
GRANTS AWARDS: N/A
SERVICE AREA: FL
COMMENTS: Must be a medical student at the University of South Florida Submit in letter form.
DEADLINES: None
OFFICERS: SunTrust Bank, Tampa Bay, TR

MCGINTY, ELLANORA SCHOLARSHIP
C/O SANFORD A. MINKOFF, TRUSTEE
1796 VIRGINIA CT.
TAVARES, FL 32778
352-343-0305

ID NUMBER: 596964815
FEDERAL REPORTING DATE: 08/01
AREAS OF INTEREST: Scholarships
CURRENT ASSETS: $166,999 PRIOR ASSETS: $165,958
TOTAL AMOUNT AWARDED: $16,571
HIGH: $2,000--Individual
MID: $1,044--Individual
LOW: $524--Individual
GRANTS AWARDS: N/A
SERVICE AREA: Tavares, Leesburg
COMMENTS: Scholarships are awarded only to graduates of Tavares High School. Contact Coranlell Glass, Tavares High School, 603 N. New Hampshire, Tavares, FL 32778, 352-343-3007. Applicants are judged on need and achievement.
DEADLINES: None
OFFICERS: Pennacchia, Claude M., TR; Vaughn, Burney A., TR; Minkoff, Sanford A., TR

MCINTOSH FOUNDATION
15840 MEADOW WOOD DR.
WELLINGTON, FL 33414-9026

ID NUMBER: 136096459
FEDERAL REPORTING DATE: 08/01
AREAS OF INTEREST: Arts & Culture, Community, Education, Environment, Health, Medicine, Religion, Research, Scholarships, Social Services
CURRENT ASSETS: $41,157,473 PRIOR ASSETS: $43,842,100
TOTAL AMOUNT AWARDED: $1,106,150
HIGH: $917,500--Conservation and Preservation (MISC)
MID: $47,550--Cultural and Civic Affairs (MISC)

LOW: $10,000--Health & Welfare
GRANTS AWARDS: Education (Misc.)--$105,000, Social
Welfare (Misc.)--$26,100
SERVICE AREA: National
COMMENTS: Gives to preselected organizations.
DEADLINES: None
OFFICERS: McIntosh, Michael A., P; McIntosh, Peter H.,
VP/T; McIntosh, Winsome D., VP/AS; McIntosh, Joan H.,
VP/AT; Terry, Frederick A. Jr.,; McIntosh, Hunter H., D

MCKINNEY, EDGAR & NONA CHARITABLE TRUST

1300 CITIZENS BLVD.
LEESBURG, FL 34748
352-326-4704

ID NUMBER: 597001925
FEDERAL REPORTING DATE: 10/01
AREAS OF INTEREST: Education, Religion, Scholarships,
Other
CURRENT ASSETS: $1,550,262   PRIOR ASSETS:
$1,373,784
TOTAL AMOUNT AWARDED: $201,500
HIGH: $45,000--First Academy Elem. & Middle School
MID: $20,000--Christian Home & Bible School
LOW: $500--Univ. of Fl.-Individual
GRANTS AWARDS: Univ. of Wisconsin Fdn.--$27,000,
Florida State--$9,000, Univ. of Fl.--$10,000, Florida A&M
Univ.--$2,500, Mars Hill College--$5,000, Univ. of Central
Florida--$1,000, Univ. of N. Florida--$1,500, Univ. of S.
Florida--$1,000, Oral Roberts Univ.--$5,000, Lake Sumter
Comm. College--$1,000, Harding Univ.--$5,000, Florida
Southern Univ.--$4,000, Stetson Univ. Scholarship Funds--
$8,000, Ctr. for Indep. Tech. & Educ.--$20,000, Sunrise Arc
of Lake Co., Inc.--$7,500
COMMENTS: Send applications to: Huntington National
Bank, 1300 Citizens Blvd., Leesburg, Fl. 34748. Attn: Karen
Bent, VP. (352)326-4704.
DEADLINES: None
OFFICERS: Huntington National Bank, TR

MEAD, EDWIN BUDGE TRUST UNDER WILL

C/O BANK OF AMERICA
P.O. BOX
JACKSONVILLE, FL 32203-0200
877-446-1410

ID NUMBER: 596190681
FEDERAL REPORTING DATE: 04/02
AREAS OF INTEREST: Scholarships
CURRENT ASSETS: $408,498   PRIOR ASSETS:
$432,566
TOTAL AMOUNT AWARDED: $29,700
HIGH: $1,100--Individual
MID: $1,000--Individual
LOW: $500--individual
GRANTS AWARDS: N/A
SERVICE AREA: Eustis High School
COMMENTS: Awards determined by committee and given to
students in the top 25% of the senior class of Eustis High
School.
DEADLINES: N/A
OFFICERS: Bank of America, TR

MEILMAN, DANIEL CHARITABLE FOUNDATION

C/O HACKER & ROMANO
3300 N. 29TH AVE., STE. 102
HOLLYWOOD, FL 33020
954-922-2207

ID NUMBER: 592706733
FEDERAL REPORTING DATE: 07/01
AREAS OF INTEREST: Community, Health, Medicine,
Scholarships
CURRENT ASSETS: $202,829   PRIOR ASSETS:
$176,840
TOTAL AMOUNT AWARDED: $10,000
HIGH: $3,000--Hollywood Florida Scholarship Foundation
MID: $2,000--Body Positive Resource Center, Inc.
LOW: $1,500--SPCA of Westchester
GRANTS AWARDS: Hollywood Fl. Scholarship Fdn.--
$3,000, Juvenile Diabetes Fdn.--$2,000
SERVICE AREA: FL
COMMENTS: Gives to preselected organizations.
DEADLINES: None
OFFICERS: Meilman, Richard, TR; Meilman Glick, Michele,
TR

MENDILLO, JOHN C. FAMILY FOUNDATION

C/O R. C. HITCHINS
325 S. OLIVE AVE.
WEST PALM BEACH, FL 33401-5619
561-832-8833

ID NUMBER: 66034882
FEDERAL REPORTING DATE: 03/02
AREAS OF INTEREST: Arts & Culture, Community,
Education, Environment, Research, Scholarships, Social
Services
CURRENT ASSETS: $275,820   PRIOR ASSETS:
$353,604
TOTAL AMOUNT AWARDED: $19,430
HIGH: $1,000--Hospital of St. Rapheal
MID: $500--John Burroughs School
LOW: $30--Belleville Labor & Industry Museum
GRANTS AWARDS: Actors' Fund of America--$200,
American Cancer Society--$100, American Heart Assn.--$250,
American Lung Association--$100, Arena Playhouse--$100,
Atlantic Theater Company--$150, Call for Help, Inc.--$100,
Cardinal Glennon NIC Unit--$150, Catholic Urban Programs-
-$100, Center for Cancer Care--$1,000, Connecticut Audubon
Society--$500, Connecticut Public Broadcasting, Inc.--$300,
Connecticut Hospice, Inc.--$300, Ethel Walker School--$500,
Foote School--$1,000
SERVICE AREA: National
COMMENTS: Should include letter stating organization
purpose and contribution use.
DEADLINES: None
OFFICERS: Mendillo, James R., VP; Mendillo, Stephen, P;
Hitchins, Richard C., T/S

MERRILL, JAMES & VIRGINIA FOUNDATION, INC.
C/O ARNOWITT
960 S.W. BAY POINTE CIR.
PALM CITY, FL 34990-1758
561-221-9494

ID NUMBER: 650136422
FEDERAL REPORTING DATE: 04/02
AREAS OF INTEREST: Education, Scholarships
CURRENT ASSETS: $518,751 PRIOR ASSETS:
$505,257
TOTAL AMOUNT AWARDED: $23,300
HIGH: $9,000--Indian River Comm College
MID: $4,000--University of Florida Foundation
LOW: $2,500--Texas A&M Development Foundation
GRANTS AWARDS: Meharry Medical College--$2,800,
George Mason University Foundation--$5,000
SERVICE AREA: National
COMMENTS: Submit in writing to Iris Arnowitt. Limited to
501(c)(3) organizations and accredited colleges for their use in
awarding scholarships and low- or no- interest loans to needy
students and/or for superior scholarship.
DEADLINES: None
OFFICERS: Arnowitt, Edwin, P/T; Arnowitt, Iris, VP/S;
Mulligan, Kim, D

MESHBERG, PHILIP & JULIA FAMILY FOUNDATION, INC.
C/O PHILIP MESHBERG
2770 OCEAN BLVD.
PALM BEACH, FL 33480-5470
561-364-0014

ID NUMBER: 591813108
FEDERAL REPORTING DATE: 12/01
AREAS OF INTEREST: Community, Health, Religion,
Scholarships, Social Services, Other
CURRENT ASSETS: $1,957,860 PRIOR ASSETS:
$1,891,956
TOTAL AMOUNT AWARDED: $97,170
HIGH: $50,000--Anti-Defamation League
MID: $10,000--Jewish Federation of Palm Beach
LOW: $20--Palm Beach PBA
GRANTS AWARDS: WPBT (PBS)--$120, Norton Museum
of Art--$250, Simon Weisenthal Ctr.--$100, Palm Beach
Community Chest--$100, Palm Beach Fellowship of Jews--
$250, Jewish Community Ctr.--$500, Anti-Defamtion League-
-$100, Care--$20, AIPAC--$1,250, JCCS--$2,500, Palm Beach
Friends of ADA--$100, Congregation B'Nai Israel--$1,000,
JCCS Schoolboy Classic--$500, Women's Auxiliary--$1,250,
Ctr. for Community Services--$2,500
SERVICE AREA: National, FL
COMMENTS: There is no carrying on of propaganda, or
otherwise attempting to influence legislation. Send applications
to: Philip Meshberg, 2770 S. Ocean Blvd., Palm Beach, Fl.
33480-5470.
DEADLINES: None
OFFICERS: Meshberg, Philip, P/D; Meshberg, Julia, D;
Meshberg, Samuel, D; Meshberg, Emil, D; Meshberg, Ronald,
D

METZ, HENRY JAMES & CHRISTINE M. FOUNDATION
1825 8TH ST., S.
NAPLES, FL 33940-7521
941-434-0674

ID NUMBER: 421324791
FEDERAL REPORTING DATE: 05/02
AREAS OF INTEREST: Arts & Culture, Community,
Education, Environment, Religion, Scholarships, Social
Services
CURRENT ASSETS: $1,221,403 PRIOR ASSETS:
$125,440
TOTAL AMOUNT AWARDED: $151,821
HIGH: $33,333--Hospice of Siouxland
MID: $25,000--Int'l Center for Biblical Counseling
LOW: $100--St. Louis Boys and Girls Club
GRANTS AWARDS: University of Florida--$10,000,
American Breeders--$11,000, Central City School Fund--
$2,000, Humane Society of Collier--$500, NHC Healthcare
Foundation--$500
SERVICE AREA: National
COMMENTS: Applications addressed to Henrry James and
Christine M. Metz Foundation (Scholarship Program)1825 oth
Street South, Naples, Fl. 34102.
DEADLINES: None
OFFICERS: Metz, Henrry J.; Metz, Christine M.

METZINGER, REVA DANIELS CHARITABLE FOUNDATION
333 SUNSET DR., STE. 407
FORT LAUDERDALE, FL 33301
954-524-5414

ID NUMBER: 656335603
FEDERAL REPORTING DATE: 05/02
AREAS OF INTEREST: Scholarships
CURRENT ASSETS: $1,059,046 PRIOR ASSETS:
$1,028,956
TOTAL AMOUNT AWARDED: $4,500
HIGH: $3,000--Individual
LOW: $1,500--Individual
GRANTS AWARDS: N/A
SERVICE AREA: FL
COMMENTS: Gives to preselected organizations.
DEADLINES: None
OFFICERS: Bowen, Irving, P; Bowen, Judy, VP

MICHAEL STEVENS SCHOLARSHIP FUND
102 STEPHEN DR.
LAKE PLACID, FL 33852
863-465-1183

ID NUMBER: 311070493
FEDERAL REPORTING DATE: 01/02
AREAS OF INTEREST: Scholarships
CURRENT ASSETS: $668 PRIOR ASSETS: $932
TOTAL AMOUNT AWARDED: $1,500
HIGH: $500--Individual
MID: $500--Individual
LOW: $500--Individual
GRANTS AWARDS: N/A
DEADLINES: None
OFFICERS: Stevens, Robert, CR; Garwood, James, M; Lang,
Karen, M

MILLER FAMILY FOUNDATION, INC.

116 GOVERNORS RD.
PONTE VEDRA BEACH, FL 32082

ID NUMBER: 593477208
FEDERAL REPORTING DATE: 06/99
AREAS OF INTEREST: Arts & Culture, Community, Education, Health, Medicine, Religion, Scholarships, Social Services, Sports & Athletics, Other
CURRENT ASSETS: $97,848 PRIOR ASSETS: $78,522
TOTAL AMOUNT AWARDED: $137,560
HIGH: $60,000--UNC Educational Fdn.
MID: $10,000--Wake Forest U.
LOW: $50--Armon/Adud Caps Junior College
GRANTS AWARDS: Gospel Films--$50,000, FCA--$100, NRCA--$2,500, YMCA of Greater Durham--$400, La Leche League--$300, Weslyn Christian--$100, Wake Forest Rolesville--$300, NWCBA--$1,000, WCA--$100, Samaritan Purse--$60, Salvation Army--$500, Children's Home--$1,000, Fellowship of Christian Athletes--$10,000, The CArolina Ear & Neuro--$200, AM Leprosy Mission--$300, Individual--$100
SERVICE AREA: National
COMMENTS: No information on application procedures given.
DEADLINES: None
OFFICERS: Miller, Deborah, D; Underwood, Robert, S; Miller, Paul, D

MILLER, R. J. FAMILY FOUNDATION

C/O ROBERT J. MILLER, 3200 N. OCEAN BLVD., STE. 271
FORT LAUDERDALE, FL 33308
954-564-5621

ID NUMBER: 586372262
FEDERAL REPORTING DATE: 05/02
AREAS OF INTEREST: Education, Religion, Scholarships
CURRENT ASSETS: $313,363 PRIOR ASSETS: $236,560
TOTAL AMOUNT AWARDED: $135,700
HIGH: $70,000--Providence Christian Academy
MID: $35,000--St. Oliver Plunkett Catholic Church
LOW: $4,000--Individual
GRANTS AWARDS: St. John the Baptist Church--$13,500, Cardinal Gibbons High School--$13,200
SERVICE AREA: National
COMMENTS: Gives to preselected organizations.
DEADLINES: None
OFFICERS: Miller, Robert J., D; Miller, Jane, D; Miller-Tong, Elizabeth, D; Miller, Robert R., D; Miller, Eric, D

MILLS, LAWRENCE & SYLVIA FOUNDATION

385 OAKVIEW DR.
DELRAY BEACH, FL 33445
561-498-0881

ID NUMBER: 592482275
FEDERAL REPORTING DATE: 06/99
AREAS OF INTEREST: Arts & Culture, Community, Health, Medicine, Religion, Research, Scholarships, Social Services

CURRENT ASSETS: $232,064 PRIOR ASSETS: $233,724
TOTAL AMOUNT AWARDED: $916
HIGH: $100--U.S. Holocaust
MID: $50--WPBT
LOW: $25--American Heart Assoc.
GRANTS AWARDS: Morse Geriatric--$50, British Museum of Art--$75, Feminist Majority--$25, US Olympics--$50, Caldwell Outreach--$30, Palm Haven--$25, Planned Parenthood--$25, Anti Defamation League--$100, UNICEF--$25, Rosary Hill Home--$100, AIDS Research--$25, Jewish Congress--$100
SERVICE AREA: SE FL
COMMENTS: Gives to preselected organizations. No unsolicited requests.
DEADLINES: None
OFFICERS: Mills, Lawrence A., P/D; Mills, Sylvia, VP/D; Mills, Steven, D

MINIACI, ALFRED & ROSE FOUNDATION, INC.

1441 S.W. 31ST AVE.
POMPANO BEACH, FL 33069
954-978-0500

ID NUMBER: 651107701
FEDERAL REPORTING DATE: 06/00
AREAS OF INTEREST: Arts & Culture, Community, Education, Health, Research, Scholarships, Social Services, Other
CURRENT ASSETS: $0 PRIOR ASSETS: $852,393
TOTAL AMOUNT AWARDED: $215,153
HIGH: $50,000--St. Anthony School
MID: $25,775--Boys Town of Italy, Inc.
LOW: $100--American Vets
GRANTS AWARDS: Adelphi Univ.--$500, Albany Univ.--$1,000, Alzheimer's Family Ctr.--$1,500, Ann Storck Ctr.--$2,500, Bard College of Liberal Arts--$1,000, Barry Univ.--$500, Binghamton Univ.--$4,000, Boston College--$1,000, Boston Univ.--$4,000, Boys & Girls Club of Broward Co.--$5,000, Broward Comm. College--$500, Broward Performing Arts Fdn.--$200, Cardinal Gibbons High School--$8,000, Children's Family Society--$1,000, Cleveland Clinic--$5,000
COMMENTS: Send applications to: Rose Miniaci, 1411 SW 31 Ave., Pompano Beach, Fl. 33069. (954)978-0500 in letter form including history of organizations & use of funds.
DEADLINES: None
OFFICERS: Miniaci, Rose, P/D; Miniaci, Dominick F., D/S; Miniaci, Albert J., D/T

MISKOFF, JOHN FOUNDATION, INC.

849 S.E. 8TH AVE., STE. 3
DEERFIELD BEACH, FL 33441
954-425-4776

ID NUMBER: 592193608
FEDERAL REPORTING DATE: 11/01
AREAS OF INTEREST: Education, Scholarships
CURRENT ASSETS: $154,797 PRIOR ASSETS: $170,976
TOTAL AMOUNT AWARDED: $15,000
HIGH: $9,000--Individual
LOW: $6,000--Individual
GRANTS AWARDS: N/A
SERVICE AREA: FL
DEADLINES: None

OFFICERS: Laker, Joyce, TR; Cahan, Sylvia, TR; Palmer, George, TR

MONTGOMERY FAMILY CHARITABLE TRUST

C/O RICHARD RAMPELL, TTEE, 122 N. COUNTY RD.
PALM BEACH, FL 33480
561-655-5855

ID NUMBER: 656285772
FEDERAL REPORTING DATE: 11/01
AREAS OF INTEREST: Arts & Culture, Community, Education, Scholarships, Sports & Athletics
CURRENT ASSETS: $3,759,960 PRIOR ASSETS: $4,181,560
TOTAL AMOUNT AWARDED: $351,000
HIGH: $177,500--Armory Art Center
MID: $51,000--Kravis Ctr. for the Perf. Arts
LOW: $2,500--Hospice Fdn. of Palm Beach Co.
GRANTS AWARDS: Anti-Defamation League--$5,000, Ballet Florida--$15,000, Dreyfoos School of the Arts--$5,000, Fl. Atlantic Univ.--$10,000, Jewish Guild for the Blind--$5,000, LIFE--$25,000, Morse Geriatric Golf--$5,000, NPR Fdn.--$15,000, Palm Beach Community--$5,000, Norton Musuem of Art--$20,000, Southern Poverty Law--$10,000
SERVICE AREA: FL, AL, DC
COMMENTS: Send applications to: Richard Rampell, 122 N. County Rd., Palm Beach, Fl. 33480. 561-655-5855. Charitable agencies serving art, music, culture, children or anti-smoking goals.
DEADLINES: None
OFFICERS: Montgomery, Robert M., Jr., TR; Montgomery, Mary M., TR; Montgomery, Courtnay E., TR; Rampell, Richard, TR

MORGAN, JOHN E. CHARITABLE TRUST II

900 S. OCEAN BLVD.
MANALAPAN, FL 33462

ID NUMBER: 521761389
FEDERAL REPORTING DATE: 05/99
AREAS OF INTEREST: Education, Health, Medicine, Scholarships
CURRENT ASSETS: $18,007 PRIOR ASSETS: $374,669
TOTAL AMOUNT AWARDED: $552,000
HIGH: $500,000--Lehigh Valley Hospital
MID: $12,000--Tamaquia Public Library
LOW: $10,000--Delaware Valley College
GRANTS AWARDS: Memorial Sloan Kettering Cancer Center--$10,000, Wingate University--$10,000, Palm Beach Atlantic College--$10,000
SERVICE AREA: PA, NY, FL
COMMENTS: Gives to preselected organizations. No unsolicited requests.
DEADLINES: None
OFFICERS: Morgan, John E., T; Loder, Harry, T; Morgan, Dorothy, T

MORGAN, RIFFAT & MARGARET FOUNDATION

4507 WATERS EDGE LN.
SANIBEL, FL 33957-2703
941-472-4718

ID NUMBER: 450423884
FEDERAL REPORTING DATE: 04/01
AREAS OF INTEREST: Education, Scholarships
CURRENT ASSETS: $52,443 PRIOR ASSETS: $49,110
TOTAL AMOUNT AWARDED: $0
GRANTS AWARDS: N/A
SERVICE AREA: ND
COMMENTS: Applications should include name, address and purpose of request.
DEADLINES: None
OFFICERS: Morgan, Margaret, S/TR; Morgan, John, P; Morgan-Fredrickson, Elaine, VP

MORRIS, HAROLD M. & MARY B. CHARITABLE FOUNDATION, INC.

437 HOLIDAY DR.
HALLANDALE, FL 33009
954-457-7355

ID NUMBER: 650540242
FEDERAL REPORTING DATE: 04/02
AREAS OF INTEREST: Arts & Culture, Community, Education, Health, Medicine, Religion, Scholarships, Social Services
CURRENT ASSETS: $381,632 PRIOR ASSETS: $338,265
TOTAL AMOUNT AWARDED: $19,622
HIGH: $3,000--Morris Rifkin Scholarship Fund
MID: $1,000--Colorado Univ. Scholarship Fund
LOW: $25--National Cancer Society
GRANTS AWARDS: Alzheimer's Assn.--$100, American Red Cross--$200, Art & Culture Center--$35, Arthritis Fdn of FL.--$200, Opera Society--$40, Father Flanagan Boys Home--$100, Jewish Women International--$100, Golden Hill Cemetary--$500, Guide Dog Fdn.--$200, Hallandale Jewish Center--$1,812, Hallandale Symphonic Orchestra--$275, Hope Center--$50, Meals on Wheels--$250, Miami Rescue Mission--$300, House of Temple Institute--$25
SERVICE AREA: National
COMMENTS: Gives to preselected organizations.
DEADLINES: None
OFFICERS: Morris, Harold M., D; Morris, Mary B., D; Shabel, Arleen, D; Morris, Barry N., D

MORRISON, GLENN W. & HAZELLE PAXSON

112 E. POINSETTIA ST.
LAKELAND, FL 33803-2919
863-683-5425

ID NUMBER: 592220612
FEDERAL REPORTING DATE: 11/01
AREAS OF INTEREST: Arts & Culture, Community, Education, Religion, Scholarships, Social Services
CURRENT ASSETS: $4,474,057 PRIOR ASSETS: $4,529,781
TOTAL AMOUNT AWARDED: $238,450
HIGH: $17,500--Lakeland Regional Medical Ctr.
MID: $8,000--Sunrise Community of Polk Co.
LOW: $1,500--Reformed Theological Seminary

GRANTS AWARDS: Polk Community College--$3,000, Polk Theatre--$5,000, Univ. of Florida--$3,000, Convenant College--$4,000, Univ. of Missouri-Columbia--$4,000, Ringling School of Art & Design--$5,000, All Saint's Academy--$5,000, Lakeland Christian School--$5,000, Santa Fe Catholic High School--$5,000, Polk Museum of Art--$3,000, Imperial Symphony Orchestra--$5,000, Florida State Univ.--$3,000, Florida Southern College--$3,000, St. Andrews Presbyterian College--$2,000, Univ. of North Florida--$4,000
SERVICE AREA: FL
COMMENTS: Submit application, answering all questions completely & attaching all requested attachments. Application should be submitted two months before the 1st of the month prior to the sem-annual meetings. Meetings are usually in May & Dec. Emphasizes on Polk Co. Area, but does not limit to that area. Student interests: Religion/Music.
DEADLINES: N/A

MURRAY, JACK & MARY FOUNDATION, INC.

P. O. BOX 14184
TAMPA, FL 33690-4184
813-223-7474

ID NUMBER: 593629657
FEDERAL REPORTING DATE: 05/02
AREAS OF INTEREST: Education, Religion, Scholarships
CURRENT ASSETS: $96,589 PRIOR ASSETS: $179,803
TOTAL AMOUNT AWARDED: $75,000
HIGH: $50,000--Univ. of Virginia Fund-Alumni Assn.
LOW: $25,000--Palma Ceia Presbyterian Church
GRANTS AWARDS: N/A
SERVICE AREA: VA
DEADLINES: N/A
OFFICERS: Murray, James K., P; Murray, Mary B., D; Murray, Sandra H., D

MURRAY, WILLIAM H. MEMORIAL SCHOLARSHIP TRUST FUND

C/O BANK OF AMERICA
P.O. BOX 40200
JACKSONVILLE, FL 32203-0200
386-673-0793

ID NUMBER: 596722136
FEDERAL REPORTING DATE: 08/01
AREAS OF INTEREST: Education, Scholarships
CURRENT ASSETS: $596,074 PRIOR ASSETS: $573,213
TOTAL AMOUNT AWARDED: $21,600
HIGH: $3,600--Individual
MID: $2,400--Individual
LOW: $1,200--Individual
GRANTS AWARDS: N/A
SERVICE AREA: Volusia County resident, Flagler County resident
COMMENTS: Request application forms from Student Financial Aid Office, Daytona Beach Community College, 12 W. Int. Speedway Blvd. Daytona Beach, FL 32114. Applicants must be enrolled in the associate degree nursing program at Daytona Beach Community College and meet criteria set by the benefactor. Phone: 94-255-8131.
DEADLINES: None
OFFICERS: Bank of America, TR

MY BROTHER'S/SISTER'S KEEPER

675 ROYAL PALM BEACH BLVD.
ROYAL PALM BEACH, FL 33411
561-793-2350

ID NUMBER: 650672664
FEDERAL REPORTING DATE: 02/02
AREAS OF INTEREST: Scholarships
CURRENT ASSETS: $32,869 PRIOR ASSETS: $23,599
TOTAL AMOUNT AWARDED: $30,500
HIGH: $1,000--Individual
MID: $750--Individual
LOW: $500--Individual
GRANTS AWARDS: N/A
COMMENTS: Eligibility restricted to students in schools located in the West Palm Beach, FL communities of Wellington, Royal Palm Beach and unincorporated Loxahatchee and The Acreage
DEADLINES: First Friday in May of each year
OFFICERS: Santamaria, Jess, P/D; Jones, Robert, D; Templeton, Stephen A., D

NALL, CAMPBELL E. SCHOLARSHIP FUND, INC.

1006 PONCE DE LEON AVE.
CLEWISTON, FL 33440
941-983-7185

ID NUMBER: 650258071
FEDERAL REPORTING DATE: 05/01
AREAS OF INTEREST: Scholarships
CURRENT ASSETS: $138,493 PRIOR ASSETS: $132,457
TOTAL AMOUNT AWARDED: $4,750
HIGH: $1,500--Individual
MID: $750--Individual
LOW: $500--Individual
GRANTS AWARDS: Individual--$1,500
SERVICE AREA: Clewiston, FL.
COMMENTS: Submit simple letter request. Must be a resident of Hendry County, FL. and initially a graduating senior of Clewiston H School. Applications should be addressed to Frances M. Nall 1006 Ponce de Leon Ave. Clewiston, FL. 33440 (941) 983-7183.
DEADLINES: 4/15
OFFICERS: Nall, Frances M., P/D; Whitehead, Joseph D., T/D; Edwards, Dr. Earl E. III, S/D; Stitt, John, VP/D

NEELY, VIRGINIA G. CHARITABLE FOUNDATION, INC.

C/O U.S. TRUST
765 SEAGATE DR.
NAPLES, FL 34103
800-554-3933

ID NUMBER: 561908500
FEDERAL REPORTING DATE: 05/02
AREAS OF INTEREST: Arts & Culture, Community, Education, Environment, Medicine, Scholarships, Social Services
CURRENT ASSETS: $4,578 PRIOR ASSETS: $6,489
TOTAL AMOUNT AWARDED: $25,775
HIGH: $5,000--Glnville-Cahiers Rescue Squad, Inc.
MID: $2,500--The Highlands Cashiers Hospital
LOW: $125--Atlanta International Museum

GRANTS AWARDS: Heffington Scholarship Fund--$2,500, Cashiers Fire Dept.--$2,500, Crystal Springs Upland School--$1,000, Holland Hall School--$3,000, The McCallie School--$600, Albert Carlton Cashiers Community Library--$1,500, The Village Green--$1,000, Cashiers Historical Society--$250, Nature Conservancy of FL.--$500, United Way of Lee Cnty.--$500, Monastery of Mary Mother of Grace--$300, Summit Charter School--$500, American Red Cross--$4,000
SERVICE AREA: National
COMMENTS: Send applications to Janice S. Berglund at P.O. Box 307, Cashiers, NC. 28717
DEADLINES: None
OFFICERS: Berglund, Janice S., D; Neely, Jack H., D; Neely, Paul, D

NEWMAN, THEODORE MEMORIAL FOUNDATION
7542 GRANVILLE DR.
TAMARAC, FL 33321
954-726-1293

ID NUMBER: 510141744
FEDERAL REPORTING DATE: 10/01
AREAS OF INTEREST: Scholarships
CURRENT ASSETS: $24,470 PRIOR ASSETS: $23,134
TOTAL AMOUNT AWARDED: $500
HIGH: $500--Univ. of Miami School of Music
GRANTS AWARDS: N/A
SERVICE AREA: Miami
COMMENTS: Send applications to: Margaret Newman Stearn, 7542 Granville Dr., Tamarac, Fl. 33321. No standard application form will be used. Recipients shall be chosen on interview & ability. Financial assistance limited to music majors from Univ. of Miami or Juliard School of Music. Give to preselected organizatios.
DEADLINES: None
OFFICERS: Stern, Margaret Newman, P; Carr, Louis C., VP; Carr, Blanche, S

NH FOUNDATION TRUST
3739 DUVAL DR.
JACKSONVILLE BEACH, FL 32250

ID NUMBER: 597063240
FEDERAL REPORTING DATE: 07/01
AREAS OF INTEREST: Arts & Culture, Education, Religion, Scholarships, Social Services, Sports & Athletics, Other
CURRENT ASSETS: $19,120 PRIOR ASSETS: $39,036
TOTAL AMOUNT AWARDED: $38,000
HIGH: $37,000--Beaches Episcopal School
LOW: $1,000--Children's Fund
GRANTS AWARDS: --$500
SERVICE AREA: FL
DEADLINES: None
OFFICERS: Hillegass, William G., TR; Hillegass, Helen N., TR

NORTH ORANGE MEMORIAL HOSPITAL TAPF
C/O SUNTRUST BANK, CENTRAL FL
P.O. BOX 3838
ORLANDO, FL 32802

ID NUMBER: 596730137
FEDERAL REPORTING DATE: 01/02

AREAS OF INTEREST: Education, Scholarships
CURRENT ASSETS: $384,741 PRIOR ASSETS: $382,753
TOTAL AMOUNT AWARDED: $15,436
HIGH: $4,686--University of Florida
MID: $1,500--University of Central FL
LOW: $250--Orange Technical Education
GRANTS AWARDS: Florida International University--$1,250, Florida Hospital College--$1,250, Union University--$500, University of Miami--$500, Miami Dade Community College--$250, University of South Florida--$750, Pensacola Christian College--$500, Wake Forest University--$250, Florida State University--$1,500, Wake Forest Univ.--$250, University of North Florida--$1,250
SERVICE AREA: FL., VA.
COMMENTS: Application standard form, include family members, transcripts, recommendation from school or employer, estimate of financial costs.
DEADLINES: March 31
OFFICERS: SunTrust Bank, TR

OATES, L. R. SCHOLARSHIP FUND TRUST UNDER WILL
FIRST UNION BANK TRUSTEE, P. O. BOX 149
ORLANDO, FL 32802-1000
407-649-5541

ID NUMBER: 596672364
FEDERAL REPORTING DATE: 10/01
AREAS OF INTEREST: Scholarships
CURRENT ASSETS: $915,931 PRIOR ASSETS: $940,025
TOTAL AMOUNT AWARDED: $39,500
HIGH: $11,000--Individual
MID: $6,000--Individual
LOW: $2,500--Individual
GRANTS AWARDS: N/A
COMMENTS: Gives to selected individuals. Send applications to: Wachovia Bank, N.A., P.O. Box 1000, MC :FL2840, Orlando, FL 32802-1000, 407-469-5541. Contact by letter or in person. Application will be provided.
DEADLINES: None
OFFICERS: Wachovia Bank, TR; McAdansm Jimmy, D; Wells, Gene, D

OHIO JUSTICE TRUST
C/O JAY HILL, P. O. BOX 516
ANNA MARIA, FL 34216-0516
941-778-4745

ID NUMBER: 311366026
FEDERAL REPORTING DATE: 03/02
AREAS OF INTEREST: Scholarships
CURRENT ASSETS: $226,096 PRIOR ASSETS: $260,750
TOTAL AMOUNT AWARDED: $8,000
HIGH: $8,000--Cincinnatti Bar Foundation
GRANTS AWARDS: N/A
SERVICE AREA: National
COMMENTS: Submit letter requesting application packet. Applicant must be an IRS 501(C)(3) organization. Contact Janet E. Hill at listed address.
DEADLINES: None
OFFICERS: Hill, Jay, TR

OLDS, CLAUDE M. UNIVERSITY OF MIAMI FOUNDATION

145 CURTISS PKWY.
MIAMI SPRINGS, FL 33166-5220
305-662-2007

ID NUMBER: 656014159
FEDERAL REPORTING DATE: 08/01
AREAS OF INTEREST: Education, Scholarships
CURRENT ASSETS: $705,094 PRIOR ASSETS:
$729,830
TOTAL AMOUNT AWARDED: $50,000
HIGH: $50,000--University of Miami Law School
GRANTS AWARDS: N/A
SERVICE AREA: Miami
COMMENTS: Gives to preselected organizations.
DEADLINES: None
OFFICERS: Carlson, Alex E., TR

OLLIFF, MATRED CARLTON FOUNDATION

P.O. BOX 995
WAUCHULA, FL 33873-0995
941-773-4131

ID NUMBER: 592241303
FEDERAL REPORTING DATE: 11/01
AREAS OF INTEREST: Arts & Culture, Community,
Education, Environment, Health, Medicine, Religion,
Research, Scholarships, Social Services, Sports & Athletics,
Other
CURRENT ASSETS: $5,746,306 PRIOR ASSETS:
$5,564,532
TOTAL AMOUNT AWARDED: $141,020
HIGH: $78,000--Charitable Organizations
MID: $56,866--Grants & Scholarships
LOW: $6,153--Grants (Individuals)
GRANTS AWARDS: N/A
SERVICE AREA: National
COMMENTS: No specific application. Submit a written
request giving details of purpose and need for a grant.
DEADLINES: July 1
OFFICERS: Carlton, Doyle E. Jr., TR; Farr, Walter S., TR;
Carlton, Doyle E. III., TR

ORANGE BOWL COMMITTEE, INC.

601 BRICKELL KEY DR.
MIAMI, FL 33131
305-371-4600

ID NUMBER: 590384382
FEDERAL REPORTING DATE: 01/02
AREAS OF INTEREST: Scholarships, Sports & Athletics
CURRENT ASSETS: $9,293,249 PRIOR ASSETS:
$6,811,453
TOTAL AMOUNT AWARDED: $0
GRANTS AWARDS: N/A
COMMENTS: Gives to preselected organizations.
DEADLINES: None
OFFICERS: Potter - Norton, Susan, P; Knight, Christopher
E., VP; Kosnitzky, Michael, S; Migoya, Carlos A., T

ORNS/MIDAS, JERRY FOUNDATION

13041 AUTOMOBILE BLVD.
CLEARWATER, FL 33762
727-572-7440

ID NUMBER: 593413420
FEDERAL REPORTING DATE: 05/01
AREAS OF INTEREST: Arts & Culture, Community,
Education, Health, Medicine, Religion, Research, Scholarships,
Social Services, Other
CURRENT ASSETS: $160,142 PRIOR ASSETS: $28,459
TOTAL AMOUNT AWARDED: $20,300
HIGH: $15,000--Florida Holocaust Museum
MID: $5,000--Jewish Federation of Pinellas County
LOW: $300--Gulf Coast jewish Services
GRANTS AWARDS: N/A
COMMENTS: Submit a letter describing the purpose and
needs of the organization.
DEADLINES: None
OFFICERS: Orns, Jerry, P/T/D; Orns, Donna, VP/S/D;
Orns, Lonnie, D; Kitenplon, Ivy, D; Morris, Pamela, D; Orns,
Jill, D

ORTEGA FOUNDATION

2000 N.W. 92ND AVE.
MIAMI, FL 33172
305-591-9785

ID NUMBER: 650014714
FEDERAL REPORTING DATE: 06/02
AREAS OF INTEREST: Education, Religion, Scholarships
CURRENT ASSETS: $5,220,637 PRIOR ASSETS:
$4,368,673
TOTAL AMOUNT AWARDED: $173,761
HIGH: $50,000--St. John Bosco Church
MID: $25,000--Creighton University
LOW: $485--Individual
GRANTS AWARDS: N/A
SERVICE AREA: National, Puerto Rico
COMMENTS: More than 30 students received scholarships.
DEADLINES: None
OFFICERS: Ortega, Jose A., TR

OTT, RICHARD F. SCHOLARSHIP FOUNDATION

C/O WILLIAM GOZA & AMSOUTH BANK
P.O. BOX 2918
CLEARWATER, FL 34617-2918
727-467-1107

ID NUMBER: 596833432
FEDERAL REPORTING DATE: 02/02
AREAS OF INTEREST: Education, Scholarships
CURRENT ASSETS: $1,125,804 PRIOR ASSETS:
$993,521
TOTAL AMOUNT AWARDED: $58,000
HIGH: $3,500--Individual
MID: $2,000--Individual
LOW: $500--Individual
GRANTS AWARDS: N/A
SERVICE AREA: Clearwater
COMMENTS: Provides college scholarships to graduates of
Clearwater High School. Awards are based on financial need,
academic standing, extracurricular activities, future goals, and

leadership ability. Scholarships are for undergraduate study only.
DEADLINES: 5/1
OFFICERS: AmSouth Bank of Florida, TR; Goza, William M., TR

OXMAN, HARRIET & THEODORE FOUNDATION, INC.
7779 ALISTER MACKENZIE DR.
SARASOTA, FL 34240

ID NUMBER: 650412800
FEDERAL REPORTING DATE: 05/01
AREAS OF INTEREST: Community, Education, Environment, Health, Medicine, Religion, Scholarships, Social Services
CURRENT ASSETS: $22,555   PRIOR ASSETS: $7,858
TOTAL AMOUNT AWARDED: $18,555
HIGH: $11,525--Temple Beth Sholom
MID: $3,500--Sarasota Cnty Library System
LOW: $10--Paralyzed Veterans of America
GRANTS AWARDS: Sarasota Manatee Jewish Federation--$300, WEDU--$25, Chabad of Sarasota--$500, Community Mobile Meals, Inc.--$50, Jewish Family & Children's Services--$25, World Wildlife Fund--$20, United Way of Sarasota--$25, Friends of Selby Public Library--$100, FJCC Children's Scolarship Fund--$100, New York Univ.--$100, Sarasota Memorial Healthcare Fdn.--$1,000, Bnai Brith--$113, Orasmus Hall High School--$100, March of Dimes--$18, American Cancer Society--$25
SERVICE AREA: National
COMMENTS: Gives to preselected organizations.
DEADLINES: None
OFFICERS: Oxman, Theodore, P/T; Oxman, Harriet, VP/S; Band, David, D

PADDOCK, JEROME & MILDRED FOUNDATION
P.O. BOX 267
SARASOTA, FL 34230
941-361-5813

ID NUMBER: 596200844
FEDERAL REPORTING DATE: 04/02
AREAS OF INTEREST: Community, Medicine, Religion, Scholarships, Social Services
CURRENT ASSETS: $5,364,957   PRIOR ASSETS: $3,150,335
TOTAL AMOUNT AWARDED: $175,140
HIGH: $20,000--Children's Haven and Adult Community
MID: $7,000--Southern Scholarship Foundation, Inc.
LOW: $9,000--Gift to Heart Wellness Ctr.
GRANTS AWARDS: Big Brothers Big Sisters of the Suncoast--$10,000, Girls, Inc.--$10,000, Pine of Sarasota--$19,040, Southern Scholarship Fdn--$15,000, Diocese of Venice--$10,000, Planned Parenthood--$20,000, Shodair Children's Hospital--$15,000, Boggy Creek Gang--$10,000, Yana Fdn.--$17,100, Child Development Ctr.--$20,000
SERVICE AREA: Sarasota County
COMMENTS: Aid to organizations that improve the quality of life for the elderly and/or underprivileged children. Funding can be for programming, operational, or emergency needs. The foundation does not favor grants for capital projects or for the arts. Must be a 51(c)(3) organization. Send applicatio to Debra Jacobs, 1800 2nd St., #750, Sarasota, FL. 34236.
DEADLINES: April 1
OFFICERS: First Union National Bank, TR

PADOLF, LOU & LILLIAN FOUNDATION
C/O AMSOUTH BANK OF FLORIDA TRUST DEPARTMENT
P.O. BOX 2918
CLEARWATER, FL 33757-2918
727-592-6907

ID NUMBER: 596190737
FEDERAL REPORTING DATE: 03/01
AREAS OF INTEREST: Education, Scholarships
CURRENT ASSETS: $958,517   PRIOR ASSETS: $864,468
TOTAL AMOUNT AWARDED: $45,100
HIGH: $2,500--Individual
MID: $1,000--Individual
LOW: $500--Individual
GRANTS AWARDS: N/A
SERVICE AREA: FL
COMMENTS: Send for application. Scholarships are limited to students attending Florida universities and colleges, and are awarded only to graduates of Pinellas County High Schools who reside within mid-Pinellas County Florida and who meet other specific criteria. Application forms are available each February.
DEADLINES: May 1st
OFFICERS: AmSouth Bank of Florida, TR

PAGLIARA CHARITABLE FOUNDATION
1370 PINEHURST RD.
DUNEDIN, FL 34698
727-736-2900

ID NUMBER: 596978261
FEDERAL REPORTING DATE: 05/02
AREAS OF INTEREST: Arts & Culture, Education, Scholarships
CURRENT ASSETS: $1,162,858   PRIOR ASSETS: $1,306,793
TOTAL AMOUNT AWARDED: $177,634
HIGH: $29,880--Everyman Theatre
MID: $12,000--Southeast Asia
LOW: $45--Individual
GRANTS AWARDS: Academy Da Vinci--$2,500, American Cancer--$100, Individual--$2,500, Boy Scouts--$2,500, Christmas--$3,673, Individual--$396, Dunedin High School--$300, Everyday Blessings--$11,110, Kids Camp--$219
SERVICE AREA: Suncoast area, Tampa Bay area
COMMENTS: Send applications to: Jack R. St. Arnold, 1370 Pinehurst Rd., Dunedin, Fl. 34698
DEADLINES: None
OFFICERS: St. Arnold, Jack R., TR; Prue, Shirley R., TR

PARETTE, LAWRENCE R. & PATRICIA P. FOUNDATION, INC.
P.O. BOX 561083
MIAMI, FL 33256-1083
305-665-6828

ID NUMBER: 650754994
FEDERAL REPORTING DATE: 07/01
AREAS OF INTEREST: Education, Research, Scholarships

CURRENT ASSETS: $237,927 PRIOR ASSETS: $234,351
TOTAL AMOUNT AWARDED: $9,345
HIGH: $5,000--Xavier High School
MID: $3,000--American Cancer Society
LOW: $345--Aerospace Education Fdn.
GRANTS AWARDS: Breukelein Institute--$1,000
SERVICE AREA: FL
COMMENTS: Gives to preselected organizations.
DEADLINES: None
OFFICERS: Paretta, Lawrence R., D/P; Paretta, Patricia A., D/S; Stamen, Robert A., D

PARISH SCHOLARSHIP TRUST
109 WOODBURN CT.
SAFETY HARBOR, FL 34695

ID NUMBER: 626195024
FEDERAL REPORTING DATE: 06/02
AREAS OF INTEREST: Scholarships
CURRENT ASSETS: $36,831 PRIOR ASSETS: $37,256
TOTAL AMOUNT AWARDED: $1
HIGH: $3,200--Individual Scholarships
GRANTS AWARDS: N/A
SERVICE AREA: IN
COMMENTS: Gives to preselected organizations. Must be a student of Morristown and in high school
DEADLINES: 4/1
OFFICERS: Thornburg, Donald, TR

PATTERSON, CHARLES & ODETTE CHARITABLE TRUST
C/O BANK OF AMERICA, TRUSTEE
P. O. BOX 40200, MC FL9-100-10-19
JACKSONVILLE, FL 32203-0200
877-446-1410

ID NUMBER: 596953716
FEDERAL REPORTING DATE: 01/02
AREAS OF INTEREST: Community, Scholarships, Other
CURRENT ASSETS: $420,156 PRIOR ASSETS: $380,663
TOTAL AMOUNT AWARDED: $19,659
HIGH: $18,159--Various Individuals-Tuition
LOW: $1,500--Annual Awards
GRANTS AWARDS: N/A
SERVICE AREA: St. Petersburg
COMMENTS: Must be employees of police or fire departments of City of St. Petersburg, FL to apply for scholarships or awards acknowledging outstanding service. Victims assistance program offers services including crisis counseling, referral to social services, for obtaining food, shelter an recovery of personal property. Fax: 813-892-1729.
DEADLINES: None
OFFICERS: Bank of America, TR

PHOTRONICS SCHOLARSHIP FOUNDATION
1061 E. INDIANTOWN RD., STE. 310
JUPITER, FL 33477
203-775-9000

ID NUMBER: 61462843
FEDERAL REPORTING DATE: 03/02
AREAS OF INTEREST: Education, Scholarships

CURRENT ASSETS: $655,243 PRIOR ASSETS: $672,978
TOTAL AMOUNT AWARDED: $43,918
HIGH: $4,000--Individual
MID: $1,250--Individual
LOW: $250--Individual
GRANTS AWARDS: N/A
SERVICE AREA: National
COMMENTS: Written form, letters of recommendation, transcripts and test scores. Must be a dependent or custodial of a current Photronics Inc. employee. Send application c/o Robert J. Bollo, to Photronics Inc. 15 Secor Road, Brookfield, CT 06804
DEADLINES: April 15
OFFICERS: Macricostas, Constantine S., C/D; Yamazzo, Michael Y., P/D; Eder, James, S/D

PINE STREET FOUNDATION
C/O TAX DEPARTMENT
3109 W. DR. MARTIN LUTHER KING JR. BLVD.
TAMPA, FL 33607
813-348-7000

ID NUMBER: 136119394
FEDERAL REPORTING DATE: 12/01
AREAS OF INTEREST: Arts & Culture, Education, Health, Medicine, Religion, Research, Scholarships, Social Services
CURRENT ASSETS: $871,697 PRIOR ASSETS: $888,028
TOTAL AMOUNT AWARDED: $0
GRANTS AWARDS: N/A
SERVICE AREA: National
COMMENTS: Give to preselected organizations. Does not accept unsolicited requests.
DEADLINES: None
OFFICERS: Kovacs, James P., P; Jourjy, Moein A., S; Starr, Samuel P., T

POE, WILLIAM F. FOUNDATION
511 W. BAY ST., STE. 400
TAMPA, FL 33606
813-259-4000

ID NUMBER: 591957094
FEDERAL REPORTING DATE: 03/02
AREAS OF INTEREST: Community, Education, Religion, Scholarships, Social Services
CURRENT ASSETS: $1,262,684 PRIOR ASSETS: $1,898,707
TOTAL AMOUNT AWARDED: $101,580
HIGH: $60,000--U. of FL Fdn.
MID: $15,000--Boys & Girls lub
LOW: $250--Plant High School
GRANTS AWARDS: Lincoln Center--$1,000, American Red Cross--$1,120, United Way--$11,000, Missionary Ventures--$1,500, Florida Council on Education--$3,000, Judea Christian--$760, Wharton High School--$250, Sickles High School--$500, Scleroderma Fdn.--$1,000, Flonda Cancer Education--$500, Bayshore Baptist--$500, Misc.--$1,700
SERVICE AREA: Tampa Bay, Tampa, Hillsborough County
COMMENTS: Letter from applicant indicating that it qualifies under Section 501(c)(3); that it is not a private foundation under Section 509; and that it is not controlled by the William F. Poe Foundation.
DEADLINES: None
OFFICERS: Poe, William F., TR; Poe, Elizabeth B., TR; Poe, Charles W., TR

POSEY, LESLIE T. & FRANCES U. FOUNDATION

P.O. BOX 267
SARASOTA, FL 34230
941-361-5813

ID NUMBER: 596832335
FEDERAL REPORTING DATE: 04/02
AREAS OF INTEREST: Scholarships
CURRENT ASSETS: $465,018   PRIOR ASSETS:
$474,794
TOTAL AMOUNT AWARDED: $22,000
HIGH: $5,000--Individual
LOW: $4,000--Individual
GRANTS AWARDS: N/A
SERVICE AREA: National
COMMENTS: Graduate level art scholarships - painting or sculpture.
DEADLINES: March 1
OFFICERS: First Union National Bank, TR

PRIOR, FRANK O. & ANN HERWIG FOUNDATION

340 ROYAL POINCIANA
PALM BEACH, FL 33480
561-833-9631

ID NUMBER: 596151187
FEDERAL REPORTING DATE: 06/99
AREAS OF INTEREST: Community, Medicine, Research, Scholarships, Social Services, Other
CURRENT ASSETS: $351,119   PRIOR ASSETS:
$360,410
TOTAL AMOUNT AWARDED: $31,500
HIGH: $2,000--St. Mary's Hospital
MID: $1,500--Palm Beach Community Chest
LOW: $500--Goodwill, Inc.
GRANTS AWARDS: American Cancer Society--$1,500, American Diabetes Association--$2,000, American National Red Cross--$1,500, American Heart Association--$2,500, Bethesda by the Sea--$1,000, Boys Club of America--$1,000, CARE--$1,500, Escondido Episcopal Church--$1,000, Good Samaritan Hospital--$2,000, Vermont State Police Contribution Fund--$2,000, National Arthritis Foundation--$1,500, Palm Beach Crippled Children--$1,000, Derby Line Fire Dept.--$2,000, Alzheimers & Related Diseases--$2,000, Cousteau Society--$1,000, Town of Palm Beach Paramedics--$1,000, Derby Line Ambulance--$2,000, North County Hospital--$2,000
SERVICE AREA: NE United States
DEADLINES: None
OFFICERS: Mettler, Thomas M., T; Prior, Ann H., T

PROGRESS VILLAGE FOUNDATION

8306 FIR DR.
TAMPA, FL 33619

ID NUMBER: 592807536
FEDERAL REPORTING DATE: 10/01
AREAS OF INTEREST: Education, Scholarships
CURRENT ASSETS: $138,065   PRIOR ASSETS:
$159,905
TOTAL AMOUNT AWARDED: $28,000
HIGH: $3,000--Individual
MID: $1,000--Individual

LOW: $75--Individual
GRANTS AWARDS: N/A
COMMENTS: Send applications to: Lois Bowers, 8306 Fir Dr., Tampa, Fl., 33619.
DEADLINES: N/A
OFFICERS: Bowes, Lois, P; Fort. Clarence, VP; Allen, Mary, T; Fort, Yvonne, Financial Sec.; Shedrick, Alberta, S; Kemp, Bertha, D

PUBLIX SUPER MARKETS CHARITIES, INC.

P.O. BOX 407
LAKELAND, FL 33802
863-688-1188

ID NUMBER: 596194119
FEDERAL REPORTING DATE: 08/01
AREAS OF INTEREST: Arts & Culture, Community, Education, Environment, Health, Medicine, Scholarships, Social Services, Sports & Athletics, Other
CURRENT ASSETS: $292,061,841   PRIOR ASSETS:
$217,957,599
TOTAL AMOUNT AWARDED: $23,956,325
HIGH: $1,223,300-United Way-Central Florida
MID: $50,000--United Way-America
LOW: $25--Clemson Univ. Fdn.
GRANTS AWARDS: Museum of Arts & Sciences--$1,000, Orlando Museum of Art--$5,500, Art League of Hilton Head--$500, Southeasten Legal Fdn.--$2,000, Martin L. King Jr. Ctr.--$4,500, Florida Sheriffs Assn.--$500, Corp-Develop Communities-Tampa--$1,500, City of Lakeland--$750, Tiger Town Pig Festival, Inc.--$2,500, Sarasota Manatee Jewish Comm.--$2,500, City of Punta Gorda--$500, City of North Charleston--$500, Junior League-Columbia--$2,500, Bartow Area Chamber Fdn.--$1,000, Boys & Girls Clubs-Lakeland--$7,500
SERVICE AREA: FL, GA, SC, AL, TN
COMMENTS: Send applications to: Carol Barnett, P. O. Box 407, Lakeland, Fl. 33802.
DEADLINES: None
OFFICERS: Barnett, Carol, C/d; Barnett, Hoyt, VP/D; Johnson, Tina, T/D; Hart, Barbara, D; Attaway, John, S/D

PUCCI FAMILY FOUNDATION

5481 PENNOCK POINT RD.
JUPITER, FL 334587
561-748-4601

ID NUMBER: 222938821
FEDERAL REPORTING DATE: 05/02
AREAS OF INTEREST: Education, Religion, Scholarships, Social Services, Sports & Athletics, Other
CURRENT ASSETS: $2,573,662   PRIOR ASSETS:
$2,460,523
TOTAL AMOUNT AWARDED: $14,153
HIGH: $5,178--In Home Care
MID: $1,175--Miami Dolphins Fdn.
LOW: $100--Easter Seals
GRANTS AWARDS: St. Mary's High School--$2,000, St. Claire's--$1,000, Cardinal Newman HS--$500, Jupiter Tequesta Women's Fund--$500, American Heart Assn.--$200, Kathleen McCarthy Fdn.--$500, People to People International--$300, Uninformed Widows & Childrens Fund--$1,000, Adam Walsh Children's Fund--$1,700
SERVICE AREA: National

COMMENTS: Send applications to: D.E. Doyle, , The Pucci Family Fdn., 5481 Pennock Pt. Rd., Jupiter, Fl. 33458. Please attach copy.
DEADLINES: None
OFFICERS: Pucci, Thomas F., P; Pucci, Yvonne, EVP; Pucci, Claudia L., VP; Vettoso, John M., VP; Doyle, Dorothy E., S/TR

PURCELL FAMILY FOUNDATION
14155 U.S. HWY 1, STE. 310
JUNO BEACH, FL 33408
561-622-2000

ID NUMBER: 161425579
FEDERAL REPORTING DATE: 05/02
AREAS OF INTEREST: Arts & Culture, Education, Medicine, Religion, Research, Scholarships, Social Services
CURRENT ASSETS: $2,540,692 PRIOR ASSETS: $2,790,973
TOTAL AMOUNT AWARDED: $75,000
HIGH: $25,000--First Presbyterian Church
MID: $10,000--Raymond F. Kravis Center
LOW: $500--St. Mark's Episcopal Church
GRANTS AWARDS: American Heart Association--$1,000, Association for Retarded Citizens--$1,500, Campus Crusade for Christ--$500, Center for Hospice Care--$5,500, Florida Atlantic University--$500, Hobe Sound Volunteer Fireman's Assoc.--$1,000, Home Safe of Palm Beach--$500, Univ. of VA School of Law--$12,000, Upledger Foundation--$15,000
SERVICE AREA: National
COMMENTS: Gives to preselected organizations.
DEADLINES: None
OFFICERS: Purcell, John R. Sr., C/P/D; Purcell, Sheryl I., VP/T/D; Gronczewski, Sandy, D; Nielsen, Patricia, H., S

QUINN FAMILY CHARITABLE FOUNDATION, INC.
PO BOX 941539
MAITLAND, FL 32794-1539
407-740-0585

ID NUMBER: 593207710
FEDERAL REPORTING DATE: 06/02
AREAS OF INTEREST: Arts & Culture, Community, Education, Environment, Health, Scholarships, Social Services
CURRENT ASSETS: $472,781 PRIOR ASSETS: $479,370
TOTAL AMOUNT AWARDED: $28,200
HIGH: $12,750--Alpha Tau Omega Fdn.
MID: $5,500--Seminole Boosters, Inc.
LOW: $100--National Heart Foundation
GRANTS AWARDS: Alzhemier's Association, Chicago--$100, American Cancer Society, Florida--$250, American Lung Association of Central Florida--$100, Boy Scouts of America, Central Florida Council--$200, Florida Special Olympics--$200, Orlando Rescue Mission--$250, St. Michael's Episcopal Church--$150, Trinity Preparatory School--$1,200, WMFE Cornnestone Society, Orlando--$1,250
SERVICE AREA: National
COMMENTS: Gives to preselected organizations.
DEADLINES: None
OFFICERS: Quinn, John H., P/T; Quinn, Hallie H., S/T/TR; Quinn, Brooks C., TR; Quinn, John H. Jr., TR; Quinn, Brooks C., TR

R & W FAMILY FOUNDATION INC.
C/O M. WALLACE RUBIN
6828 PARISIAN WAY
LAKE WORTH, FL 33467
203-366-5876

ID NUMBER: 61531915
FEDERAL REPORTING DATE: 03/02
AREAS OF INTEREST: Arts & Culture, Community, Education, Health, Religion, Scholarships, Social Services
CURRENT ASSETS: $1,078,020 PRIOR ASSETS: $1,054,770
TOTAL AMOUNT AWARDED: $54,250
HIGH: $13,500--Deerfield Academy
MID: $3,000--Milford Hospital
LOW: $50--Perlman Hebrew Day School
GRANTS AWARDS: Columbus House--$2,000, Amherst College--$3,500, Helps International--$1,000, Highland Elementary School--$1,000, Jewish Chautauqua Society--$1,400, Jewish Home for Aged of New Haven--$2,000, Orchestra University of New Haven--$100, Red Cross Diaster Relief--$2,500, Ronald McDonald--$1,600, USO--$2,000, United Way Milford--$2,000, University of New Haven--$4,000
SERVICE AREA: National
COMMENTS: Gives to preselected organizations.
DEADLINES: None
OFFICERS: Rubin, M. Wallace, P; Rubin, Rita E., VP; Rubin, David R., T; Rubin, Anne D., S; Hurwitz, Sally, D; Lerman, Deborah R., D

RASMUSSEN, SUSAN O. TWPF
P. O. BOX 3838
ORLANDO, FL 32802

ID NUMBER: 596521640
FEDERAL REPORTING DATE: 01/02
AREAS OF INTEREST: Education, Health, Scholarships
CURRENT ASSETS: $327,761 PRIOR ASSETS: $249,642
TOTAL AMOUNT AWARDED: $46,889
HIGH: $46,889--University of Florida, College of Medicine
GRANTS AWARDS: N/A
COMMENTS: Submit letter describing scholarship program & need.
DEADLINES: None
OFFICERS: Suntrust Bank, TR

RAYNI FOUNDATION, INC.
C/O RAUL F. RODRIGUEZ
300 S.W. 124 AVE.
MIAMI, FL 33184
305-227-1264

ID NUMBER: 650838191
FEDERAL REPORTING DATE: 04/02
AREAS OF INTEREST: Education, Religion, Scholarships
CURRENT ASSETS: $3,498,571 PRIOR ASSETS: $3,833,800
TOTAL AMOUNT AWARDED: $174,600
HIGH: $5,650--Individual
MID: $2,400--Individual
LOW: $1,150--Individual
GRANTS AWARDS: N/A
SERVICE AREA: FL
COMMENTS: Gives to preselected organizations.
DEADLINES: None

OFFICERS: Rodriguez-Perez, Raul, D; Rodriguez, Nidia M., D; Rodriguez, Raul F., D

OFFICERS: Reinhold, Gary, TR; Reinhold, Robert, TR; Fleming, Marie, TR

REED, ELSIE SELLER CHARITABLE TRUST

P.O. BOX 944
DE BARY, FL 32713
407-668-6625

ID NUMBER: 596836787
FEDERAL REPORTING DATE: 05/02
AREAS OF INTEREST: Community, Education, Scholarships
CURRENT ASSETS: $286,750 PRIOR ASSETS: $284,630
TOTAL AMOUNT AWARDED: $10,920
HIGH: $2,000--Citizens 4 De Bary
MID: $1,400--Individual
LOW: $1,000--De Bary Elementary School
GRANTS AWARDS: Individual--$1,100, Individual--$1,000, Individual--$1,100, Individual--$1,400, Individual--$1,400
SERVICE AREA: DeBary
COMMENTS: See application form restricted to residents of DeBary only.
DEADLINES: None
OFFICERS: Wilson, Pete, C; Potter, Janet, S; Rollings, Joe, TR; Cappizzi, Jeanne T; McAllister, Peggy, TR

REINHEART, FRANK A. SCHOLARSHIP FUND

C/O GLENN CALHOUN
P.O. BOX 641083
MIAMI, FL 33164-1083
305-471-2042

ID NUMBER: 650495979
FEDERAL REPORTING DATE: 08/01
AREAS OF INTEREST: Scholarships
CURRENT ASSETS: $16,518 PRIOR ASSETS: $15,806
TOTAL AMOUNT AWARDED: $500
HIGH: $500--International Association for Identification
GRANTS AWARDS: N/A
COMMENTS: Application form must be requested from trustee. Only FDIAI Members & defendents attending college or university as a full time student may apply.
DEADLINES: 8/15
OFFICERS: Calhoun, Glen, TR; Bryant, Karen, TR; Fisher, Debbie, TR

REINHOLD, GRACE FLAMING SCHOLARSHIP

C/O CARL D. REINHOLD
629 INERTIA ST., UNIT H
SANIBEL, FL 33957-6808
941-472-2682

ID NUMBER: 391682031
FEDERAL REPORTING DATE: 04/02
AREAS OF INTEREST: Scholarships
CURRENT ASSETS: $5,756 PRIOR ASSETS: $8,628
TOTAL AMOUNT AWARDED: $1,500
HIGH: $1,500--Individual
GRANTS AWARDS: N/A
SERVICE AREA: FL
COMMENTS: Gives to preselected organizations.
DEADLINES: None

RELIGIOUS INSTITUTIONAL FINANCE CORPORATION OF AMERICA

C/O BROOKS HUEY
1901 PRINCESS CT.
NAPLES, FL 34110-1018
941-597-4309

ID NUMBER: 621183570
FEDERAL REPORTING DATE: 05/01
AREAS OF INTEREST: Scholarships
CURRENT ASSETS: $166,611 PRIOR ASSETS: $162,040
TOTAL AMOUNT AWARDED: $8,000
HIGH: $8,000--Individual
GRANTS AWARDS: N/A
SERVICE AREA: NC, FL
COMMENTS: Write to: Religious Institutional Finance Corp. of America P.O. Box 120957, Nashville, TN 37212 for application form and complete rules regarding grants.
DEADLINES: None
OFFICERS: Huey, Brooks T., P; Huey, Sandra P., S; King, Frank S., D; Thompson, David E., D; Huey, Gwen P., D

RICHARDI, RICHARD SCHOLARSHIP TRUST

501 S. RIDGEWOOD AVE.
DAYTONA BEACH, FL 32114
386-252-4499

ID NUMBER: 5970620490
FEDERAL REPORTING DATE: 10/01
AREAS OF INTEREST: Scholarships
CURRENT ASSETS: $2,306,115 PRIOR ASSETS: $2,123,176
TOTAL AMOUNT AWARDED: $189,000
HIGH: $5,000--Individual
MID: $3,000--Individual
LOW: $2,000--Individual
GRANTS AWARDS: N/A
SERVICE AREA: MA
COMMENTS: Gives to preselected organizations. Must be a graduate of Walpole, MA High School.
DEADLINES: 4/1
OFFICERS: Hawkins, Donald E., Co-TR; First Union National Bank, Co-TR

RICHARDSON SCHOLARSHIP FOUNDATION, INC.

P.O. BOX 370
VERO BEACH, FL 32961
561-567-1151

ID NUMBER: 650064113
FEDERAL REPORTING DATE: 05/01
AREAS OF INTEREST: Community, Education, Health, Scholarships
CURRENT ASSETS: $215,815 PRIOR ASSETS: $228,969
TOTAL AMOUNT AWARDED: $104,960
GRANTS AWARDS: N/A

SERVICE AREA: National
COMMENTS: Recipients are selected from general public on basis of recommendations solicited by the foundation from educational institutions and other parties. Most solicitations will be done in Indian River County, FL, but shall not be limited to that geographic area. Write Gary Lindsey, c/o Richardson Foundation, Inc., P.O. Box 339, Vero Beach, FL 32961-339.
DEADLINES: May 10
OFFICERS: Richardson, Danforth K., P; Hopkins, Carter W., D; Richardson, Marjorie H., VP; Luther, Nancy R., T; Hopkins, Susan R., AS; Perez, Tomas Rene, AT

RIEGEL, JOHN L. & MARGARET FOUNDATION

C/O JOHN RIEGEL, 2341 CAMPBELL RD.
CLEARWATER, FL 33765
727-797-3972

ID NUMBER: 136154512
FEDERAL REPORTING DATE: 06/01
AREAS OF INTEREST: Arts & Culture, Education, Health, Medicine, Scholarships, Social Services, Other
CURRENT ASSETS: $243,284   PRIOR ASSETS: $213,098
TOTAL AMOUNT AWARDED: $6,500
HIGH: $2,000--Museum of Fine Arts, Boston
MID: $1,000--All Children's Hospital
LOW: $200--Richard Barruta Fund
GRANTS AWARDS: Association of Childrens Services--$600, Planned Parenthood--$500, Deerfield Academy--$2,000
SERVICE AREA: FL
COMMENTS: Gives to preselected organizations.
DEADLINES: None
OFFICERS: Locknart, Mary Ann, T; Riegel, William, T; Riegel, John L., T

RIGSBY, JOHN & DAVID MEMORIAL FUND

9013 POINT CYPRESS DR.
ORLANDO, FL 32836
407-660-5501

ID NUMBER: 593398973
FEDERAL REPORTING DATE: 12/01
AREAS OF INTEREST: Scholarships
CURRENT ASSETS: $89,018   PRIOR ASSETS: $91,336
TOTAL AMOUNT AWARDED: $8,000
HIGH: $1,000--Individual
MID: $1,000--Individual
LOW: $1,000--Individual
GRANTS AWARDS: N/A
SERVICE AREA: FL
COMMENTS: Submit completed application form including applicant's biographical information (education and family), financial needs statement, transcript, letter of recommendation, and essay explaining the applicant's clear vision of how this scholarship would help.
DEADLINES: March 28
OFFICERS: Rigsby, John N., P; Rigsby, Virginia B., D; Rigsby, John M., D

ROBERTS, CRAIG & FLORI FAMILY FOUNDATION, INC.

1241 GULF OF MEXICO DR., STE. 801
LONGBOAT KEY, FL 34228
941-383-3655

ID NUMBER: 650402203
FEDERAL REPORTING DATE: 05/01
AREAS OF INTEREST: Arts & Culture, Community, Education, Environment, Religion, Research, Scholarships, Social Services
CURRENT ASSETS: $357,169   PRIOR ASSETS: $320,629
TOTAL AMOUNT AWARDED: $14,737
HIGH: $5,687--Asolo Center for Performing Arts
MID: $3,000--Jewish Federation
LOW: $100--American Jewish Community
GRANTS AWARDS: AIPAC--$250, Boys & Girls Clubs of Sarasota Co., Inc.--$100, Florida West Coast Symphony--$1,000, Jewish Family Service--$2,000, S. Waxman Cancer Research--$1,000, Sarasota County Arts Council--$250, Sarasota Opera--$350, Harvard College Parents Fund--$500
SERVICE AREA: National
COMMENTS: Submit application in the form of a letter.
DEADLINES: None
OFFICERS: Roberts, Craig N., P/TR; Roberts, Florence, VP/S; Roberts, Bruce, D; Roberts, Douglas, D

ROBERTSON, LOIS & EDWARD FOUNDATION

691 LAKE SUE AVE.
WINTER PARK, FL 32789
407-647-0234

ID NUMBER: 366146685
FEDERAL REPORTING DATE: 06/01
AREAS OF INTEREST: Scholarships
CURRENT ASSETS: $57,880   PRIOR ASSETS: $59,969
TOTAL AMOUNT AWARDED: $3,750
HIGH: $1,250--Individual, Winter Park
MID: $1,250--Individual, Winter Park
LOW: $1,250--Individual, Winter Park
GRANTS AWARDS: N/A
SERVICE AREA: Winter Park
COMMENTS: Grants limited to graduates of Winter Park High School.
DEADLINES: 3/31
OFFICERS: Robertson, Lois M., P; Munns, Harry P., VP; Robertson, Edward, T; Munns, Jane, S

ROBEY CHARITABLE TRUST

2986 MEADOW HILL DR.
CLEARWATER, FL 33761-2825
912-598-8202

ID NUMBER: 596961615
FEDERAL REPORTING DATE: 03/02
AREAS OF INTEREST: Education, Scholarships
CURRENT ASSETS: $175,942   PRIOR ASSETS: $73,913
TOTAL AMOUNT AWARDED: $38,400
HIGH: $18,250--Hillsdale College
MID: $13,250--Thomas More College
GRANTS AWARDS: N/A
SERVICE AREA: NH, MI, NM
COMMENTS: Submit informal verbal or written contact to L.J. Robey, 9 Brisbane court, Savannah, GA 31411, 912-598-

8202. Current practice is to orient programs to students of small colleges
DEADLINES: None
OFFICERS: Robey, E.W., TR; Robey, L.J., TR; Robey, A.M., TR

ROBINSON, JIM A. FOUNDATION, INC.

C/O FERRELL SCHULTZ CARTER ZUMPANO
201 S. BISCAYNE BLVD., STE. 3400
MIAMI, FL 33131
305-371-8585

ID NUMBER: 650415399
FEDERAL REPORTING DATE: 12/01
AREAS OF INTEREST: Education, Health, Religion, Scholarships, Other
CURRENT ASSETS: $2,175,565   PRIOR ASSETS: $1,507,718
TOTAL AMOUNT AWARDED: $175,000
HIGH: $50,000--Helping Hands for the Poor
MID: $25,000--Episcopal Aids Ministry
LOW: $10,000--Ashville School
GRANTS AWARDS: Our Lady of Belen Jesuit--$20,000, Jackson Memorial Fdn.--$25,000, Mercer Univ.--$25,000, Recovery Fdn.--$10,000, Venezuela W/O Boundries--$10,000
COMMENTS: Gives to preslected organizations.
DEADLINES: None
OFFICERS: Robinson, Jaime A., P/TR; Ferrell, Milton M. Jr., VP/TR; Forshee, William H., S/T

ROLLNICK, WILLIAM D. & NANCY ELLISON FOUNDATION

7733 FISHER ISLAND DR.
FISHER ISLAND, FL 33109
818-981-2240

ID NUMBER: 954394898
FEDERAL REPORTING DATE: 02/01
AREAS OF INTEREST: Arts & Culture, Community, Environment, Religion, Scholarships
CURRENT ASSETS: $114,296   PRIOR ASSETS: $1,441,695
TOTAL AMOUNT AWARDED: $506,802
HIGH: $340,000--Metropolitan Opera
MID: $90,000--American Ballet Theater
LOW: $500--United Pegasus
GRANTS AWARDS: Martha's Vineyard Community Service--$32,250, Rainforest Alliance--$15,000, National Gallery of Art--$10,000, Children's Diabetes Fdn.--$5,552, God's Love We Deliver--$3,500, National Museum of Catholic Art--$3,000, Broadway Cares--$2,000, Sir Rex Harrison Scholarship Fund--$2,000, Aperture Fdn.--$1,000, Marlborough School--$1,000, The Drawing Center--$1,000
SERVICE AREA: FL
COMMENTS: Gives to preselected organizations.
DEADLINES: None
OFFICERS: Rollnick, William D., D

ROSENBERG, WILLIAM FAMILY FOUNDATION

C/O GERSON PRESTON & CO.
666 71 ST.
MIAMI BEACH, FL 33141
305-868-3600

ID NUMBER: 592675613
FEDERAL REPORTING DATE: 11/01
AREAS OF INTEREST: Education, Health, Religion, Scholarships, Social Services
CURRENT ASSETS: $3,684,134   PRIOR ASSETS: $3,630,038
TOTAL AMOUNT AWARDED: $173,551
HIGH: $104,550--Dana Farber Cancer Inst. of Harvard Univ.
MID: $16,500--National Alliiance for Mental Illness
LOW: $100--Jimmy Fund of Dana Farber Cancer Inst.
GRANTS AWARDS: Temple Beth Elohim--$1,500, Facing History Boston Benefit--$2,500, Grow Clinic @ Boston Medical Ctr.--$1,000, Rivers School Annual Fund--$250, Combined Jewish Philanthropies--$5,000, Rashi School--$250, Univ. of Vermont--$500, Synagogue 2000--$5,500, Leukemia & Lyphoma Society--$250, Animal Rescue League of Boston--$1,000, Tulane A. B. Freeman School of Business--$7,000, Hospice by the Sea--$3,750, Salvation Army--$2,750, American Red Cross--$2,750, Handy--$1,000
COMMENTS: Gives to preselected organizations.
DEADLINES: None
OFFICERS: Rosenberg, Ann M., P/D; Rosenberg, William, C/TR; Rosenberg, Robert, TR; Silverstein, Carol, VP/TR; Rosenberg, Donald, TR; Rosenberg, James, TR/T

ROSENSON FAMILY FOUNDATION

C/O HAROLD ROSENSON,
13332 VERDUN DR.
PALM BEACH GARDENS, FL 33410-1473

ID NUMBER: 363677314
FEDERAL REPORTING DATE: 10/01
AREAS OF INTEREST: Arts & Culture, Community, Education, Environment, Health, Medicine, Religion, Scholarships, Social Services
CURRENT ASSETS: $323,172   PRIOR ASSETS: $397,896
TOTAL AMOUNT AWARDED: $94,365
HIGH: $5,000--Ravinia Festival Assn.
MID: $1,500--Duncan YMCA
LOW: $15--Illinois Charity
GRANTS AWARDS: 11 10 02 Fdn.--$300, ACLU Fdn.--$500, Adam Walsh Fdn.--$300, Adler Planetarium--$1,000, AFOBIS--$300, Alzheimers Assn.--$1,000, American Assn. of Ben Gurion--$600, American Cancer Society--$500, American Committee for Weisman Inst.--$600, American Friends of Israel--$600, American Friends of Livnot--$1,000, American Heart Assn.--$500, American Jewish Congress--$500, American Jewish World Service--$300, American Technion Society--$600
SERVICE AREA: National
COMMENTS: Gives to preselected organizations.
DEADLINES: None
OFFICERS: Rosenson, Harold, D; Rosenson, Linda J., D; Rosenson, Alan D., D; Rosenson, Kenneth B., D; Rosenson, Michael E., D

ROSS, JOSEPH & FRIEDA FOUNDATION, INC.

P.O. BOX 114007
MIAMI, FL 33111-4007
305-377-4228

ID NUMBER: 650919356
FEDERAL REPORTING DATE: 04/02
AREAS OF INTEREST: Arts & Culture, Community, Education, Environment, Health, Religion, Scholarships
CURRENT ASSETS: $3,369,543 **PRIOR ASSETS:** $3,382,937
TOTAL AMOUNT AWARDED: $163,020
HIGH: $43,650--Temple Samuel / or Olom
MID: $18,000--Florida Hillel Council
LOW: $480--Augustine Fellowship
GRANTS AWARDS: Beth Jacob Congregation--$37,150, Boggie Creek Camp--$1,000, First Baptist Church--$1,000, Grace Lutheran Church--$2,500, High County United Way--$5,000, Holocaust Memorial Committee--$7,000, Humaine Society of Wautaga County--$2,000, Miami Palmetto Senior High--$1,000, Prep Arts Dept Lees-Mcrae College--$4,500, Ruach Hoariti--$10,000
SERVICE AREA: National
COMMENTS: Gives to preselected organizations.
DEADLINES: None
OFFICERS: Hornik, Peter F., P; Hornik, Todd A., VP; Hornik, Steven R., VP; Sax, William L., S

ROSS, RICHARD M. & ELIZABETH M. FOUNDATION

2145 14TH AVE., STE. 16
VERO BEACH, FL 32960
772-978-9686

ID NUMBER: 311480761
FEDERAL REPORTING DATE: 05/02
AREAS OF INTEREST: Arts & Culture, Community, Education, Environment, Health, Medicine, Religion, Scholarships, Social Services, Other
CURRENT ASSETS: $12,458,598 **PRIOR ASSETS:** $12,844,856
TOTAL AMOUNT AWARDED: $747,000
HIGH: $60,500--Food for the Poor
MID: $20,000--Boys Hope/ Girls Hope
LOW: $1,000--St. Matthew's Episcopal Church
GRANTS AWARDS: Anglican Frontier Missions--$25,000, Camp Wingmann--$7,500, Childrenss Place Association--$10,000, Davidson College Annual FUnd--$1,000, Fellowship St. James--$13,000, El Buen Samaritano--$14,000, Evans Scholars Foundation--$10,000
SERVICE AREA: National
COMMENTS: Applications should be sent to Marcia Blackburn, 2145 14th Avenue, Suite 16, Vero Beach, FL 32960. Email questions to rossfund@earthlink.net The Ross Fdn. does not accept any unsolicited proposals.
DEADLINES: September 1
OFFICERS: Ross, Elizabeth M., P/TR; Blackburn, Marcia Ross, S/TR/M/T; Soter, Sarah Ross, TR; Ross, George A., TR; Ross, Richard M., Jr., TR; Ziegler, Sarah W., TR

ROTARY CLUB OF NAPLES CHARITABLE FOUNDATION

501 GOODLETTE RD., N.
NAPLES, FL 34102-5666
941-261-7055

ID NUMBER: 656165341
FEDERAL REPORTING DATE: 08/01
AREAS OF INTEREST: Education, Scholarships, Social Services
CURRENT ASSETS: $10,551 **PRIOR ASSETS:** $30,934
TOTAL AMOUNT AWARDED: $49,874
HIGH: $21,000--Naples Highschool
MID: $1,000--Rotary International
LOW: $540--Naples Bay Rotary
GRANTS AWARDS: Individual--$13,334, Baron Collier High School--$1,000, Lely High School--$1,000, St. John Newman--$1,000, Gulf Coast High School--$1,000, University of Central Florida--$1,000, Gift of Giving--$4,000
SERVICE AREA: Naples
COMMENTS: Gives to preselected organizations.
DEADLINES: None
OFFICERS: Atzingen, Hal; Hendry, Peggy; Mediavilla, Leo; Geshay, John; Kelly, Charles

RUBENS FAMILY FOUNDATION

5114 WINDSOR PARK DR.
BOCA RATON, FL 33496-1636
561-997-9667

ID NUMBER: 656235868
FEDERAL REPORTING DATE: 03/02
AREAS OF INTEREST: Arts & Culture, Education, Health, Medicine, Religion, Scholarships, Social Services
CURRENT ASSETS: $832,442 **PRIOR ASSETS:** $827,173
TOTAL AMOUNT AWARDED: $18,900
HIGH: $3,500--Crohns & Colitis Foundation of America, Inc
MID: $1,000--Temple Brith Kodesh
LOW: $100--Southern Poverty Law Center
GRANTS AWARDS: Bailey-Boushay House--$500, Seneca Park Zoo Society--$500, American Civil Liberties Union--$500, NASDAQ Disaster Relief Fund, Inc.--$3,000, Chicago Public Radio--$1,000, Chichago Cultural Center--$900, Northwest Burn Foundation--$500, Garth Fagan Dance, Inc.--$750, Jewish Federation of South Palm Beach County--$1,200, EISMA--$1,000, Theatre in the Round Players, Inc.--$1,000, Minneapolis Institute of the Arts--$1,000
SERVICE AREA: National
COMMENTS: Gives to preselected organizations.
DEADLINES: None
OFFICERS: Rubens, Jack, C/TR; Rubens, Helen, S/TR; Robfogel, Nathan, TR; Kanter, Suzanne Rubens, TR; Druckman, Nicole E., TR; Rubens, Margaret, TR

RUBIN, J.M. FOUNDATION, INC.

505 S. FLAGLER DR., STE. 1320
WEST PALM BEACH, FL 33401
561-833-3309

ID NUMBER: 591958240
FEDERAL REPORTING DATE: 06/02
AREAS OF INTEREST: Arts & Culture, Community, Education, Environment, Health, Medicine, Scholarships, Social Services
CURRENT ASSETS: $26,467,256 **PRIOR ASSETS:** $26,736,999

TOTAL AMOUNT AWARDED: $2,127,025
HIGH: $125,000--Palm Beach Atlantic College
MID: $50,000--Palm Beach Community Chest
LOW: $100--Shrine Circus Fund
GRANTS AWARDS: Adopt-A-Family of Palm Beaches, Inc.--$25,000, Alzheimer's Assn.--$2,250, Alzheimer's Community Care Assn.--$17,500, American Heart Assn.--$10,000, Boys & Girls Clubs of Palm beach Cnty.--$25,000, Communities In Schools--$10,000, Coral Reef Society, Inc.--$500, Convenant House Florida, Inc.--$500, Friends of Abused Children, Inc.--$27,000, FL. Sherrif's Youth Ranches--$25,000, United Negro College Fund, Inc.--$5,000, Instrumental Society of Palm Beach Cnty--$6,000, Lynn University--$300, Lighthouse for the Blind--$500, Make A Wish Fdn.--$500
SERVICE AREA: National
COMMENTS: Send applications to the J. M. Rubin Foundation at 505 S. Flagler Drive, Suite 1320, West Palm Beach, FL. 33401
DEADLINES: March 1
OFFICERS: Owens, Robert T., P; Harper, Mary S., VP/S; Carpenter, Charles M., T

RUMSEY, MURIEL FOUNDATION

BANK ONE, FLORIDA
3399 PGA BLVD., STE. 100
PALM BEACH GARDENS, FL 33410
561-627-9400

ID NUMBER: 656047139
FEDERAL REPORTING DATE: 05/00
AREAS OF INTEREST: Education, Scholarships
CURRENT ASSETS: $375,712 **PRIOR ASSETS:** $344,902
TOTAL AMOUNT AWARDED: $39,000
HIGH: $13,000--Purdue University
MID: $13,000--University of Florida
LOW: $13,000--University of Michigan
GRANTS AWARDS: N/A
SERVICE AREA: FL, MI, IN
COMMENTS: Must be a charitable organization. Applications should have an outline of the proposed budget and its objectives and a photocopy of exempt status letter from the IRS. Contact Gary W. Gomoll, Bank One, Florida, Palm Beach Gardens, FL 33410; 561-627-9400
DEADLINES: None
OFFICERS: Bank One, FL, TR; Wertenberger, J.W., TR

RUSSACK FAMILY FOUNDATION

4445 ALTON RD.
MIAMI BEACH, FL 33140
305-532-2028

ID NUMBER: 596152314
FEDERAL REPORTING DATE: 12/01
AREAS OF INTEREST: Arts & Culture, Community, Education, Health, Medicine, Research, Scholarships, Social Services
CURRENT ASSETS: $156,712 **PRIOR ASSETS:** $161,749
TOTAL AMOUNT AWARDED: $12,000
HIGH: $2,000--Miami Rescue
MID: $1,000--School for Special Children
LOW: $1,000--Saleasean Mission
GRANTS AWARDS: Covenant House--$1,000, St. Jude Research--$2,000, The Hope School--$1,000, Cumberland--$1,000, Guiding Eyes for the Blind--$1,000, --$1,000
SERVICE AREA: FL

COMMENTS: Submit written request with purpose of grants and qualifications to Michael Abraham at the above address. Preference given to Florida charities.
DEADLINES: None
OFFICERS: Abraham, Michael

RYAN FOUNDATION

207A STATE RD. 434
WINTER SPRINGS, FL 32708
407-327-2306

ID NUMBER: 592950299
FEDERAL REPORTING DATE: 06/01
AREAS OF INTEREST: Education, Health, Medicine, Religion, Scholarships, Social Services
CURRENT ASSETS: $4,022,008 **PRIOR ASSETS:** $3,792,594
TOTAL AMOUNT AWARDED: $145,890
HIGH: $17,000--Alzheimer Resource Center
MID: $9,055--Beter Living for Seniors
LOW: $1,000--Winter Springs High School
GRANTS AWARDS: Central Florida Chapter IBWC--$5,000, Children's Rights Foundation--$10,000, CITE--$7,500, Coalition for the Homeless of Central FL--$10,000, Crooms School of Choice--$1,000, Foundation for Seminole Co. Public Schools--$10,500, Habatit for Humanity in Seminole Country, Inc.--$5,880, Jeppesen Vision Quest, Inc.--$2,500, Kids House of Seminole, Inc.--$4,355
SERVICE AREA: National, Seminole County
COMMENTS: Apply with preprinted foundation application, financial statements, and tax status letter. Preference given to organizations residing in the Seminole County area.
DEADLINES: None
OFFICERS: Ryan, Maria, VP; Young, Shirley, P/S; Ryan, Dennis, VP; Kisling, Sheryl, S; Ohab, Pamela, VP/TR; Ryan, Jennifer, VP

RYDER SYSTEM CHARITABLE FOUNDATION

C/O CORPORATE TAX
3600 N.W. 82ND AVE.
MIAMI, FL 33166
305-500-4088

ID NUMBER: 592462315
FEDERAL REPORTING DATE: 05/02
AREAS OF INTEREST: Arts & Culture, Community, Education, Environment, Health, Medicine, Religion, Research, Scholarships, Social Services, Sports & Athletics, Other
CURRENT ASSETS: $896,777 **PRIOR ASSETS:** $83,949
TOTAL AMOUNT AWARDED: $974,127
HIGH: $635,210--Civic Organizations (misc.)
MID: $91,000--Cultural Organizations (misc.)
LOW: $15,000--Disaster Relief.
GRANTS AWARDS: Educational Organizations (misc.)--$212,442, Health & Welfare Organizations (misc.)--$19,675
SERVICE AREA: National
COMMENTS: Submit request in letter form. Proposals should be concise yet contain adequate information about the specific project. Include organization's financial status, its management, board of directors, and scope of service to the community. Particular emphasis should be placed on why it would be appropriate for the foundation to support a given request.
DEADLINES: 6/29

OFFICERS: Swienton, Gregory T., P; Goode, R. Ray, ED, CA; Nelson, Corliss J., VP; Lowe, Challis M., VP/T; Susik, W. Daniel, VP/T; Nguy, Alfred C., AT

SAMPLE, A.M. SCHOLARSHIP
P.O. BOX 14728
FORT LAUDERDALE, FL 33302

ID NUMBER: 596490788
FEDERAL REPORTING DATE: 05/01
AREAS OF INTEREST: Scholarships
CURRENT ASSETS: $3,225,050 PRIOR ASSETS: $3,220,761
TOTAL AMOUNT AWARDED: $181,000
HIGH: $3,000--Individual
MID: $2,000--Individual
LOW: $400--Individual
GRANTS AWARDS: N/A
SERVICE AREA: Fl.
COMMENTS: Must be a resident of St. Lucie or Okeechobee counties and attend a Florida College or Davidson College, NC. A form must be submitted by a Protestant Minister. Obtain application form from Margaret G. Sample at 14050 Fairway Willow Lane, Winter Garden, FL 34787. (407) 877-9901
DEADLINES: 4/15
OFFICERS: SunTrust Bank Inc., TR

SAMSTAG, GORDON FINE ARTS TRUST
C/O BANK OF AMERICA
P.O. BOX 40200
JACKSONVILLE, FL 32203-0200
904-464-3664

ID NUMBER: 656064217
FEDERAL REPORTING DATE: 08/01
AREAS OF INTEREST: Scholarships
CURRENT ASSETS: $8,600,906 PRIOR ASSETS: $8,519,021
TOTAL AMOUNT AWARDED: $390,249
HIGH: $44,126--Individual
MID: $14,534--Individual
LOW: $118--Individual
GRANTS AWARDS: N/A
SERVICE AREA: South Australia
COMMENTS: Foundation is just starting to disburse funds. Gives to fine arts students of the University of South Australia who wish to continue their study outside Australia. Awards would cover all expenses for travel, materials, and tuition. Apply to the University of South Australia.
DEADLINES: 6/3
OFFICERS: Bank of America, TR; Wolfe, Ross, D; Wicks, Jane, D

SANTO, JAMES M. & DONNA B., FOUNDATION, INC.
3301 BAYSHORE BLVD.
TAMPA, FL 33629
813-258-8545

ID NUMBER: 593275370
FEDERAL REPORTING DATE: 06/01
AREAS OF INTEREST: Arts & Culture, Education, Health, Medicine, Religion, Scholarships, Social Services

CURRENT ASSETS: $54,252 PRIOR ASSETS: $74,432
TOTAL AMOUNT AWARDED: $22,690
HIGH: $10,000--University of Tampa
MID: $5,000--Vanderbilt University Law School
LOW: $50--University of Notre Dame
GRANTS AWARDS: Child Reach--$240, Highlands Cashiers Hospital--$6,000, Make-A-Wish Foundation--$100, Baskin Louise Gallery--$300, St. John's Episcopal--$1,000
SERVICE AREA: FL
COMMENTS: Apply by letter describing purpose and needs of the organizations.
DEADLINES: None
OFFICERS: Santo, James M., D; Santo, Donna B., D; Kelly, Peter, D

SCHACKNOW, MAX & EVELYN FOUNDATION, INC.
10481 N.W. 17TH ST.
PLANTATION, FL 33322
954-474-5240

ID NUMBER: 650464694
FEDERAL REPORTING DATE: 06/01
AREAS OF INTEREST: Arts & Culture, Community, Scholarships, Social Services
CURRENT ASSETS: $1,151,445 PRIOR ASSETS: $2,161,905
TOTAL AMOUNT AWARDED: $1,325,823
HIGH: $1,324,803-The Schacknow Museum
MID: $1,000--Museum of Discovery
LOW: $20--Florida Sherriff's Assoc.
GRANTS AWARDS: N/A
SERVICE AREA: FL.
COMMENTS: Gives to preselected organizations.
DEADLINES: None
OFFICERS: Schacknow, Max, D; Schacknow, Evelyn, D; Schacknow, Paul, D; McLean, Frederick, S; Schacknow, Sharma, D

SCHEINMAN, ROSLYN FOUNDATION, INC.
5640 COLLINS AVE.
MIAMI BEACH, FL 33140

ID NUMBER: 650327950
FEDERAL REPORTING DATE: 05/01
AREAS OF INTEREST: Education, Health, Medicine, Religion, Scholarships
CURRENT ASSETS: $112,959 PRIOR ASSETS: $112,938
TOTAL AMOUNT AWARDED: $7,835
HIGH: $4,000--Kent State Univ. Museum
MID: $2,000--Temple Beth Am
LOW: $15--Museum of Natural History
GRANTS AWARDS: Simone Wiesenthal Ctr.--$100, New York State Troopers--$25, Westchester Oratorio Society--$200, WNET, 13--$200, Westchester Co. Corrections--$20, Scarsdale Hadassah--$1,000, Carter Ctr--$25, Worldwide Wildlife Foundation--$50, March of Dimes--$25, American Cancer Research--$25, UJA of NY--$100, American Heart Assn.--$25, Lighthouse International--$25
SERVICE AREA: NY, FL
COMMENTS: Gives to preselected organizations. Send applications to: Roslyn Scheinman, 5640 Collins Ave., Miami Beach, Fl. 33140
DEADLINES: Prior to 9/30

OFFICERS: Scheinman, Roslyn, P; Lucas, Vicki S., VP; Scheinman, Diane M., S/TR

SCHENCK, VIRGIL & VIRGINA FOUNDATION
5440 SCHENCK AVE.
ROCKLEDGE, FL 32955
321-636-7826

ID NUMBER: 593411693
FEDERAL REPORTING DATE: 05/02
AREAS OF INTEREST: Education, Medicine, Religion, Scholarships, Social Services
CURRENT ASSETS: $818,574 PRIOR ASSETS: $1,028,537
TOTAL AMOUNT AWARDED: $85,230
HIGH: $26,600--Florida A&M University
MID: $11,000--Florida State University
LOW: $100--American Life League
GRANTS AWARDS: American Red Cross--$100, Bethlehem Lutheran Church--$500, Heritage Foundation--$1,000, Institute of Human Studies--$250, Jewish Federation of Greater Orlands--$1,500, Kenan-Flagler Business Campus--$350
SERVICE AREA: National
COMMENTS: For scholarship applicants, a biographical outline is requested. A scholastic history, the need for the scholarship, and the amount requested. Also, what the applicant plans to do in college, the field of study, and the reason they want to attend college. Does the applicant have other sources of funds? If so, how much?
DEADLINES: None
OFFICERS: Schenck, L. Virgil Jr., P; Schenck, Jay G.M., VP/S/T

SCHOENBAUM FAMILY FOUNDATION
P.O. BOX 580
SARASOTA, FL 34230-0580
941-366-1708

ID NUMBER: 650043921
FEDERAL REPORTING DATE: 06/02
AREAS OF INTEREST: Arts & Culture, Community, Education, Environment, Health, Medicine, Religion, Scholarships, Social Services
CURRENT ASSETS: $23,321,899 PRIOR ASSETS: $24,528,553
TOTAL AMOUNT AWARDED: $1,037,076
HIGH: $282,250--Kanawha County Commission
MID: $100,000--Pinellas Co. Jewish Day School
LOW: $1,000--American Jewish Committe
GRANTS AWARDS: Pinellas County Jewish Day School--$125,000, Ohio State University--$200,000, Nature Conservancy of West VA--$50,000, Natl. Conference on Soviet Jewry--$3,500, Mary's Center for Maternial And Representing--$5,000, Life Pieces to Masterpieces--$5,000, Jewish Theological Seminary--$1,500, Florida West Coast Symphony--$50,000
SERVICE AREA: National
COMMENTS: Submit applications to Raydel Walston, Schoenbaum Family Fdn., P.O. Box 580, Sarasota, FL 34230-0580; 941-366-1708
DEADLINES: None
OFFICERS: Schoenbaum, Betty, P/S-T/T; Schoenbaum, Jeffry F., VP/T; Schoenbaum, Raymond D., VP/T; Schoenbaum, Emily, VP/T; Schoenbaum Miller, Joann, VP/T

SECOND CHANCE FOUNDATION
208 RIDGE DR.
NAPLES, FL 34108
941-592-9300

ID NUMBER: 592708392
FEDERAL REPORTING DATE: 06/01
AREAS OF INTEREST: Education, Environment, Health, Scholarships, Social Services
CURRENT ASSETS: $6,131,186 PRIOR ASSETS: $5,807,847
TOTAL AMOUNT AWARDED: $118,145
HIGH: $89,750--Care
MID: $8,440--X-Mas Fund
LOW: $50--Collier County Historical Society
GRANTS AWARDS: Port Washington Sauleville Schoo District--$2,500, Wishing Well Fdn.--$500, Classic Chamber Orchestra--$600, City of Naples Parks--$765, Naples Art Assn.--$60, Conservancy of South West Florida--$90, Tyme Out--$2,000, Leukemia Society--$500, Nancy Forresters Secret Garden--$100, Quest Education Fund--$1,490, Pewaukee Yaught Club--$100, Vivian Rolle Fdn.--$2,000, Society for Handicapped Acheivement--$6,700, Wisconsin Breast Cancer Coalition--$200, All Sports Comm. Svc.--$1,250
SERVICE AREA: FL
COMMENTS: Submit written request to Bruce Conley, 2338 Immokalee Road, #147, Naples, FL 33942. No special application necessary.
DEADLINES: None
OFFICERS: Conley, Bruce, TR

SELINGER EDUCATIONAL FUND
P. O. BOX 14728
FORT LAUDERDALE, FL 33302

ID NUMBER: 596501141
FEDERAL REPORTING DATE: 05/01
AREAS OF INTEREST: Education, Scholarships
CURRENT ASSETS: $336,902 PRIOR ASSETS: $338,127
TOTAL AMOUNT AWARDED: $6,000
HIGH: $1,000--Tulane Univ. A/R Dept.
MID: $1,000--Univ. of Miami
LOW: $1,000--Florida Atlantic Univ.
GRANTS AWARDS: Office of Financial Aid--$1,000, Duke Univ.--$1,000, Univ. of Central Florida--$1,000
SERVICE AREA: Broward County (south)
COMMENTS: Broward County Superintendent submits names of honor students to a committee of trustees for selection for an award. Selection is based on GPA and financial need.
DEADLINES: 6/1
OFFICERS: SunTrust Bank Inc., TR

SETA, DON & ANGIE FOUDATION
6400 E. ROGERS CIR.
BOCA RATON, FL 33499-0001
561-994-2260

ID NUMBER: 656265708
FEDERAL REPORTING DATE: 05/02
AREAS OF INTEREST: Community, Education, Health, Medicine, Religion, Scholarships, Social Services
CURRENT ASSETS: $94,721 PRIOR ASSETS: $98,851
TOTAL AMOUNT AWARDED: $5,020
HIGH: $3,000--Son's of Italy, OH

MID: $1,000--St. Francis Seraph
LOW: $70--Township Lodge
GRANTS AWARDS: Seton High School Scholarship
Program--$2,000, Christopher Reeve Paralysis Fund--$1,000,
Son's of Italy Fdn., FL--$2,000, Kidney Fdn.--$1,050, Ocean
Ridge Dept.--$200, Order SOns of Italy, Boca Raton--$2,000,
LaSalle High School--$500, Xavier Univ.--$1,000, FL. Fdn.--
$1,000, Epic House--$500, Sacred Heart Catholic Church--
$500, La Societa Fusfuscaldese Fem--$1,000, Advisory Council
to Juveniles--$2,000, Il Circolo--$710, Ascension Catholic
Church--$400
SERVICE AREA: National
COMMENTS: Gives to preselected organizations.
DEADLINES: None
OFFICERS: Seta, Don, TR; Seta, Angelina, TR

SHANE FAMILY FOUNDATION

4101 PINETREE DR., STE. 1804
MIAMI BEACH, FL 33140
305-532-7311

ID NUMBER: 650715198
FEDERAL REPORTING DATE: 07/01
AREAS OF INTEREST: Arts & Culture, Education, Health,
Religion, Scholarships
CURRENT ASSETS: $1,334,840   PRIOR ASSETS:
$1,330,917
TOTAL AMOUNT AWARDED: $30,315
HIGH: $2,750--Florida A & M University
MID: $1,000--Florida International University
LOW: $25--Consumers Union
GRANTS AWARDS: Univ. of Miami--$2,000, Fisher Island
Philantropic Fund--$350, Mount Sinai Medical Ctr. Fdn.--
$1,000, Consumers Union--$25, New World Symphony--
$115, Univ. of Miami Hurricane Club--$500, Temple Beth
Shalom--$75, Muhlenberg College--$200, Parc--$2,000,
Miami Beach Watersports Ctr., Inc.--$1,000, American Heart
Assn.--$50, Kiwanis Club of Miami Beach--$2,400, Cancer
Lifeline of Mount Siani--$500, Florida Atlantic Univ.--$1,000, .
Univ. of Florida--$2,000
COMMENTS: Gives to preselected organizations.
DEADLINES: None
OFFICERS: Nusbaum, Ira, P; Shane-Nusbaum, Stacey, VP;
Cheema, Balwant, S/T

SHELTZ FINANCIAL ASSISTANCE CORP.

C/O PENNY P. SHELTZ
1033 COUNTRY CLUB DR.
NORTH PALM BEACH, FL 33408-3715
561-626-7031

ID NUMBER: 651012305
FEDERAL REPORTING DATE: 05/02
AREAS OF INTEREST: Scholarships
CURRENT ASSETS: $120   PRIOR ASSETS: $787
TOTAL AMOUNT AWARDED: $3,126
HIGH: $1,043--Individual
MID: $540--Individual
LOW: $500--HighSchool Essay Contest
GRANTS AWARDS: N/A
DEADLINES: N/A
OFFICERS: Sheltz, Penny P., P; Sheltz, Walker W., Jr., D;
Anderson, John B., D

SHERBURNE, GEORGE & KARLA EDUCATIONAL FUND

C/O BANK OF AMERICA
P.O. BOX 40200
JACKSONVILLE, FL 32203-0200
877-446-1410

ID NUMBER: 592667373
FEDERAL REPORTING DATE: 12/01
AREAS OF INTEREST: Scholarships
CURRENT ASSETS: $821,296   PRIOR ASSETS:
$852,350
TOTAL AMOUNT AWARDED: $33,000
HIGH: $3,750--Individual
MID: $1,500--Individual
LOW: $750--Individual
GRANTS AWARDS: N/A
SERVICE AREA: FL
COMMENTS: Gives to preselected organizations.
DEADLINES: None
OFFICERS: Bank of America, TR

SHIMBERG, HINKS & ELAINE FOUNDATION, INC.

C/O M. SHIMBERG
611 BAY ST.
TAMPA, FL 33606
813-254-7567

ID NUMBER: 591432870
FEDERAL REPORTING DATE: 12/01
AREAS OF INTEREST: Arts & Culture, Community,
Health, Religion, Scholarships, Other
CURRENT ASSETS: $873,346   PRIOR ASSETS:
$849,859
TOTAL AMOUNT AWARDED: $59,150
HIGH: $11,000--United Way
MID: $5,000--Andover School of Montessori
LOW: $900--TPA Bay Super Bowl Task Force
GRANTS AWARDS: Tampa Bay Performing Arts Ctr.--
$10,000, Tampa Bay Male Club--$1,500, USF Fdn.--$2,000,
WEDU--$10,000, St. Joseph's Hospital of Tampa Fdn.--
$2,500, Kid City--$6,250, Tampa JCC/Federation Inc.--
$5,000, Community Fdn.--$5,000
SERVICE AREA: FL
COMMENTS: Gives to preselected organizations.
DEADLINES: None
OFFICERS: Shimberg, M., P/T; Shimberg, E., S; Wineberg,
Harvey, TR; Shimberg-Kelly, Kasey, TR; Shimberg, Scott, TR;
Shimberg-Shaw, Betsy, TR

SILVERSTEIN FOUNDATION, INC.

6696 VERSAILLES CT.
LAKE WORTH, FL 33467-5015
561-968-6530

ID NUMBER: 592747181
FEDERAL REPORTING DATE: 05/01
AREAS OF INTEREST: Community, Education, Medicine,
Religion, Scholarships, Social Services
CURRENT ASSETS: $19,853   PRIOR ASSETS: $6,816
TOTAL AMOUNT AWARDED: $48,010
HIGH: $10,700--Haddash
MID: $5,000--B'Nai Zion Fdn.
LOW: $500--D.R.E.D.

GRANTS AWARDS: Temple Beth Tikvah--$1,030, Yishuv Matzas--$2,000, Anti- Defamation League--$5,000, Women's American ORT--$5,000, Keepers of the Gate--$1,000, Palm Beach Jewish Community Campus--$5,000, JAFCO--$800, Jewish Fund for Justice--$1,000, Misc.--$980
SERVICE AREA: National
COMMENTS: Gives to preselected organizations.
DEADLINES: None
OFFICERS: Silverstein, Herman J., P/T; Silverstein, Pauline, S; Silverstein, Robert, VP; Silverstein, Michael, VP

SIMON, HAROLD E. CHARITABLE FOUNDATION

12380 S.W. 82ND AVE.
MIAMI, FL 33156
305-234-2797

ID NUMBER: 592747958
FEDERAL REPORTING DATE: 09/01
AREAS OF INTEREST: Education, Health, Medicine, Religion, Research, Scholarships, Social Services
CURRENT ASSETS: $340,635   PRIOR ASSETS: $294,841
TOTAL AMOUNT AWARDED: $5,106
HIGH: $1,471--Temple Judea
MID: $268--Anti-Defamation League
LOW: $10--Elder Hostel
GRANTS AWARDS: Amer. Auto Immune Disease--$25, Americans for Safe Israel--$100, Arthritis Fdn.--$30, B'Nai B'Reith--$170, Camera--$100, Ctr. for Science--$20, Etta Ress Inst.--$50, Flame--$25, Florida Atlantic Univ.--$183, Florida Society of Middle East--$20, Hillel--$50, International Waldenstrom Fdn.--$1,265, International Myeloma Fdn.--$25, JCC Boynton--$48, Jewish Federation--$125
SERVICE AREA: National
DEADLINES: None
OFFICERS: Simon, Harold E., P/D; Simon, David F., VP/S; Simon, Susan L., D

SKELLY, GERTRUDE E. CHARITABLE FOUNDATION

4600 N. OCEAN BLVD., STE. 206
BOYNTON BEACH, FL 33435-7365
561-243-6725

ID NUMBER: 656085406
FEDERAL REPORTING DATE: 05/02
AREAS OF INTEREST: Arts & Culture, Community, Education, Health, Medicine, Research, Scholarships, Social Services
CURRENT ASSETS: $18,530,630   PRIOR ASSETS: $18,643,574
TOTAL AMOUNT AWARDED: $689,200
HIGH: $50,000--Florida Institute of Technology
MID: $25,000--Indian River Community College Fdn., Inc.
LOW: $700--Palm Beach Community College Fndn. Coalition
GRANTS AWARDS: Alzheimer's Community Care Assn.--$10,000, American Cancer Society, Inc.--$10,000, Colby-Sawyer College--$50,000, American Red Cross Brevard County Chapter--$10,000, Florida Atlantic University--$50,000, American Red Cross National Headquaters--$20,000, ARC--$15,000, Binghamton Univ.--$50,000, Full Circle Therapeutic Riding--$5,000, Broward Community College Fdn.--$25,000, Polk Community College Foundation, Inc.--$25,000, Westcare Health System--$10,000, Children & Families First--$15,000, Children's Aid & Family Services, Inc.--$15,000

SERVICE AREA: National
COMMENTS: Submit on organization's letterhead the details of the organ purpose, function, and methods used to accomplish objectives. Send applications to: Erik Edward Joh, 4600 N. Ocean Blvd., Suite 206, Boynton Beach, Fl. 33435
DEADLINES: 7/31
OFFICERS: Suntrust Bank South Florida, TR; Joh, Erik Edward, TR

SMITH, ALICE F. SCHOLARSHIP TRUST

P.O. BOX 1207
ENGLEWOOD, FL 34295-1207
941-474-7768

ID NUMBER: 656202829
FEDERAL REPORTING DATE: 05/01
AREAS OF INTEREST: Scholarships
CURRENT ASSETS: $272,599   PRIOR ASSETS: $269,912
TOTAL AMOUNT AWARDED: $0
GRANTS AWARDS: N/A
SERVICE AREA: Englewood, FL
COMMENTS: Submit application to R. Earl Warren, 359 West Dearborn St. Englewood, FL 34295-1207. Gives to students educated in Englewood, FL school systems.
DEADLINES: 5/15
OFFICERS: Warren, R. Earl, TR

SMITH, GARNETT A. FAMILY FOUNDATION, INC.

3100 GIN LN.
NAPLES, FL 34102
941-434-7027

ID NUMBER: 582316808
FEDERAL REPORTING DATE: 05/02
AREAS OF INTEREST: Community, Education, Environment, Health, Medicine, Religion, Scholarships, Social Services, Sports & Athletics
CURRENT ASSETS: $4,182,327   PRIOR ASSETS: $1,447,139
TOTAL AMOUNT AWARDED: $153,415
HIGH: $65,250--Community Fdn.-Greater Atlanta
MID: $10,000--Univ. of North Carolina
LOW: $100--100 Club of Raburn
GRANTS AWARDS: All Saints Church--$10,000, American Cancer Society--$100, Community Fdn.-Lake Rabun Fund--$440, Atlanta Youth Academics Fdn.--$500, Link Counseling Ctr.--$300, Hospice of Chattanooga--$100, Univ. of Georgia--$2,500, Baylor School--$10,000, Art Reach Fdn.--$500, Care--$5,275, March of Dimes--$100, Christchurch School--$1,500, American Diabetes--$100, Dixie Golden Retriever--$200, Samaritan House of Atlanta--$1,000
SERVICE AREA: National
COMMENTS: Submit a written summary of no more than two pages. Send applications to: Garnett A.Smith, 3100 Gin Lane, Naples, Fl., 34102 941-434-7027
DEADLINES: N/A
OFFICERS: Smith, Garnett A., D/P; Smith, Emily H.,S

SMITH, MCGREGOR & ELIZABETH WILSON FOUNDATION

200 S. BISCAYNE BLVD., 40TH FL.
MIAMI, FL 33131-2398
305-667-4952

ID NUMBER: 591038572
FEDERAL REPORTING DATE: 05/02
AREAS OF INTEREST: Community, Education, Environment, Health, Scholarships, Other
CURRENT ASSETS: $1,455,886 PRIOR ASSETS: $1,676,388
TOTAL AMOUNT AWARDED: $64,315
HIGH: $26,000--Florida Methodist Children's Home
MID: $5,000--Phi Gamma Delta Educational Support
LOW: $20--FL. Sheriff's Assn.
GRANTS AWARDS: Individual--$3,900, Philanthropy Round Table--$500, Florida Swamplands Operating Foundation--$123, Lawyers for Children--$100, Care Resource--$1,500, American Heart Association--$150, WPBT Channel 2--$640, Komen Race for the Cure--$150, New World for the Performing Arts--$800, Metropolitan Museum of Art--$225, WLRN Public Radio--$200, The Nature Conservancy--$100
SERVICE AREA: National
COMMENTS: Send applications to Wilson-Smith, Pres. at 200 S. Biscayne Blvd., 40th Floor, Miami, FL. 33131.
DEADLINES: None
OFFICERS: Smith, Wilson, Esq., P/D; Mirman, Charles B., Esq., S/D; Mirman, Beverly, VP/T/D

SNOW WHITE FOUNDATION, INC.

600 S. SANDLAKE CT.
MOUNT DORA, FL 32757
352-735-4866

ID NUMBER: 593603616
FEDERAL REPORTING DATE: 04/02
AREAS OF INTEREST: Community, Education, Medicine, Religion, Research, Scholarships, Sports & Athletics
CURRENT ASSETS: $179,148 PRIOR ASSETS: $216,091
TOTAL AMOUNT AWARDED: $19,500
HIGH: $3,000--Community Church Boulder
MID: $1,000--American Cancer Society
LOW: $500--Childrens Hospital Foundation
GRANTS AWARDS: Univ. of Northern IA.--$2,500, Fellowship Christian Athletes--$2,500, First Baptist Church of Mt. Dora--$3,000, Lance Armstrong Fdn.--$1,000, Boy Scouts of America--$1,000, Citizens Scholarship Fdn.--$3,000, A G Bell Florida, Inc.--$2,000
SERVICE AREA: National
COMMENTS: Gives to preselected organizations.
DEADLINES: None
OFFICERS: Edwins, Lynn H., VP/D; Reece, Kandy H., VP/D; Henderson, Jennifer H., S/D; Hart, Jonathan A., VP/D; Hart, Donald E., P/D; Hart, Frances I., T/D

SNOW, GEORGE SCHOLARSHIP FUND, INC.

998 S. FEDERAL HWY., STE. 203
BOCA RATON, FL 33432
561-347-6799

ID NUMBER: 592162597
FEDERAL REPORTING DATE: 11/01

AREAS OF INTEREST: Education, Scholarships
CURRENT ASSETS: $887,562 PRIOR ASSETS: $923,880
TOTAL AMOUNT AWARDED: $194,791
HIGH: $33,334--Florida Atlantic Univ.
MID: $750--Individual
LOW: $250--Individual
GRANTS AWARDS: N/A
SERVICE AREA: Palm Beach County
COMMENTS: Send applications to: Timothy Snow, George Snow Scholar- ship Fund, Inc., 998 S. Federal Hwy., #203, Boca Raton, Fl. 33432.
DEADLINES: 3/15
OFFICERS: Cryan, Gregory J., C; Snow, Timothy G., P; Snow, Jeffrey E., VP; Jones, Rexann H., S., T; Bowman, Richard E., TR; Briggs, C. Norman, TR

SNYDER, ALICIA MATCHORN FOUNDATION

305 LIVE OAK RD.
VERO BEACH, FL 32963
772-231-3882

ID NUMBER: 237049760
FEDERAL REPORTING DATE: 05/02
AREAS OF INTEREST: Arts & Culture, Community, Education, Environment, Health, Medicine, Religion, Research, Scholarships, Social Services
CURRENT ASSETS: $906,093 PRIOR ASSETS: $856,387
TOTAL AMOUNT AWARDED: $44,608
HIGH: $8,065--Community Church
MID: $2,860--American Cancer Society
LOW: $50--Kids Wish Network
GRANTS AWARDS: American Bible Society--$1,000, American Heart Assn.--$500, American Red Cross--$100, Barry Univ.--$100, Bolle's School Scholarship Fund--$150, Brevard College--$100, Brewster Academy--$1,000, Cedarville College--$500, CARE--$500, Coastal Conservation Assn.--$100, Coral Ridge Ministries--$2,000, Davison College--$250, Florida Fdn.--$200, Gow School--$500, Habitat for Humanity--$1,000
SERVICE AREA: National
COMMENTS: Gives to preselected organizations.
DEADLINES: None
OFFICERS: MacMillan, R.J., P; MacMillan, David G., VP; MacMillan, Randy, S/TR

SOLOMON LEVEL 8 FOUNDATION

4925 BAY WAY PL.
TAMPA, FL 33629
813-222-4608

ID NUMBER: 593539126
FEDERAL REPORTING DATE: 02/02
AREAS OF INTEREST: Arts & Culture, Community, Education, Health, Scholarships, Social Services
CURRENT ASSETS: $152,173 PRIOR ASSETS: $134,971
TOTAL AMOUNT AWARDED: $1,358
HIGH: $200--University of Michigan
MID: $100--Salvation Army
LOW: $25--Charles Darwin
GRANTS AWARDS: Andersen Fdn.--$180, WUSF--$145, Phi Beta Kappa Scholarship Fund--$100, Dian Fossey Gorilla Fund--$50, Berkeley Carroll School--$100, American Red Cross--$180, WEDU--$98, University of Illinois--$180

SERVICE AREA: National
COMMENTS: Send applications to Martin & Maxine Solomon at 4925 Bay Way Place, Tampa, FL. 33629
DEADLINES: None
OFFICERS: Solomon, Martin B., TR; Solomon, Maxine, TR

SOUTHWEST FLORIDA COMMUNITY FOUNDATION

PO BOX 9326
FORT MYERS, FL 33902-9326
941-334-0377

ID NUMBER: 596580974
FEDERAL REPORTING DATE: 06/96
AREAS OF INTEREST: Arts & Culture, Community, Education, Environment, Religion, Scholarships, Social Services
CURRENT ASSETS: $10,195,011 PRIOR ASSETS: $7,873,174
TOTAL AMOUNT AWARDED: $653,193
HIGH: $31,100--Fort Myers Comm. Concert Assoc.
MID: $5,000--Hope Hospice
LOW: $350--Goodwill Industries
GRANTS AWARDS: Canterbury School Designated Fund--$11,811, Cape Coral Police Dept. PBA--$10,317, Community Cooperative Ministries--$12,408, E.C.H.O., Inc.--$5,000, Dr. Ella Piper Center Fund--$12,181, Ft. Myers Christian School Fund--$12,138, Greater Ft. Myers Chamber of Commerce--$17,765, Lee Co. Alliance of the Arts Scholarship Fund--$11,312, Lee Co. Mission Fund--$11,647, Lee Healthcare Resources Fund--$11,504, Rhea B. Mike Fund--$10,861, Octagon Sequence of Eight, inc.--$11,978, Ruth Cooper Center Fund--$11,490, Untied Way of Lee Co. Fund--$11,304, VIP/Margaret Fox Fund--$11,503
SERVICE AREA: Lee County and contiguous counties, Charlotte County, Hendry County, Collier County, Glades County
COMMENTS: Written applications available at the foundation office. Grants awarded to 501(c)(3) organizations only. Major grants deadline is March; mini-grants September. Scholarships are awarded to Lee County graduating high school seniors only and are handled through each individual high school. No funds for administration or start up costs. Fax: 941-334-92
DEADLINES: 3/15, 9/15
OFFICERS: Sheppard, John, P; Nathan, James, VP; Barrett, Thomas, S/T; Flynn, Paul B., ED; Shimp, Kathleen, AD; Robinson, Sue, AA

SPARKMAN FOUNDATION

P.O. BOX 58
LAKE PANASOFFKEE, FL 33538
352-793-4040

ID NUMBER: 593378332
FEDERAL REPORTING DATE: 05/02
AREAS OF INTEREST: Community, Education, Scholarships, Social Services, Sports & Athletics
CURRENT ASSETS: $228,220 PRIOR ASSETS: $276,318
TOTAL AMOUNT AWARDED: $59,500
HIGH: $25,000--Sumter County Youth Center
MID: $5,000--Sumter County Special Olympics
LOW: $1,000--Sumter Schools Enhancement
GRANTS AWARDS: SCARC, Inc.--$1,000, Join effort of Town of Lady Lake--$2,500
SERVICE AREA: Sumter County, FL

COMMENTS: Submit letter including the name of the charitable org., the corporate structure and copy of determination letter and the purpose for which donation will be used. Specifically for those charitable organizations and causes in Sumter County, FL.
DEADLINES: None
OFFICERS: Thornton, Randall N., P; Suber, William A., TR; Dew, Bernard, VP/S

ST. PETERSBURG TIMES SCHOLARSHIP FUND, INC.

P.O BOX 1121
ST. PETERSBURG, FL 33731
727-892-2219

ID NUMBER: 596142547
FEDERAL REPORTING DATE: 05/00
AREAS OF INTEREST: Education, Scholarships
CURRENT ASSETS: $2,601,520 PRIOR ASSETS: $2,470,742
TOTAL AMOUNT AWARDED: $207,635
HIGH: $120,200--Scholarships
MID: $21,435--Matching Grants to Education
LOW: $4,000--Fellowships
GRANTS AWARDS: Grants--$62,000
COMMENTS: Scholarship applications must be journalism and newspaper oriented. Send applications to Andy Corty at 490 1st Ave. S St. Petersburg, FL 33701.
DEADLINES: 7/1
OFFICERS: Barnes, Andrew E., P; Corty, Andy, S; Rahdert, George K., TR; Maxwell, Bill, TR; Grinstead, Jeanne, TR; Clark, Roy Peter, TR

STARK, PAUL FOUNDATION, INC.

C/O CAROLE STARK, TRUSTEE
981 SAND CASTLE RD.
SANIBEL, FL 33957
941-489-0100

ID NUMBER: 351939122
FEDERAL REPORTING DATE: 05/00
AREAS OF INTEREST: Scholarships
CURRENT ASSETS: $1,066,348 PRIOR ASSETS: $1,022,293
TOTAL AMOUNT AWARDED: $0
GRANTS AWARDS: N/A
COMMENTS: Four year college scholarships are granted to high school seniors who attend Indiana public schools. Send applications to Paul Stark, 160 Olde Mill Circle S. Dr., Indianapolis, IN 46260; 317-255-8580 Applicants are submitted by the school administration to the foundation.
DEADLINES: N/A
OFFICERS: Stark, Paul, D; Stark, Carole, D; Koehler, Charles, D; Smith, Ron Esq., D; Peter, Arthur, D; Loft, Mona, D

STROH, CORA TESTAMENTARY SCHOLARSHIP TRUST

P.O. BOX 1207
ENGLEWOOD, FL 34295-1207
941-474-7768

ID NUMBER: 596214629
FEDERAL REPORTING DATE: 05/01
AREAS OF INTEREST: Scholarships

CURRENT ASSETS: $411,494 PRIOR ASSETS:
$412,431
TOTAL AMOUNT AWARDED: $2,000
HIGH: $1,000--Individual
LOW: $1,000--Individual
GRANTS AWARDS: N/A
SERVICE AREA: National
COMMENTS: Applications should be addressed to R. Earl
Warren at 359 W. Dearborn St.: PO BOX 1207, Englewood,
FL. 34295-1207. Limited to students educated in Englewood,
FL. school system attending manatee Community College.
DEADLINES: 5/15
OFFICERS: Warren, R. Earl, TR

STUART, EDWARD C. FOUNDATION, INC.
P.O.BOX 250
BARTOW, FL 33830
863-533-4196

ID NUMBER: 596142151
FEDERAL REPORTING DATE: 01/02
AREAS OF INTEREST: Education, Scholarships
CURRENT ASSETS: $3,283,639 PRIOR ASSETS:
$3,096,217
TOTAL AMOUNT AWARDED: $116,538
HIGH: $116,538--Erskine College
GRANTS AWARDS: N/A
SERVICE AREA: S.C., N.C.
COMMENTS: Preprinted applications available by writing to
the foundation.
DEADLINES: None
OFFICERS: Terry, Jean R., T/D; Stuart, William H., P/D;
Boswell, C.A., D; Stuart, Nancy S., D; Terry, Nelle S., VP/D;
Satterfield, Kennedy, D

SUNBURST FOUNDATION, INC.
P. O. BOX 812155
BOCA RATON, FL 33481-2155
561-995-7755

ID NUMBER: 592637289
FEDERAL REPORTING DATE: 11/01
AREAS OF INTEREST: Scholarships
CURRENT ASSETS: $2,153,905 PRIOR ASSETS:
$2,143,552
TOTAL AMOUNT AWARDED: $90,525
HIGH: $6,000--Individual
MID: $2,750--Individual
LOW: $1,275--Individual
GRANTS AWARDS: N/A
SERVICE AREA: FL, CA
COMMENTS: Send applications to: James M. Hankins, P. O.
Box 812155, Boca Raton, Fl. 33481-2155. Submit written
application detailing academic performance, financial need &
field of interest.
DEADLINES: None
OFFICERS: Hankins, James M., P/TR; Wenzel, Kenneth A.,
S/T; Baker, Donald E., VP/T

SWISHER, CARL S. FOUNDATION, INC.
1301 RIVERPLACE BLVD., STE. 2640
JACKSONVILLE, FL 32207
904-399-8000

ID NUMBER: 590998262
FEDERAL REPORTING DATE: 05/02
AREAS OF INTEREST: Arts & Culture, Community,
Education, Health, Medicine, Religion, Scholarships, Social
Services
CURRENT ASSETS: $7,319,451 PRIOR ASSETS:
$7,365,887
TOTAL AMOUNT AWARDED: $339,050
HIGH: $60,000--Jacksonville Univ.
MID: $10,000--Museum of Science & History (MOSH)
LOW: $1,000--ARC(Duval Assn. for Retarded Citizens)
GRANTS AWARDS: Alzheimer's Assn.--$2,500, Baptist
Wolfson Children Hospital--$3,500, Big Brothers/Big Sisters--
$1,000, Boys Home Assn.--$1,000, Cathedral Arts Project,
Inc.--$2,050, Cerebral Palsy Assn.--$3,500, Children Home
Society of Florida--$10,000, City Rescue Mission--$5,000,
Clara While Mission--$2,000, Community Connection--
$4,500, Cummer Museum of Art & Gardens--$5,000, Daniel
Fdn.(Educational Prog.)--$2,500, Diabetes Fdn.--$10,500,
Downs Syndrome Assn.--$2,500, Downtown Ecumenical
Council--$10,000
SERVICE AREA: National
COMMENTS: Send applications to: Kenneth G. Anderson,
1301 River- Place Blvd., , Suite 2640, Jax, Fl. 32207.
(904)399-8000. Must be a qualifying Section 501(c)(3)
organization.
DEADLINES: None
OFFICERS: Anderson, Kenneth G., P/TR; Lindsey, John,
TR; Charbonnet, Carolyn, S/T/TR; Stevens, James P., TR

TAPPER, GEORGE G. & AMELIA G. TRUST FOUNDATION
P.O. BOX 280
PT. ST. JOE, FL 32457-0280
850-227-1111

ID NUMBER: 592639039
FEDERAL REPORTING DATE: 05/02
AREAS OF INTEREST: Arts & Culture, Education,
Scholarships, Social Services
CURRENT ASSETS: $1,641,874 PRIOR ASSETS:
$1,599,068
TOTAL AMOUNT AWARDED: $16,426
HIGH: $5,000--Gulf Coast Community College
MID: $1,250--Gladys Chapman Golf Tournament
LOW: $500--Individual
GRANTS AWARDS: Ruth & Billy Graham Children's
Health Center--$1,000, The Hampton School--$3,500, Junior
Service League--$3,676
SERVICE AREA: National
COMMENTS: Organization must qualify as an organization
set forth in IRC Section 170(C), 2055 (A).
DEADLINES: 12/31
OFFICERS: Johnson, Greg, TR; McSpadden, Robert, TR;
Warriner, Patricia T., TR/M; Gander, Bubba, TR; Gaskin,
David, TR; Warriner, David P., TR

TARR CHARITABLE FAMILY FOUNDATION

P.O. BOX 49948
SARASOTA, FL 34230
941-366-6660

ID NUMBER: 650416098
FEDERAL REPORTING DATE: 04/02
AREAS OF INTEREST: Arts & Culture, Community, Education, Environment, Health, Medicine, Religion, Research, Scholarships, Social Services, Sports & Athletics
CURRENT ASSETS: $4,626,466 PRIOR ASSETS: $4,692,829
TOTAL AMOUNT AWARDED: $133,683
HIGH: $12,500--Comm Center Project of San Francisco
MID: $2,600--Sarasota Blood Bank
LOW: $50--Leukemia & Lymphoma Society
GRANTS AWARDS: Cat Woman's Shelter--$250, All Faiths Food Bank--$1,000, Ringling Redskins--$1,000, Boys and Girls Club--$2,500, Sarasota Film Festival--$7,500, Caring Children's Charities--$10,000, Sarasota Ballet--$6,500, United Way--$2,500, Breast Health--$833, Education Foundation--$1,500, Booker High School--$500
SERVICE AREA: National
COMMENTS: Applications should be addressed to David Band-Abel, Band Russell, Collier, Pitchford & Gordon at PO BOX 49948, Sarasota, FL. 34230 in no specified form.
DEADLINES: None
OFFICERS: Band, David S., P/S; Doerr, Kenneth D., VP/S/T; Dascenzo, Veronica, T

TAUNTON FAMILY CHILDREN'S HOME

P.O. BOX 870
WEWAHITCHKA, FL 32465

ID NUMBER: 592335556
FEDERAL REPORTING DATE: 08/01
AREAS OF INTEREST: Scholarships
CURRENT ASSETS: $652,183 PRIOR ASSETS: $552,634
TOTAL AMOUNT AWARDED: $18,838
HIGH: $6,945--Individual
MID: $2,513--Individual
LOW: $730--Individual
GRANTS AWARDS: N/A
COMMENTS: Gives to preselected individuals.
DEADLINES: None
OFFICERS: Tounton, David, D

TAYLOR FAMILY FOUNDATION, INC.

314 PINE AVE.
ANNA MARIA, FL 34217-0798
941-778-7668

ID NUMBER: 396058301
FEDERAL REPORTING DATE: 10/01
AREAS OF INTEREST: Community, Education, Environment, Medicine, Religion, Research, Scholarships, Social Services
CURRENT ASSETS: $17,756,851 PRIOR ASSETS: $824,675
TOTAL AMOUNT AWARDED: $178,890
HIGH: $36,500--Sisters of Mercy
MID: $10,000--Russian Ministries

LOW: $250--Celebrate Anna Maria
GRANTS AWARDS: Haywood Christian Ministries--$300, Doctors Without Borders--$3,000, Island Baptist Church--$1,000, Lexington Shriner's Hospital--$2,000, AHMO-ALT. Help Ministries Outreach--$26,000, Nobody's Children--$23,000, St. Francis House--$4,000, Manatee Youth for Christ--$25,000, Haywood County Dare--$1,000, Missionaries of Charity--$500, Educational Support--$3,000, Michael J. Fox Fdn.--$5,000, St. PJ'S Children's Home--$10,000, Little Sisters of the Poor--$5,000, EKO, C/O Life Ctr. Church--$2,500
SERVICE AREA: National
COMMENTS: Gives to preselected organizations.
DEADLINES: None
OFFICERS: Taylor, Ritchey Nelson, D; Huettig, Chris, P; Kittsmiller, Katherine, S; Huettig, Edward, VP

THELEN, GEORGE J. & MARY SUSAN FAMILY FOUNDATION, INC.

5393 GULF OF MEXICO DR., STE. 112B
LONGBOAT KEY, FL 34228
941-366-3600

ID NUMBER: 650533389
FEDERAL REPORTING DATE: 04/02
AREAS OF INTEREST: Scholarships
CURRENT ASSETS: $15,322 PRIOR ASSETS: $16,162
TOTAL AMOUNT AWARDED: $1,000
HIGH: $1,000--Univ. of Cincinnati
GRANTS AWARDS: N/A
SERVICE AREA: OH
COMMENTS: Gives to preselected organizations.
DEADLINES: None
OFFICERS: Thelen, George, P/T/D; Harper, Maribeth, D; Thelen, Jay Paul, D; Cipollone, Rebeca, D; Regan, Jennifer, D

THOMSEN FOUNDATION, INC.

701 E. COMMERCIAL BLVD., STE. 300
FORT LAUDERDALE, FL 33334
954-776-6323

ID NUMBER: 592070983
FEDERAL REPORTING DATE: 03/02
AREAS OF INTEREST: Arts & Culture, Education, Health, Medicine, Scholarships, Social Services
CURRENT ASSETS: $359,451 PRIOR ASSETS: $318,410
TOTAL AMOUNT AWARDED: $22,000
HIGH: $5,000--Mayo Fdn.
MID: $5,000--Michigan State U.
LOW: $2,000--WPBT Channel 2
GRANTS AWARDS: Univ. of Miami--$5,000, Univ. of Fl.--$5,000
SERVICE AREA: National
COMMENTS: Gives to preselected organizations.
DEADLINES: None
OFFICERS: Thomsen, Carl J., P/T; Thomsen, Frances D., S; Thomsen, Nancy L., VP

THRUSH, ROBERT A. CHARITABLE TRUST

2810 E. OAKLAND PARK BLVD.
FORT LAUDERDALE, FL 33306
954-563-1000

ID NUMBER: 650136688
FEDERAL REPORTING DATE: 06/01
AREAS OF INTEREST: Scholarships
CURRENT ASSETS: $859,300 PRIOR ASSETS:
$817,222
TOTAL AMOUNT AWARDED: $44,046
GRANTS AWARDS: N/A
SERVICE AREA: Dade County, Palm Beach County,
Broward County
COMMENTS: Submit formal pre-printed application: name,
address, family income, grade point average, outside
employment. Scholarship is restricted to students in Dade,
Broward and Palm Beach Counties. GPA must be 3. or higher.
Must be a student who is working his way through college.
DEADLINES: None
OFFICERS: Case, James L., Esq., TR

TOUSSAINT, PIERRE/RADLOFF, ROGER FOUNDATION

10017 S.W. 41T RD.
GAINESVILLE, FL 32608
352-336-5181

ID NUMBER: 656083720
FEDERAL REPORTING DATE: 08/01
AREAS OF INTEREST: Education, Scholarships
CURRENT ASSETS: $235,135 PRIOR ASSETS:
$273,050
TOTAL AMOUNT AWARDED: $57,016
HIGH: $17,500--Individual
MID: $5,000--Individual
LOW: $500--Individual
GRANTS AWARDS: N/A
DEADLINES: None
OFFICERS: McInerney, Vincent D., TR; McInerney, Evelyn,
TR; Gallagher, Myrna, TR

TROIANO, JOHN G. & ANNA MARIA FOUNDATION

435 L'AMBIANCE DR., STE. K-805
LONGBOAT KEY, FL 34228
941-383-4570

ID NUMBER: 650716854
FEDERAL REPORTING DATE: 05/02
AREAS OF INTEREST: Arts & Culture, Community,
Education, Health, Medicine, Religion, Scholarships, Social
Services
CURRENT ASSETS: $95,484 PRIOR ASSETS: $89,480
TOTAL AMOUNT AWARDED: $48,450
HIGH: $10,000--St. Martha's Pallottine Father
MID: $4,900--Cardinal Mooney High School
LOW: $250--Smith Center for Therap. Riding
GRANTS AWARDS: Sarasota Council of the Arts--$500, St.
Martha's School--$1,000, Wellness Community--$500, YMCA
Fdn. of Sarasota, Inc.--$500, WEDU--$300, Pace University--
$3,000, Sarasota Memorial Hospital Ctr.--$500, Sarasota Ballet
of Florida--$1,500, Mote Marine Laboratiries--$500, John &
Mable Ringling Museum--$5,000, Ringling School of Art and
Design--$500, Sarasota Opera--$5,000

SERVICE AREA: National
COMMENTS: Application should be addressed to John G.
Troiano to the adresss listed.
DEADLINES: None
OFFICERS: Troiano, John G., P/D; Troiano, Anna Maria,
S/T/D; Russo, Marie A., D

TWEED, ETHEL & GEORGE W. SCHOLARSHIP ENDOWMENT TRUST

C/O BANK OF AMERICA
P.O. BOX 40200
JACKSONVILLE, FL 32203-0200
877-446-411

ID NUMBER: 596145533
FEDERAL REPORTING DATE: 02/02
AREAS OF INTEREST: Scholarships
CURRENT ASSETS: $175,588 PRIOR ASSETS:
$249,764
TOTAL AMOUNT AWARDED: $11,470
HIGH: $4,595--Individual
MID: $125--Individual
LOW: $125--Individual
GRANTS AWARDS: N/A
SERVICE AREA: St. Petersburg
COMMENTS: No formal application - include financial need
and academic achievements.
DEADLINES: 6/1
OFFICERS: Bank of America, TR

TWIN TREES FOUNDATION, INC.

C/O THOMAS H. SCHWALM
5983 S.E. MOURNING DOVE WAY
HOBE SOUND, FL 33455
561-560-3548

ID NUMBER: 912092293
FEDERAL REPORTING DATE: 05/02
AREAS OF INTEREST: Arts & Culture, Community,
Education, Scholarships, Social Services
CURRENT ASSETS: $520,385 PRIOR ASSETS:
$528,442
TOTAL AMOUNT AWARDED: $26,250
HIGH: $5,000--Jefferson Historical Society
MID: $1,000--United Way of Martin County
LOW: $500--Hamilton College
GRANTS AWARDS: Vanderbilt University--$4,000,
Samaritan Foundation of Northern NY--$1,000, River
Foundation--$500, Abaco Medical Clinic--$500, Greenwich
Hospital--$1,250, Brunswick School--$1,500, Thousand
Islands Land Trust--$1,000, Oshkosh Area Community--
$2,500
SERVICE AREA: National
COMMENTS: Gives to preselected organizations.
DEADLINES: None
OFFICERS: Schwalm, Thomas H., P/D; Schwalm, JoAnn F.,
S/T; Schwalm, J. Bradford, D; Schwalm, Matson F., D

UNCLE LARRY'S FUND
C/O WINTERER
P.O. BOX 640
BOKEELIA, FL 33922
941-283-7406

ID NUMBER: 316653673
FEDERAL REPORTING DATE: 05/02
AREAS OF INTEREST: Education, Scholarships
CURRENT ASSETS: $706,218 PRIOR ASSETS:
$250,000
TOTAL AMOUNT AWARDED: $25,000
HIGH: $15,000--Miss Hall's School
MID: $10,000--Miss Hall's School
GRANTS AWARDS: N/A
SERVICE AREA: National
COMMENTS: Gives to preselected organizations.
DEADLINES: None
OFFICERS: Winterer, Victoria T., TR; Winterer, William G.,
TR

VASSET, GEORGE J. & MARGARET I. MEMORIAL FOUNDATION
C/O FIRST UNION
P. O. BOX 9333
BRADENTON, FL 34206
941-795-3103

ID NUMBER: 237320718
FEDERAL REPORTING DATE: 08/01
AREAS OF INTEREST: Religion, Scholarships
CURRENT ASSETS: $246,105 PRIOR ASSETS:
$236,045
TOTAL AMOUNT AWARDED: $1,468
HIGH: $1,468--Individual, First Presbyterian Church
GRANTS AWARDS: N/A
COMMENTS: Financial assistance is limited to candidates
preparing for service in presbyterian church, USA. Send
application to: First Union Nation Bank, PO BOX 9333,
Bradenton, Fl. 34206.
DEADLINES: None
OFFICERS: First Union National Bank, TR

VEITIA, DIEGO J. FOUNDATION
250 PARK AVE., S.
WINTER PARK, FL 32789
407-629-1400

ID NUMBER: 593150010
FEDERAL REPORTING DATE: 05/01
AREAS OF INTEREST: Education, Scholarships, Social
Services
CURRENT ASSETS: $701,943 PRIOR ASSETS:
$462,412
TOTAL AMOUNT AWARDED: $18,000
HIGH: $5,000--Hamilton Holt School Scholarship Fund
MID: $3,000--Big Oak Ranch
LOW: $2,500--The Iowa State University Fdn.
GRANTS AWARDS: The Thunderbird Fund--$2,500, The
Salvation Army--$5,000
SERVICE AREA: National
DEADLINES: None
OFFICERS: Veitia, Diego J., P; Halliday, Don, VP; Veitia,
Tresa, TR/S

VENICE FOUNDATION
601 TAMIAMI TRAIL, S.
VENICE, FL 34285
941-486-4600

ID NUMBER: 591052433
FEDERAL REPORTING DATE: 06/00
AREAS OF INTEREST: Arts & Culture, Community,
Education, Environment, Health, Medicine, Religion,
Research, Scholarships, Social Services, Sports & Athletics
CURRENT ASSETS: $163,817,207 PRIOR ASSETS:
$161,391,270
TOTAL AMOUNT AWARDED: $8,000,000
HIGH: $341,402--Senior Friendship Centers
MID: $25,000--Sarasota County Arts Council
LOW: $1,450--The Vision Foundation
GRANTS AWARDS: Cardinal Mooney High School--
$250,000, Communities in Schools of Manasota--$30,350,
Community Presbyterian Church--$24,854, Dreams are Free--
$30,000, Diocese of Venice--$11,275, Englewood Helping
Hand--$2,100, Alzheimer's Lifeliners--$52,500, Bon Secours
Venice Hospital--$20,000, Child Protection Center--$11,000,
Children's Haven and Adult Center, Inc.--$100,000, Coalition
to Assist Supported Living, Inc.--$125,000, Friends of the
Myakka River--$25,000, Mote Marine Laboratory--$41,130,
Big Brothers/Big Sisters of the Sn Coast, Inc.--$76,500,
Ballroom Dancesport Theatre--$50,000, Circus Sarasota--
$96,963, Gulf Coast Heritage Association--$10,000, Lemon
Bay Playhouse--$26,927, Bay Life Community Church--
$15,000, Venice Youth Soccer Association--$2,000, Sarasota
Opera--$100,000, Venice Concert Band--$6,883, Volunteering
Connections--$12,300, Mothers Helping Mothers--$6,000,
Safe Place & Rape Crisis Network--$79,000
SERVICE AREA: South Sarasota County, Englewood, Boca
Grande
COMMENTS: Submit a two-page letter of intent for funding
requests. The format is available by contacting Beth Harrison,
Director of Administrative and Grant Services. Website:
www.tvf.org
DEADLINES: 8/24, 1/2, 4/2
OFFICERS: Collins, Judy; Wilcox, Judy D; Killorin, Jamie,
CPA

VICTORY FOUNDATION, INC.
C/O ROBERT M. FRANZBLAU
5401 HANGAR CT.
TAMPA, FL 33634-5341

ID NUMBER: 593536437
FEDERAL REPORTING DATE: 05/02
AREAS OF INTEREST: Arts & Culture, Community,
Education, Environment, Religion, Scholarships, Social
Services, Other
CURRENT ASSETS: $2,189,813 PRIOR ASSETS:
$2,455,161
TOTAL AMOUNT AWARDED: $383,975
HIGH: $215,000--Victory Ship, Inc.
MID: $101,250--New York Maritime College Alumn. Assoc.
LOW: $25--Florida Wildlife Federation
GRANTS AWARDS: ASPCA--$5,000, Avon Breast Cancer 3
Day--$1,000, Barbara Ann Karramosw Cancer Ins.--$500,
Berkley Prep School--$7,500, Congregation of Schaari Zedek--
$12,500, Direct Marketing Association Council--$500, Friends
of the Danish Jewish Museum--$1,000, Girl Scouts of America
Suncoast--$500, Guide Dog Foundation--$12,600, H. Lee
Moffit Cancer Center--$1,500, Harvard College Fund--$500,
Humane Society of Tampa Bay--$750, Junior Achievement--
$850, Moffit Foundation--$1,000
SERVICE AREA: National

COMMENTS: Gives to preselected organizations.
DEADLINES: None
OFFICERS: Franzblau, Robert M., D; Franzblau, Jo, D; Dorr, Alix F., D; Franzblau, Charles A., D

WAGNER FUND TRUST
100 S.E. 2ND ST., STE. 2300
MIAMI, FL 33131-2135
305-372-1260

ID NUMBER: 596234167
FEDERAL REPORTING DATE: 04/02
AREAS OF INTEREST: Education, Scholarships
CURRENT ASSETS: $322,123 PRIOR ASSETS: $315,250
TOTAL AMOUNT AWARDED: $14,000
HIGH: $5,000--Individual loan
MID: $5,000--Individual loan
LOW: $4,000--Individual loan
GRANTS AWARDS: N/A
SERVICE AREA: FL
COMMENTS: Loans only. Apply through Dean of Student Affairs. Available only to medical students in Florida medical schools. These awards are loans for medical studies. They must be repaid.
DEADLINES: None
OFFICERS: Fiduciary International Trust, TR

WAHLSTROM FOUNDATION
3055 CARDINAL DR., STE. 106
VERO BEACH, FL 32963
561-231-0373

ID NUMBER: 66053378
FEDERAL REPORTING DATE: 05/02
AREAS OF INTEREST: Arts & Culture, Community, Education, Health, Scholarships, Social Services
CURRENT ASSETS: $7,834,534 PRIOR ASSETS: $8,609,869
TOTAL AMOUNT AWARDED: $682,822
HIGH: $194,698--Center for the Arts
MID: $50,000--St. Edward's School
LOW: $50--AIDS Walk New York
GRANTS AWARDS: Academy of Entrepreneurship, Inc.--$250, Alliance for Young Artists & Writers--$250, American Cancer Society--$350, Agneta Liljesahl Ballet School Scholarship Fund--$500, American Red Cross North Treasure Coast Chap.--$200, Antique Boat Museum--$2,500, Bertram R. MacMannis Memorial Fund--$100, Boys & Girls Club of Indian River--$1,000, Bridgeport Area Fdn.--$5,000, Camp Areadia Scholarship Fund--$500, Canter Fitzgerald Rehef Fund--$100, Ctr for the Arts--$10,000, Sacred Heart Univ.--$1,000, Citizens Scholarship Fund--$5,000, Community Child Care Resources, Inc.--$1,000
SERVICE AREA: Indian River Cnty, FL., Bridgeport area, CT
COMMENTS: Mail inquiries to Leonora A Richie, Executive Director, The Wahlstrom Foundation, P.O. Box 3276, Vero Beach, FL. 32964.
DEADLINES: March 31
OFFICERS: McCabe, Eleonora W., P; Hughes, Lois J., VP; Johnson, Bruce R., VP; McCabe, Robert F., VP; Kaufman, Charles B. III, S; Machen, Jim D., T

WALLACH FOUNDATION
1201 S. OCEAN DR., 1904N
HOLLYWOOD, FL 33019
954-921-9633

ID NUMBER: 232494924
FEDERAL REPORTING DATE: 11/01
AREAS OF INTEREST: Community, Education, Environment, Health, Medicine, Religion, Scholarships, Social Services, Sports & Athletics
CURRENT ASSETS: $885,023 PRIOR ASSETS: $872,968
TOTAL AMOUNT AWARDED: $40,761
HIGH: $12,000--Lower Merion Synagogue-Bldg. Fund
MID: $2,000--Torah Academy
LOW: $36--Yeshivah Shearis Yisrogi
GRANTS AWARDS: Aish Hatorah--$200, American Friends Shalva--$200, American Red David for Israel--$100, AMIT--$180, Anti-Defamation League--$100, B'Nai B'Rith Fdn.--$100, Bayit Layeled--$150, Beth Oloth--$100, Beth RivKah School--$100, Big Brothers / Big Sisters Montgomery Co.--$500, Birkur Cholim Hospital--$180, Boys Town Jerusalem--$500, Broward Outreach Ctr.--$50, Chai Lifeline / Camp Simcha--$500, Chamah--$180
SERVICE AREA: National
COMMENTS: Gives to preselected organizations.
DEADLINES: None
OFFICERS: Wallach, Janet, TR; Wallach, Michael C., TR; Wallach, Eileen D., TR; Levene, Rabbi Abraham, TR

WATSON, CLERMONT & KATHRYN SCHOLARSHIP TRUST
C/O BANK OF AMERICA
P.O. BOX 40200
JACKSONVILLE, FL 32203-0200
877-446-1410

ID NUMBER: 656300887
FEDERAL REPORTING DATE: 04/02
AREAS OF INTEREST: Education, Scholarships
CURRENT ASSETS: $414,830 PRIOR ASSETS: $446,154
TOTAL AMOUNT AWARDED: $16,911
HIGH: $5,637--Central High School
MID: $5,637--Ishpeming High School
LOW: $5,637--Grinnell High School
GRANTS AWARDS: N/A
SERVICE AREA: National
COMMENTS: Gives to preselected organizations.
DEADLINES: None
OFFICERS: Bank of America N.A., TR

WAYGOOD FAMILY FOUNDATION
4215 CALOOSA DR.
PALMETTO, FL 34221
941-729-9751

ID NUMBER: 650967432
FEDERAL REPORTING DATE: 12/00
AREAS OF INTEREST: Arts & Culture, Education, Health, Scholarships
CURRENT ASSETS: $1,171,232 PRIOR ASSETS: $1,171,232
TOTAL AMOUNT AWARDED: $70,000
HIGH: $10,000--All Children's Hospital Fdn.
MID: $5,000--Manatee Community College, Bradenton, FL
LOW: $2,000--Manatee Community College, Bradenton, Fl

GRANTS AWARDS: For All Kids Foundation, Ramsey, NJ--$7,000, Shriner's Hospital of Tampa--$7,000, Gloria's Place of Hope, Oak Ridge, NJ--$10,000, America's Promise, Alexandria, VA--$5,000, Briarcliff Manor Education Fdn., Briarcliff, NY--$5,000, Pinellas County Education Fdn--$7,000, St. Petersburg Junior College--$7,000
SERVICE AREA: Fl, NJ, VA, NY
COMMENTS: Gives to preselected organizations.
DEADLINES: N/A
OFFICERS: Waygood, Caroyln R., P/Ch; Hierak, Robert J., VP/T; Waygood, Charles M. , S; Waygood, Carole B., S; Borho, Constance Waygood, D; Waygood Jr., Charles M., D

WEIDEN, NORMAN & VIVIAN FOUNDATION, INC.

100 SUNRISE AVE.
PALM BEACH, FL 33480
561-833-0396

ID NUMBER: 136131592
FEDERAL REPORTING DATE: 03/02
AREAS OF INTEREST: Arts & Culture, Community, Education, Environment, Health, Medicine, Religion, Research, Scholarships, Social Services, Other
CURRENT ASSETS: $1,032,943 PRIOR ASSETS: $1,029,681
TOTAL AMOUNT AWARDED: $47,425
HIGH: $9,000--Mr. Sinai Medical School
MID: $5,350--Jewish Federation of Palm Beach
LOW: $60--Fraternal Order of Police
GRANTS AWARDS: St. Luke-Roosevelt--$4,000, Cardiovascular Institute--$2,000, Guiding Eyes for the Blind--$500, Greater Palm Beach Philharmonic--$3,200, Make A Wish Fdn.--$100, Riverside Park Fdn.--$2,000, Temple Emanuel--$1,385, Eastern Paralyzed Vets--$100, Oregon Ballet--$1,500, Palm Beach Opera--$1,900, Cystic Fibrosis--$1,000, Salvation Army--$500, Cancer Resrarch Institute--$1,000, International Society of Philanthropists--$3,000, National Fderation of the Blind--$100
SERVICE AREA: National
DEADLINES: None
OFFICERS: Weiden, Vivian, P; Schwartz, Barbara, S; Weiden, Jacqueline, VP

WEIGLE, FLORENCE C. TRUST UNDER WILL

C/O BANK OF AMERICA, TRUSTEE 8361305
P. O. BOX 40200
JACKSONVILLE, FL 32203-0200
877-446-1410

ID NUMBER: 596487752
FEDERAL REPORTING DATE: 11/01
AREAS OF INTEREST: Education, Religion, Scholarships
CURRENT ASSETS: $248,442 PRIOR ASSETS: $260,802
TOTAL AMOUNT AWARDED: $17,926
HIGH: $17,926--St. Petersburg Junior College
GRANTS AWARDS: N/A
SERVICE AREA: FL
COMMENTS: Send applications to: Private Bank Ctr. 1-800-832-9071. Restricted to: Scholastic achivements, recommendations, students residing in Pinellas co., Fl.
DEADLINES: None
OFFICERS: Bank of America, TR

WELDON FOUNDATION, INC.

3200 N. OCEAN BLVD., STE 2610
FORT LAUDERDALE, FL 33308-7139
954-561-5196

ID NUMBER: 650715451
FEDERAL REPORTING DATE: 04/02
AREAS OF INTEREST: Community, Education, Medicine, Religion, Research, Scholarships, Social Services
CURRENT ASSETS: $5,147,672 PRIOR ASSETS: $5,331,596
TOTAL AMOUNT AWARDED: $152,500
HIGH: $23,500--Florida International University Fdn.
MID: $5,000--United Home Care
LOW: $500--Metro Food Bank, CO
GRANTS AWARDS: Purdue University--$20,000, Junior Achievement--$10,000, First Plymouth Congregational Church--$7,000, United Way of Broward County--$2,500, Salvation Army--$1,000, University of Colorado, CO--$2,500, Cooke Foundation--$500, Newton County Fnd.--$500, Good Shepard Hospice--$1,000
SERVICE AREA: National
COMMENTS: Gives to preselected organizations.
DEADLINES: None
OFFICERS: Weldon, Norman R., P/T/D; Cassidy, Karen I., S/D; Weldon, Thomas D., VP/D; Weldon, Cynthia M., VP/D

WELLS, LILLIAN S. FOUNDATION, INC.

600 SAGAMORE RD.
FORT LAUDERDALE, FL 33301
954-462-8639

ID NUMBER: 237433827
FEDERAL REPORTING DATE: 05/02
AREAS OF INTEREST: Education, Health, Medicine, Research, Scholarships
CURRENT ASSETS: $11,196,734 PRIOR ASSETS: $11,351,004
TOTAL AMOUNT AWARDED: $8,200,000
HIGH: $155,000--Univ. of Florida
MID: $50,000--Susan B. Anthony
LOW: $1,000--Philanthropy Round Table
GRANTS AWARDS: James Madison Inst.--$25,000, Miss Porters School--$10,000, Intercollege Studies Inst.--$130,000, Heritage Fdn.--$139,000, Capital Research Ctr.--$100,000, Memorial Sloan Kettering Cancer Ctr.--$100,000, Garden County Fdn.--$100,000, Children First America--$10,000
SERVICE AREA: National
COMMENTS: Send applications to: Barbara Van Fleet, 600 Sagamore Rd., Ft. Lauderdale, Fl. (954)462-8639. Gives to medical or educational institutions.
DEADLINES: None
OFFICERS: Van Fleet, Barbara, P; Wells, Preston A., Jr., VP; Wells, Marion G., S

WERTZBERGER, FRANCES R. TRUST

C/O DR. J. EUGENE GLENN, M.D.
1308 WINDSOR PL.
JACKSONVILLE, FL 32205
904-724-4020

ID NUMBER: 597158689
FEDERAL REPORTING DATE: 03/02
AREAS OF INTEREST: Scholarships

CURRENT ASSETS: $839,266 PRIOR ASSETS: $917,767
TOTAL AMOUNT AWARDED: $60,808
HIGH: $21,143--Georgia Institute of technology Scholarship
MID: $9,576--Eastern Carolina Univ. Scholarship
LOW: $6,182--Western Carolina Univ. for Scholarship
GRANTS AWARDS: Univ. of South Carolina--$15,992
SERVICE AREA: National
COMMENTS: Send applications to the Office of Scholarship, Francis Wertzberger Trust, P.O. Box 6688, Raleigh, NC. 27628-6688. Colleges, universities, or grad schools located in the US only apply.
DEADLINES: December 1
OFFICERS: Glenn, J. Eugene, MD, TR; Stites, Arthur J., CPA, TR; Glenn, Sharon M., TR

WHITE, HARVEY & DOROTHY CHARITABLE TRUST

13315 N.W MAPLEWOOD RD.
PALM CITY, FL 34990-8078
561-336-3486

ID NUMBER: 56017835
FEDERAL REPORTING DATE: 05/02
AREAS OF INTEREST: Arts & Culture, Community, Education, Environment, Health, Medicine, Religion, Research, Scholarships, Social Services, Sports & Athletics
CURRENT ASSETS: $265,011 PRIOR ASSETS: $203,667
TOTAL AMOUNT AWARDED: $37,773
HIGH: $22,500--Miles Health Care
MID: $2,540--Dartmouth 1946
LOW: $3--UNICEF
GRANTS AWARDS: American Cancer Society--$200, Island Institute--$40, American Red Cross--$200, AMVETS--$25, Arthritis Fdn.--$25, Brigham & Women's Hospital--$750, Dana-Farber Cancer Institute--$150, Kieve--$50, Dartmouth Athletic Sponsor Program--$100, Dartmouth Educational Assn.--$40, Disabled American Veterans--$25, Doctors Without Borders--$100, Easter Seal Society--$20, Farnsworth Art Museum--$40, Florida Oceanographic Society--$30
SERVICE AREA: National
COMMENTS: Applications should be addressed to Harvey White at PO BOX 1006 Palm City, FL. 34991, (561) 366-3486. Request in writing for donation under $500.
DEADLINES: None
OFFICERS: White, Harvey, TR

WIGGINS, J. J. MEMORIAL TRUST

P. O. BOX 1111
MOORE HAVEN, FL 33471
863-946-3400

ID NUMBER: 592675273
FEDERAL REPORTING DATE: 09/01
AREAS OF INTEREST: Education, Scholarships
CURRENT ASSETS: $5,666,007 PRIOR ASSETS: $5,782,027
TOTAL AMOUNT AWARDED: $59,000
HIGH: $9,000--Edison Comm. College
MID: $5,250--Fl. Gulf Coast Univ.
LOW: $750--Central Fl. Comm. College
GRANTS AWARDS: Univ. of So. Fl.--$2,250, Fl. State Univ.--$1,500, Univ. of Fl.--$6,750, Indian River Comm. College--$3,500, Warner Southern College--$1,500, Union College--$1,500, Fl. A & M Univ.--$2,250, Fl. Inst. of Tech.--$1,500, Univ. of Central Fl.--$3,000, Cumberland College--

$1,500, Santa Fe Comm. College--$1,500, Webber College--$2,250, Mcneese State Univ.--$1,500, Univ. of North Fl.--$1,500, Univ. of West Alabama--$750
SERVICE AREA: FL, AL
DEADLINES: None
OFFICERS: Holbrook, John H., TR; Strope, L. E., TR; Branch, Joseph P., TR

WILLIAMS FAMILY FOUNDATION

C/O LEONARD E. WILLIAMS
P.O. BOX 563845
ORLANDO, FL 32853-6846
407-896-6911

ID NUMBER: 593688456
FEDERAL REPORTING DATE: 02/02
AREAS OF INTEREST: Scholarships, Social Services
CURRENT ASSETS: $256,877 PRIOR ASSETS: $9,457
TOTAL AMOUNT AWARDED: $8,000
HIGH: $4,000--Individual
MID: $3,000--Individual
LOW: $1,000--Individual
GRANTS AWARDS: N/A
SERVICE AREA: FL
COMMENTS: Send a financial affidavit and a written statement of the purpose of the grant to apply. Any person related to Leonard E. or Marjorie H. Williams or an employee, officer, or director of the foundation is not entitled to reciede a grant.
DEADLINES: None
OFFICERS: Williams, Leonard E., P; Williams, Marjorie H., VP; Williams, Leonard E., Jr., D; Williams, John A., D; Williams, Michael J., D

WILLIAMS, MARGARET MCCARTNEY CHARITABLE FOUNDATION

C/O SUNTRUST BANK
P. O. BOX 620005
ORLANDO, FL 32862-0005
407-237-4354

ID NUMBER: 597162849
FEDERAL REPORTING DATE: 04/01
AREAS OF INTEREST: Scholarships, Social Services
CURRENT ASSETS: $5,142,579 PRIOR ASSETS: $0
TOTAL AMOUNT AWARDED: $0
GRANTS AWARDS: N/A
DEADLINES: N/A
OFFICERS: Suntrust Bank, TR

WINN-DIXIE STORES FOUNDATION

5050 EDGEWOOD CT.
JACKSONVILLE, FL 32254
904-783-5429

ID NUMBER: 590995428
FEDERAL REPORTING DATE: 04/02
AREAS OF INTEREST: Arts & Culture, Community, Education, Environment, Health, Medicine, Religion, Research, Scholarships, Social Services, Sports & Athletics, Other
CURRENT ASSETS: $218,820 PRIOR ASSETS: $40,364
TOTAL AMOUNT AWARDED: $1,832,804

HIGH: $139,615--American Cancer Society
MID: $10,000--Salvation Army
LOW: $50--University of South Florida Fndn.
GRANTS AWARDS: University of Florida Fndn.--$1,150,
Boy Scouts of America--$2,500, Leukemia & Lymphoma
Society--$633, United Way--$25,000, American Red Cross--
$2,500, Furman University--$1,000, Gainesville Care Center--
$500, Audubon Institute--$1,000, Mobile Opera--$1,000,
National Multiple Sclerosis Society--$4,033
SERVICE AREA: National
DEADLINES: None
OFFICERS: Toscano, A.B., D/P; Rowland, A.R., D/VP; Ross,
K.D., D/T/VP; Dixon, Judith W., S; Sheehan, J.R., VP;
Byrum, D.M., D/S/VP

WINTER PARK MEMORIAL HOSPITAL ASSOCIATION, INC.

D/B/A WINTER PARK HEALTH FOUNDATION
1870 ALOMA AVE., STE. 200
WINTER PARK, FL 32789
407-644-2300

ID NUMBER: 590669460
FEDERAL REPORTING DATE: 11/01
AREAS OF INTEREST: Arts & Culture, Community,
Education, Health, Religion, Scholarships
CURRENT ASSETS: $128,726,789 PRIOR ASSETS:
$112,372,682
TOTAL AMOUNT AWARDED: $1,223,528
HIGH: $167,555--Orange Co. Healthy Start Coalition, Inc.
MID: $60,000--Alzheimer's Assn.
LOW: $6--Individual
GRANTS AWARDS: Orange Co. School Board--$29,877,
Orlando Museum of Art--$9,035, Central Florida YMCA--
$10,000, Jewish Community Ctr.--$12,000, Boggy Creek
Gang Camp, Inc.--$53,000, Easter Seals, Camp Challenge--
$8,150, American Lung Assn. of Central Florida--$7,692, Bach
Festival of Winter Park, Inc.--$24,800, Boys & Girls Clubs of
Central Florida, Inc.--$25,000, Catholic Charities--$25,000,
Children's Home Society of Florida--$68,171, Church Street
Counseling Ctr.--$65,175, CITE- Ctr. for Independence--
$25,000, ESTEEM, Inc.--$53,753, Florida Hospital /
Adventist Health System--$60,903
COMMENTS: Please see website: WWW.WPHF.ORG
DEADLINES: N/A
OFFICERS: Walker, William A. II, C; Ackley, Suzanne M.,
TR; Bernstein, Raymond, M.D., TR; Castro, Ivan J., M.D.,
TR; Grammer, Leslie C. Jr., TR; Guameri, John D., M.D., TR

WOLFE, FRANK M. FOUNDATION, INC.

505 N. ORLANDO AVE., STE. 304
COCOA BEACH, FL 32931
321-783-2834

ID NUMBER: 593482977
FEDERAL REPORTING DATE: 05/02
AREAS OF INTEREST: Scholarships, Other
CURRENT ASSETS: $754,581 PRIOR ASSETS:
$744,407
TOTAL AMOUNT AWARDED: $11,784
HIGH: $7,500--Individual
MID: $1,687--Individual
LOW: $1,097--Individual
GRANTS AWARDS: N/A
SERVICE AREA: FL

COMMENTS: Limit on awards shall be the applicant or their
family's inability to provide the assistance being sought. Send
written communication outlining applicant's background and
aspirations for which they desire assistance to Frank M. Wolfe,
505 N. Orlando Ave., Suite 304 Cocoa Beach, Fl 32931.
DEADLINES: None
OFFICERS: Wolfe, Frank M., P/TR/T; LeBlanc, Jennifer,
TR; Medina, Maria, TR; Baugher, Robert, TR

WOLLOWICK, RUBIN & GLADYS FOUNDATION, INC.

C/O MELLON TRUST
2875 N.E. 191ST ST., STE. 800
NORTH MIAMI BEACH, FL 33180
305-521-9008

ID NUMBER: 592469452
FEDERAL REPORTING DATE: 12/01
AREAS OF INTEREST: Community, Education, Health,
Religion, Research, Scholarships, Social Services
CURRENT ASSETS: $6,673,781 PRIOR ASSETS:
$7,292,983
TOTAL AMOUNT AWARDED: $920,900
HIGH: $100,000--Wollowick Lab. for Multiple Sclerosis
Resrch.
MID: $50,000--Bar-Ilan Univ.
LOW: $2,000--Alzheimer's Assn.
GRANTS AWARDS: Temple B'Nai Torah--$2,500,
American Friends of Beit--$15,000, Coconut Grove Playhouse-
-$20,000, Miami Children's Hospital--$5,000, Nat'l Jewish
Ctr. for Immunology & Respiratory--$10,000, Nat'l Multiple
Sclerosis--$5,000, Appaloosa Pleasure Horse Assn.--$5,000,
Guys & Dolls Auction Gala for Cystic Fibrosis--$5,000,
Women's Cancer League--$5,000, Parents TV Council--
$2,500, Anti-Defamation League--$3,500, South Palm Beach
Jewish Federation--$10,000, Univ. of Florida--$20,000, Univ.
of Miami--$25,000, Weizmann Inst. of Science--$25,000
COMMENTS: Send applications to: Edward Levnson, 407
Lincoln Rd., Miami Beach, Fl. 33139. (305)534-6171 in the
form of a letter stating name, address, tax exempt status,
purpose, amount & term.
DEADLINES: None
OFFICERS: Wollowick, Patricia, P/S; Levinson, Edward, VP;
Stein, Rhoda, D; Lowe, Sandra Lois, D; Wollowick, Janet
Amy, D; Lowe, Richard, D

WOZNIAK, VIC & VERMELL DREAMLAND TRUST

P.O. DRAWER 13207
PENSACOLA, FL 32591-3207
850-435-8300

ID NUMBER: 596973290
FEDERAL REPORTING DATE: 11/98
AREAS OF INTEREST: Education, Scholarships
CURRENT ASSETS: $54,288 PRIOR ASSETS: $53,835
TOTAL AMOUNT AWARDED: $600
HIGH: $600--Pensacola Junior College
GRANTS AWARDS: N/A
SERVICE AREA: FL
DEADLINES: None
OFFICERS: Gund, Charles F., T; Gund, Theodore G., T;
Gund, Charles F., Jr., T

WURTH, SUSAN ROYAL FOUNDATION

324 S.W. 16TH ST.
BELLE GLADE, FL 33430
561-996-6581

ID NUMBER: 650647302
FEDERAL REPORTING DATE: 05/02
AREAS OF INTEREST: Community, Education, Religion, Scholarships, Social Services
CURRENT ASSETS: $909,902 PRIOR ASSETS: $925,884
TOTAL AMOUNT AWARDED: $44,789
HIGH: $15,000--Glades Day School
MID: $2,500--PB Cty Athletic League
LOW: $250--Life Builders
GRANTS AWARDS: Salvation Army--$600, Auburn University--$12,039, Christian Veterinary Mission--$1,000, Belle Glade Alliance--$500, Episcopal Diocese od SW FL--$400, First Care Program--$5,000, Hospice of Palm Beach County--$1,000, Land of God Ministries--$500, Open Homes Ministries--$5,000, Historical Society of PB--$1,000
SERVICE AREA: National
COMMENTS: Submit written letter stating purpose. Address application to John C. Royal and mail to listed Address.
DEADLINES: None
OFFICERS: Royal, George L. Jr., P; Royal, George M., VP; Royal, John C., S/T; Royal, Jeffrey L., TR

Y.E.S. OPPORTUNITIES, INC.

8828 S.E. 140 LN. RD.
SUMMERFIELD, FL 34491
352-307-6691

ID NUMBER: 593656796
FEDERAL REPORTING DATE: 02/02
AREAS OF INTEREST: Education, Scholarships
CURRENT ASSETS: $850,256 PRIOR ASSETS: $1,015,119
TOTAL AMOUNT AWARDED: $86,263
HIGH: $6,000--Individual
MID: $2,000--Individual
LOW: $500--Individual
GRANTS AWARDS: N/A
SERVICE AREA: National
COMMENTS: Send applications to Dorothy Rice-Cobbs, 13889 Del Webb Blvd., Summerfield, FL. 34491 34491 (352)307-2694. 1-800-297-7272
DEADLINES: N/A
OFFICERS: Rice-Cobbs, Dorothy, P/TR; Payne, Mary W., VP; Holmes, Particia Ann, VP; Jefferson, Mary J., VP

YODER, JOSHUA MEMORIAL SCHOLARSHIP FUND

11952 COLLIER'S RESERVE DR.
NAPLES, FL 34110

ID NUMBER: 341848189
FEDERAL REPORTING DATE: 05/01
AREAS OF INTEREST: Scholarships
CURRENT ASSETS: $309,536 PRIOR ASSETS: $183,725
TOTAL AMOUNT AWARDED: $21,000
HIGH: $2,500--Individual
MID: $1,000--Individual
LOW: $500--Individual

GRANTS AWARDS: Individual--$2,500, Individual--$2,500, Individual--$1,000, Individual--$500, Individual--$10,000
SERVICE AREA: Ohio
COMMENTS: Gives to preselected organizations.
DEADLINES: None
OFFICERS: Menosky, John J., T; Menosky, Theresa, T; Yoder, Timothy, T; Yoder, Kara, T

YOUNGER, JOHN O. & HELEN CHARITABLE TRUST

201 CENTER RD., STE. 2
VENICE, FL 34292
941-493-3600

ID NUMBER: 650314860
FEDERAL REPORTING DATE: 02/02
AREAS OF INTEREST: Education, Scholarships
CURRENT ASSETS: $784,932 PRIOR ASSETS: $818,954
TOTAL AMOUNT AWARDED: $53,041
HIGH: $109,096--Lawrence University
GRANTS AWARDS: N/A
SERVICE AREA: WI
COMMENTS: Gives to preselected organizations.
DEADLINES: None
OFFICERS: Caldwell Trust Co., TR

ZEITZ FOUNDATION

6711 N. OCEAN BLVD.
OCEAN RIDGE, FL 33435-3326
561-737-4417

ID NUMBER: 650190440
FEDERAL REPORTING DATE: 05/00
AREAS OF INTEREST: Arts & Culture, Community, Education, Environment, Medicine, Religion, Research, Scholarships, Social Services
CURRENT ASSETS: $121,412 PRIOR ASSETS: $118,293
TOTAL AMOUNT AWARDED: $5,765
HIGH: $1,000--Jewish Federation of New Bedford
MID: $250--New Bedford Whaling Museum
LOW: $35--MADD
GRANTS AWARDS: Anti-Defamation League--$50, Buttonwood Park Zoo--$70, CAP of Palm beach County--$50, Columbia University--$250, Friends of Abused Children--$750, Individual--$50, Planned Parenthood Federation--$50
SERVICE AREA: FL, MA
COMMENTS: Gives to preselected organizations.
DEADLINES: None
OFFICERS: Zeitz, Kenneth, TR; Zeitz, Vivian, TR

CHAPTER FOUR

MINORITY AND WOMEN'S ASSISTANCE PROGRAMS

MINORITY AND WOMEN'S ASSISTANCE PROGRAMS

Scholarships for minorities and women are more plentiful than you may think. Most are awarded through private organizations that have some type of professional or civic affiliation with the minority it serves. Below are programs available to minorities and women in Florida:

Actuarial Scholarships for Minority Students provides scholarships for under-represented minority students that plan actuarial careers and are studying mathematics or actuarial science. Financial need and academic performance are considered. The deadline for applications is April 15. For details, contact Minority Scholarship Coordinator, Society of Actuaries, 475 N. Martingale Road, Schaumburg, IL 60173-2226; 847/705-3500. Email: flupo@casact.org Website: http://www.beanactuary.com/minority/scholarship.cfm

ADHA Institute Scholarship Program assists students interested in pursuing a career in dental hygiene. The program provides financial assistance to those who can demonstrate a commitment to further the discipline of dental hygiene through academic achievement, professional excellence, and a desire to improve the public's overall health. The deadline for scholarships is May 1 and June 30 for fellowships. ADHA Institute Scholarship Program, 444 N. Michigan Avenue, Suite 3400, Chicago, IL 60611 or call 800/735-4916. Website: http://www.adha.org/institute/

American Architectural Foundation Minority/Disadvantaged Scholarship Program provides 20 annual awards for minority or disadvantaged students studying architecture. Students must be nominated by a practicing architect or firm or other AIA affiliate, your guidance counselor or dean, or the director of a community-based civic organization. The average award is between $500 and $2,500. Nominations must be in by early December of each year: http://www.archfoundation.org/scholarships/index.htm

American Association of University Women Education Foundation provides a variety of fellowships for women in graduate school, dental school, medical school, veterinary school, law school and business school. Postdoctoral fellowships are also available. For information, write to the American Association of University Women Educational Foundation, Dept. 60, 2201 N. Dodge Street, Iowa City, IA 52243-4030.
Website: http://www.aauw.org/fga/fellowships_grants/

American Association of Women Dentists Hayden (Gillette) Memorial Foundation Loans are available to third- and fourth-year women studying dentistry. Loans up to $2,000 with 5% interest are available based on either merit or financial need. Students in graduate dental programs are also eligible. For more information, write to the Gillette Hayden Memorial Foundation, American Association of Women Dentists, 645 North Michigan Avenue, Chicago, IL 60611 or call 312/644-6610.

American Council of Independent Laboratories Scholarship Alliance provides tuition assistance up to $2,000 to juniors and seniors who are majoring in chemistry or biology with financial assistance. For details about this program, write to the Scholarship Chairperson, American Council of Independent Laboratories, Inc., 1629 K Street NW, Suite 400, Washington DC 20006. Website: http://www.acil.org/

American Dental Association Scholarships provide funding for second-year minority students enrolled in a dental school full-time. Financial need and academic performance are considered. The deadline is May 1. For details, contact the Director of Programs, ADA Foundation, 211 East Chicago Avenue, Chicago, IL 60611-2678 or call 312-440-2547. http://www.ada.org/ada/prod/adaf/prog_scholarship.asp

American Geological Institute Minority Geoscience Scholarships provide minority students studying the geosciences with scholarship awards. Undergraduate and graduate students are eligible to receive a scholarship. Recipients are chosen based on financial need and academic performance. Funding ranges from $250 to $10,000 annually. The deadline is early March. For more information, write to AGI Minority Geoscience Award, American Geological Institute, 4220 King Street, Alexandria, VA 22302. Website: http://www.agiweb.org/mpp/

American Foundation for the Blind Scholarships provide a variety of financial assistance programs to prospective undergraduates and graduates who are blind or visually impaired. Awards are for $1,000 to $2,500 annually. The deadline for application submissions is April 30. For details about these programs, write to Julie Tucker, AFB Information Center, American Foundation for the Blind, 11 Penn Plaza, Suite 300 New York, NY, 10011. Applicants can also call 212-502-7661 or visit the website at: http://www.afb.org/scholarships.asp

American Institute of Certified Public Accountants Minority Awards provide a variety of funding for minority students studying accounting at either the undergraduate (with at least 30 credit hours) or graduate level (with at least 12 credit hours earned). Awards are up to $5,000. Application deadlines vary, so contact for more information. For details, write to the Manager, Minority Recruitment, American Institute of C.P.A.'s, 1211 Avenue of the Americas, New York, NY 10036-8775. Website: http://www.aicpa.org/nolimits/become/ships/AICPA.htm

American Medical Women's Association Medical Education Loan Program provides first, second, or third-year female medical students with financial aid. Applicants must be U.S. citizens or permanent residents and members of the American Medical Women's Association. The deadline for applications is April 30. For details about this program, write to the American Medical Women's association Medical Education Loan Program, 801 N. Fairfax Street, Suite 400, Alexandria, VA 22314, 703/838-0500. Website: http://www.amwa-doc.org/Foundation/wf_scholarship.htm

American Political Science Association provides a variety of assistance to minority students enrolled in graduate programs for political science. To receive more information about this program, write to the American Political Science Association, 1527 New Hampshire Avenue, NW, Washington, DC 20036-1206. Website: http://www.apsanet.org/about/minority/fellows.cfm

American Psychological Association Minority Fellowship Program provides fellowships for minority students enrolled in doctoral programs in psychology who are committed to a mental health career, research or service for minority groups. Recipients are chosen for academic performance and motivation. For information, write to the American Psychological Association, Minority Fellowship Program, 750 First Street, NW, Washington, DC 20002-4242. Website: http://www.apa.org/mfp/

American Sociological Association Minority Fellowship Program provides fellowships for minority students enrolled in doctoral programs in sociology. Applications are due late January, annually. To receive information about this program, write to the American Sociological Association, Minority Fellowship Program, 1307 New York Avenue, NW, Suite 700 Washington, DC 20005-4701. Website: http://www.asanet.org/student/mfp.html

American Society of Women Accountants provides scholarships to women studying accounting. Applicants must be in their junior or senior year. Deadlines vary from chapter to chapter. For details about this program, write to the Scholarship Committee, American Society of Women Accountants, 1595 Spring Hill Road, Suite 330, Vienna, VA 22182. Website: http://www.aswa.org/scholarship.html

American Women in Radio and Television Guber (Sid) Memorial Award provides funding for undergraduate and graduate women studying the performing arts. Applicants must be members of American Women in Radio and Television, Inc. For more information about this program, write to the Foundation of American Women in Radio and Television, 8405 Greensboro Drive, Suite 800, McLean, VA 22102. 703/506-3290. Website: http://www.awrt.org/foundation.html

Arts Recognition and Talent Search (ARTS) Program offers competitions for cash awards to be used for continuing education in five artistic disciplines: dance, music, theater, visual arts, and writing. Up to $300,000 is available for awards annually; selection is based on artistic expression rather than grades. Must be in high school and a senior, whatever the age. The June 1 deadline requires a $25 fee while the October 1 deadline requires a $35 fee. For more information, call or write the National Foundation for Advancement of the Arts, 800 Brickell Avenue, Suite 500, Miami, FL 33131. Website: http://www.nfaa.org/aboutarts.htm

Association of University Programs in Health Administration provides internship programs for minority students. Applicants must be second- or third-year students with demonstrated academic ability. For more information, write to the Association of University Programs in Health Administration, 2000 N. 14th Street, Suite 780, Arlington, VA 22201. Website: http://www.aupha.org/

Association of Women in Science provides assistance of up to $1,000 to undergraduate women studying physical and social sciences. To receive more information about this program, write to the Association of Women in Science, 1200 New York Avenue, Suite 650, Washington, DC 20005. Website: http://www.awis.org/resource/scholarships.html

Auzenne (Delores) Fellowship is available to black graduate and professional students who are U.S. citizens and are enrolled full-time an accredited university. Students must maintain full-time enrollment status for the academic year in which the fellowship is awarded. Selections are made in the spring term for the next academic year in which the fellowship is awarded. Applicants must complete a graduate fellowship application to receive the $5,000 annual award. Contact your university's affirmative action office for application information.

Bell (Alexander Graham) Association for the Deaf Scholarships are provided for deaf students attending hearing colleges. Awards range from $250 to $1,000 annually. For more information, visit http://www.agbell.org/financialaid.cfm

Business and Professional Women's Foundation sponsors a wide variety of need-based scholarship and loan programs designed to assist women in health professions, schools, engineering, and graduate business programs. For details about the various financial assistance programs, write to the Business and Professional Women's Foundation, 2012 Massachusetts Avenue, NW, Washington, DC 20036 or call 202/293-1200 ext. 169. Website: http://www.bpwusa.org/content/BPWFoundation/scholarships_introtext.htm

Consortium for Graduate Study in Management Fellowships provide fellowships for students pursuing a career in business. Awards provide tuition and also a stipend for living expenses. For more information, write to the Consortium for Graduate Study in Management, 5585 Pershing, Suite 240, St. Louis, MO 63112-4621. Website: http://www.cgsm.org/apply.asp

Daughters of the American Revolution Scholarships are available for women students. Local DAR chapters administer many of the scholarship programs including the American History Scholarship, Enid Hall Griswald Memorial Scholarship, Caroline E. Holt Educational Fund Scholarship and the Occupational Therapy Scholarship. Deadlines vary. For more information, contact a local DAR chapter or write to the Committee Services Office, Attn: Scholarships, 1776 D Street, NW, Washington, DC 20006-5303. Website: http://www.dar.org/natsociety/edout_scholar.html

Dow Jones Newspaper Fund Minority Reporting Award provides $1,000 to minority students who compete for this award. Recipients are chosen based on talent shown during a reporting internship, an essay and recommendations. Applications deadlines vary. For program information and a list of participating newspapers, write to the Dow Jones Newspaper Fund, P.O. Box 300, Princeton, NJ 08543-0300. Website: http://djnewspaperfund.dowjones.com/fund/hss_summer_workshop.asp

Harkness (Georgia) Scholarship Award assists female seminary students over 35 preparing for ordained ministry in the United Methodist Church. Ten grants of $5,000 will be awarded and the deadline for applications is March 1 of each year. For more information about this program, write to the Georgia Harkness Scholarship Award Program, Division of Ordained Ministry, The United Methodist Church, P.O. Box 340007, Nashville, TN 37203-0007 or call 615/340-7409. Website: http://www.gbhem.org/Harkness.html

Hispanic Scholarship Fund partners with various corporations and other non-profit groups to award a wide variety scholarship programs to Hispanic-American undergraduates enrolled full time at accredited U.S. colleges and universities. Application deadlines vary. For more information contact the Hispanic Scholarship Fund, Southeast Regional Office, 960 Holcomb Bridge Road, Suite 5, Roswell, GA 30076 or call 770/922-8841. Website: http://www.hsf.net.

International Furnishings and Design Association Scholarships provide women with scholarships to pursue careers in the areas of design, arts and crafts. Applications are due March 31. An annual competition is held to determine the recipients of these scholarships. For more information, visit: http://www.ifdaef.org/scholarships.html

Japanese-American Citizens' League (JACL) Scholarship Program offers scholarships to students at the entering freshman, undergraduate and graduate levels. In addition, the program provides special awards to individuals involved in creative projects that reflect the Japanese-American experience. Scholarships range in the amounts of $1,000 to $5,000. Applicants may apply under only one scholarship category, and only one application needs to be submitted to be considered for any of the awards listed under each category heading. JACL members and their families may apply for a JACL Scholarship or Award. Deadline for freshmen is March 1 and for all others is April 1. Address correspondence to JACL National Scholarship Awards, 1765 Sutter Street, San Francisco, CA 94115. Website: http://www.jacl.org/scholarships.html

League of United Latin American Citizens National Scholarship Fund is a community based scholarship program that awards over half a million dollars each year to outstanding Hispanic students in communities served by participating Councils of the League of United Latin American Citizens. To qualify, an applicant must be a US citizen or legal resident and enrolled or planning to enroll in a two-year or four-year college or university. An applicant must apply directly to participating LULAC Council in his/her community. A list of participating LULAC Councils can be obtained by sending a self-addressed stamped envelope to the LULAC National Education Service Centers at the following address: LULAC National Educational Service Centers, Department of Scholarship Inquiries, 2000 L Street, NW, Suite 610, Washington, DC 20001. 202/835-9646 Website: http://www.lulac.org/Programs/Scholar.html

Mexican American Legal Defense and Educational Fund provides assistance to needy, full-time Hispanic students enrolled in law school. Scholarships range from $2,000 to $6,000. For more information, write to the Mexican American Legal Defense and Education Fund, 634 S. Spring Street, 11th Floor, Los Angeles, CA 90014. Website: http://www.maldef.org/education/scholarships.htm

National Merit Scholarship Corporation provides recognition and encouragement for over 600 promising black high school students nationwide each year. To qualify for consideration, you must take the Preliminary Scholastic Aptitude Test/National Merit Scholarship Qualifying Test (PSAT/NMSQT) during your junior year of high school. For more information, see your high school guidance counselor or contact the National Merit Scholarship Corporation, 1560 Sherman Avenue, Suite 200, Evanston, Illinois 60201-4897, 847/866-5100. Website: http://www.nationalmerit.org/

National Black Nurses Association Scholarships are available to African-American. The applicant must qualify for financial aid at his/her college; have successfully completed at least one year of college courses; be accepted into the nursing program; have a GPA of at least 2.5; be a full-time student; and be a member of NBNA or of their local chapter. To apply, submit an application, three letters of reference, and appear at the NBNA meeting at the request of the chairperson for an interview. The deadline for applications is April 15 each year. For more information, contact the National Black Nurses Association, 8630 Fenton Street, Suite 330, Silver Spring, MD 20910-3803. Website: http://www.nbna.org/scholarship.htm

National Council of Negro Women (Pensacola Section) Scholarship is offered to a black graduating high school senior who plans to attend a two- or four-year college or university. Selection is based on a high school GPA of 2.0, an essay and planned full-time attendance in college. The applicant must be single. One award is offered annually and it varies in amount from $500 to $1,200. For more information, contact the National Council of Negro Women/Pensacola, 765 Berkley Drive, Pensacola, FL 32503.

National Federation of the Blind provides financial assistance in the form of scholarships to legally blind undergraduate and graduate students. For more information, contact the National Federation of the Blind, 1800 Johnson Street, Baltimore, MD 21230. Website: http://www.nfb.org/sch_intro.htm

National Medical Fellowships offer a wide variety of scholarship and fellowship programs dedicated to increase the representation of minority physicians, educators, researchers, and policymakers in the United States. Deadlines vary. For more information about any of the following programs contact National Medical Fellowships, 5 Hanover Square, 15th Floor, New York , NY 10004; phone 212-483-8880; email: info@nmfonline.org; or online at http://www.nmf-online.org/Programs/programs.htm

National Scholarship Service and Fund for Negro Students (NSSFNS) Supplementary Scholarship Assistance is available to Miami-area minority high school students who have been counseled by the NSSFNS. For more information, see your high school guidance counselor or write to NSSFNS, 250 Auburn Avenue NE, Suite 500, Atlanta, GA 30303.

National Society of Professional Engineers provides assistance for women or minority students enrolled in engineering programs. Recipients are chosen based on academic performance. For information, contact the National Society of Professional Engineers, 1420 King Street, Alexandria VA, 22314. Call 703/684-2800.

Native American Education Grants are for Native Americans and Alaska Natives pursuing full-time postsecondary education. Students must be U.S. citizens and members of the Presbyterian Church (USA). They must have completed at least one semester/quarter of work at an accredited institution of higher education. Preference will be given to members of Native American Tribes or Alaska Native Corporations who are studying at the undergraduate level. Awards range from $200 to $1,500 per academic year. The deadline for this program is June 1, 1996. For further information, write to Native American Education Grant, Financial Aid for Studies, 100 Witherspoon Street; Louisville, KY 40202-1396.

Nurses Educational Funds scholarships are available to students pursuing a career in nursing. To be eligible, you must be a registered nurse, a member of the American Nurses' Association, and a U.S. citizen or permanent resident. Doctoral students may pursue nursing or nursing-related study. Awards are for fulltime study or part-time study. Awards range from $2,500-$10,000 annually. The deadline for applications is March 1. For more information, contact Nurses Educational Funds, Inc., 304 Park Avenue South, 11th Floor, New York, New York 10010, 212/582-8820, ext. 806. Website: http://www.n-e-f.org/

Rankin (Jeanette) Foundation assists women over age 35 who are enrolled in undergraduate or
vocational/technical programs. Seven to ten awards of $1,000 are given annually to women across the country. For more information, write to the Jeannette Rankin Foundation, P.O. Box 6653, Athens, GA 30604-6653. 706/208-1211. Website: http://www.rankinfoundation.org/

Society of Women Engineers Scholarships provide seventy $1,000 to over-$5,000 annual scholarships to females majoring in engineering and enrolled in an accredited engineering program. Awards are made during sophomore, junior, and senior years of college; a minimum GPA is required. The deadline for applications is May 15. For more information, contact the Fund Development Director, Society of Women Engineers, 230 E. Ohio Street, Suite 400, Chicago, IL 60611-3265 or call 312/596-5223. Website: http://www.societyofwomenengineers.org/partners/corporateScholarship.aspx.

United Methodist Scholarships/Loans are available to minority students that are active members of the United Methodist church. Scholarship and loan programs are available for graduate and undergraduate students. Deadlines vary. For more information, write to the General Board of Higher Education and Ministry, Office of Loans and Scholarships, P.O. Box 340007, Nashville, TN 37203-0007. Website: http://www.gbhem.org/gbhem/loans2.html

United Negro College Fund (UNCF) Scholarships offer financial assistance to students interested in attending independent, accredited, predominately black senior colleges and universities nationwide. To be considered for assistance, you must graduate from high school with a strong academic performance and demonstrate financial need. High school juniors may be considered if they demonstrate an outstanding academic record. The individual schools administer some scholarships; however most are awarded directly by UNCF. Florida colleges and universities eligible for UNCF assistance include Bethune-Cookman College in Daytona Beach and Florida Memorial College in Miami. For more information, contact the respective schools or visit: http://www.uncf.org/

University of Florida Phi Alpha Delta Scholarships offer $500 to members of Phi Alpha Delta Fraternity who have completed two years of law school. Applicants must be U.S. citizens or permanent residents and attend school full-time. Ten recipients will be chosen for this award. For more information, contact the University of Central Florida, College of Law, Financial Aid Office, Gainesville, FL 32611. Website: http://www.law.ufl.edu/

University of Florida Wohlgemuth Scholarship is available to black undergraduate and graduate students majoring in business at the University of Florida. Applicants must be United States citizens and attend school full-time. This $1,000 scholarship will be awarded to a recipient based on his/her academic achievement and financial need. All areas of business will be accepted. For information, contact the University of Florida, College of Business Administration, Scholarship Committee, P.O. Box 117150, Gainesville, FL 32611-7160.

University of South Florida offers a variety of funding programs for black community college graduates who have received their A.A. or an approved A.S. degree and have been accepted at USF. **USF Black Scholars Award** provides $1,500 in tuition assistance and **"Success" Award by Metropolitan** sponsors a $750 award for a black graduate of Hillsborough Community College. The individual must be a business major with a 3.0 GPA. For more information, contact the Office of Financial Aid, University of South Florida, 4202 Fowler Ave., Tampa, FL 33620.

Warren (Earl) Legal Training Program provides assistance to black students enrolled in law school. Applications may be requested between November 30 and February 15. Completed applications are due March 15. For more details about this program, write to the Earl Warren Legal training Program, 99 Hudson Street, New York, NY 10013. Website: http://www.naacpldf.org/scholarships/e_w_l_training.html

Whitehead (Lettie Pate) Foundation provides scholarship support directly to schools in the Southeastern United States. The charter of the foundation is to provide funding for "Christian ladies who might not otherwise be able to afford an education." Contact the financial aid department of your school to determine whether funding is available. Website: http://www.lpwhitehead.org/

Woodrow Wilson (Woodrow) National Fellowship Foundation offers a variety of scholarship and fellowship programs centered on education in the arts and sciences. For more information write to WWNFF, CN 5281, Princeton, NJ 08543-5281 or visit: http://www.woodrow.org

Zanders (Marvin C.) Scholarship is available to black residents of Zellwood, Apopka, Plymouth and Tangerine located in Orange County who have at least a 2.5 high school GPA. One high school senior will be chosen on the basis of academic achievement, recommendations and an essay. Applicants must also submit evidence of acceptance at a post-secondary school. The award amount is $500 and can be used toward study at a two or four-year college or vocational school. For more information, contact Scholarship Coordinator, Zanders Funeral Home, 232 W. Michael Gladden, Boulevard, Apopka, FL 32703.

Zonta International Scholarships are provided to women studying in the field of aerospace engineering and science. Awards are for graduate students. For more information, write to Zonta International, 557 W. Randolph Street, Chicago, IL 60601. Website: http://www.zonta.org

CHAPTER FIVE

APPLYING FOR FINANCIAL ASSISTANCE

APPLYING FOR FINANCIAL ASSISTANCE

It has been said that the best defense is a good offense. This adage applies directly to you if you are attempting to finance your college education. Now that you are aware of the millions of dollars in unused financial aid available to Florida students, you must plan your strategy to show scholarship recommendation boards and financial aid directors that you deserve the available funds.

The following list of suggestions will help you increase your chances of winning financial assistance:

Begin your financial planning as early as possible. Do not wait until you have selected a school; you may not be able to afford the school of your choice. Instead, make the financial aid program at two or three different schools work for you. Review the financial aid programs and the availability of scholarships at each school and then negotiate for more. For parents, the state of Florida currently offers a Pre-Paid Tuition Program, which allows parents to begin financial planning for their child's education while the child is still an infant.

Understand the application forms. Read over each of the forms you must complete *before* you begin filling in the blanks. If you do not understand something, ask the agency what type of answer they expect. Many scholarship applications are denied because the applicant failed to complete the form properly. If this happens to you, by the time you re-submit the application package, the funds may have already been awarded or the deadline has passed. Most colleges and universities have financial aid advisors who can assist you.

Submit all necessary forms. The paperwork required to apply for scholarship aid can be very complicated. Often multiple forms are required from the federal government, state government, college or private program. Make sure that you read the requirements and complete the required documents. Once again, your financial aid advisor can help make sure that you do not overlook anything.

Keep copies of all applications. While it may seem obvious, this is important, While it takes only a few minutes to make copies of your applications, it takes a great deal of time to recreate an application form in the event that it is lost or needs to be amended. This simple step can give you peace of mind. Also, because most financial aid applications contain similar information, you can use the information that you initially researched over and over again.

Know your deadlines. Many financial assistance programs have open application periods; applications are date- and time-stamped, and are reviewed in the order of receipt. Plan to submit your completed application on the first day permitted.

Improve your writing skills. Many financial assistance forms and applications require a demonstration of your writing skills. Learn to be concise and complete when you write. Make sure you have addressed the subject completely in a logical, smooth-flowing format. And *always, always* let someone else proofread your work before you submit it.

Write to the evaluators. Whether you are applying to your local VFW Post for a scholarship or to the financial aid evaluators at your school, learn to present your financial picture in a manner that will leave the financial aid evaluators with a clear understanding of your need for financial assistance. Make sure you investigate all available discipline-based scholarship programs.

Apply for every financial aid program for which you are eligible. Millions of dollars of financial aid remain unspent each year because no one applied to receive them. Check with the department of your major at each school to find out what financial assistance is available.

Capitalize on your abilities. You do not have to score a 1600 on your SAT or have a 4.0 GPA to win a scholarship. Think about your interests and special skills. Scholarships are available for everything from art to zoology. If you have a special talent such as public speaking or musical skills, find out what your schools of choice have to offer in the way of assisted tuition.

Make the most of your family and social associations. Opportunities for scholarships and grants may be as close as a phone call to your local fraternal organization. Many corporations have scholarship programs for employees and children of employees; ask your parents to contact the benefits office at their company to find out what programs are available. Additionally, you may want to talk with local, military and civic organizations to locate scholarship programs. Most of these groups promote education through some type of scholarship program. Religious groups also offer a great number of scholarships.

Sail into a scholarship. Or swing. Or spike. Or dive. Many schools have scholarship programs for sports such as sailing, golfing, volleyball, swimming, tennis, gymnastics, rowing, and soccer. Even if you are not a world-class athlete, find out what your school has to offer. Many athletic departments have money to supplement student athletes' tuition; while a full scholarship may not be a reality, a partial scholarship or supplemental tuition funds *will* help fund your education.

Take advantage of your ethnic background or sex. Minorities and women qualify for scholarships that other students do not. Local chapters of minority and women's business associations often provide scholarship programs to members, their families, or a target group such as high school students.

Keep your grades up. Most financial assistance programs have minimum academic requirements. It is your responsibility to maintain your academic standing within the administering agency's requirements.

Don't estimate financial information. Although it is tempting to estimate financial information, it is important to be accurate. Make sure to keep a file containing the documentation needed to back up your financial statements if needed.

Remember to apply each year. Your freshman year is not the only time to search for scholarship funding. Every year you should pursue available funding. Even reapplying for some programs that denied your application the first time makes sense. It is possible that the amount you are eligible for will differ depending on your current financial status, school funding and federal regulations.

Sample Application Letters

The cover letter you include with your financial assistance application provides the reviewer with his or her first impression of you. As with any form of business correspondence, your correspondence with administering organizations should be clear and concise. Your letters should be structured so that the reviewer knows who you are, what you want and where to find you.

This section provides six types of sample letters for approaching different types of financial assistance programs:

- Privately-sponsored assistance
- School-sponsored assistance
- Federally-sponsored assistance
- Organization-sponsored assistance
- State-sponsored assistance
- Graduate research grants

Letters to private organizations and individuals should follow the general rules of business correspondence. You may include brief background information about yourself and your educational history and goals so that the reviewer knows something about you. Private scholarship program reviewers tend to be more subjective in the award process, so personalizing your letters will improve your chances of success.

Letters to schools, state and federal assistance agencies must be clear and direct. Unless the agency specifically asks you for a subjective statement as to why you need assistance, give them only the facts they need to provide you with application forms, guidelines and other information.

Remember to always include a self-addressed, stamped envelope when corresponding with potential scholarship funding organizations. Doing so will more than likely get you a response, and more importantly, accelerate the time you hear back from them.

Privately Sponsored Assistance

(Foundation, Trust Department, Religious Affiliation)

September 30, 2001
1234 Shady Oaks Lane
Jacksonville, FL 09876

Mrs. Jane K. Jones, President
The Carrie Jones Memorial Scholarship Foundation, Inc.
4567 St. John's Road
Jacksonville, FL 09865

Re: Scholarship Application

Dear Mrs. Jones,

I am writing to request a copy of the application procedures for the Carrie Jones Memorial Scholarship. I understand that this scholarship is available to undergraduate women studying in the field of medicine. As you read on, I hope that you will find my accomplishments qualify me for consideration for this prestigious award.

I am currently a senior at Duval County High School and will be graduating in June 1994. I am scheduled to begin my undergraduate studies at the University of Florida in August 1994, provided I can obtain financial assistance to help pay for my tuition and fees.

Throughout high school (grades 9-11), I have maintained a 3.8 grade point average. All of the courses in my curriculum have been rated as college-bound, but I excel in science and mathematics. My extracurricular activities include the National Honor Society, Fellowship of Christian Athletes, participating on the school swimming team and volunteering as a Candy Striper at General Hospital. I am also a member of Phi Beta, a national honor society for chemistry students.

To help save money for my college education, I work Saturdays for our local retirement community running errands for the homebound residents.

You may address all correspondence to me at the address shown above. I look forward to receiving your application materials, Mrs. Jones. Pursuing a career in geriatric medicine is very important to me and I am hopeful that you will consider me for your foundation's assistance.

Sincerely Yours,

Karen Hobbs

Organization Sponsored Assistance
(Civic Group, Professional Association, Fraternal Organization)

January 15, 2002
4567 Palm Court
Pensacola, FL 87654

Mr. Lawrence P. Jefferson, Programs Director
The American Veteran's Association
2345 Main Highway
Pensacola, FL 87632

Re: Scholarship Program Application

Dear Mr. Jefferson,

The purpose of this letter is to provide an introduction to the scholarship application package contained herein. For your reference, I have enclosed my completed essay, entitled "Why I'm Proud to be an American," a copy of my high school transcripts, and the completed application form. In addition, I have provided three letters of reference.

I am currently a sophomore at the University of Florida in Gainesville, Florida; my field of study is engineering sciences, with a concentration in aeronautical science. My career goal is to become a P-3 pilot in the United States Navy. As you read on, I hope that you will find my accomplishments qualify me for consideration for this important community scholarship.

As a senior at George Washington Carver High School, I excelled in science and mathematics. My extracurricular activities included volunteer work for the local Veteran's Hospital and participating in the NROTC unit at school. Since enrolling at the University of Florida, I have maintained a 3.8 grade point average. I currently receive some financial assistance through a partial NROTC scholarship and campus work-study program.

However, I will begin engineering flight school during my junior year and either financial aid program does not cover these costs. I will not be able to complete my education, or reach my career goal, without this training. My father is a Korean War veteran and retired from the United States Army in 1983; it is very important to me to continue our family tradition of a career in the United States military forces. I appreciate your attention to my application; if I receive this award, you can rest assured that I will do my best to maintain the high standards of the American Veteran's Association.

I look forward to receiving your response to this application, Mr. Jefferson. Thank you in advance for your consideration.

Sincerely Yours,

Jackson C. Williams

Enclosures

School Sponsored Assistance
(Student Financial Assistance/Scholarship Offices)

September 30, 2001

Route 5, Box 234
Titusville, FL 34567

Director, Student Financial Aid Office
The Community College of Brevard County
5689 College Drive
Cocoa, FL 34892

Re: Student Financial Aid Programs

Dear Sir or Madam:

Please send me the available information and application materials for the financial assistance programs available to students at the Community College of Brevard County (CCBC). Currently, I am a senior at Titusville High School and have applied for acceptance to CCBC for next fall.

I am interested in all of the available information regarding scholarships and financial aid programs for CCBC students. If a separate office administers scholarships, please forward a copy of this letter to the appropriate individual.

Thank you for your assistance. Please address all correspondence to me at the above address.

Sincerely Yours,

Lee Davis

State Sponsored Assistance
(Florida Department of Education)

January 15, 2002
6789 Village Way, Apt. 4568
Miami, FL 33456

Director, Office of Student Financial Assistance
Florida Department of Education
Florida Education Center
325 West Gaines Street
Tallahassee, FL 32399-0400

Re: Student Financial Aid Program

Dear Sir or Madam:

I would like to request information and application materials for the financial assistance programs available to minority/disabled students attending college in Florida. I am a Florida resident planning to study elementary education, but first plan to attend Miami-Dade Community College to obtain my Associate of Arts degree.

Please send me all of the available information regarding scholarships and financial aid programs for Florida students. I have requested similar information regarding scholarships and financial assistance from Miami-Dade Community College.

Thank you for your assistance. Please address all correspondence to me at the above address.

Sincerely Yours,

Patricia Miller

Federally Sponsored Assistance
(Federal Government Agencies)

July 14, 2001

4632 First Street
St. Augustine, FL 34567

Director, Harry S. Truman Scholarship Program
Harry S. Truman Scholarship Foundation, Inc.
712 Jackson Place, NW
Washington, DC 20006

Re: Scholarship Nomination

Dear Sir or Madam:

Please send me all available information about the nomination procedures for the Harry S. Truman Scholarship Program. I attend a small private college in Florida and I understand that my school must nominate me; however, the administration advised me to write to you to obtain the procedures.

My major is public administration (with a 3.8 grade point average); upon graduation I plan to pursue a career in public service at the municipal level. I am currently serving a summer internship at the city manager's office in my hometown, where I am assisting in the preparation of the city's five-year development plan. I have consistently ranked in the top 20 percent of my class since my junior year of high school.

On behalf of Flagstone College and myself, thank you in advance for your assistance.

Sincerely Yours,

Carolyn Gaines

Graduate Research Grants
(Federal Government Agencies)

January 15, 2002

975 Collins Hall-Robotics Lab
University of Southwest Florida
9870 Kennedy Drive
Ft. Myers, FL 33600

Director, Division of Research Grants
National Institutes of Health
Bethesda, MD 20892

Re: *Food and Drug Administration (FDA) Research Grants-Medical Devices*

Dear Sir or Madam:

I am writing to request information about graduate research grants that provide funding for medical prosthetic devices. I am currently working on my doctoral degree in medical robotics engineering at the University of Southwest Florida and believe that my doctoral research project has the potential for full-scale medical development and eventual submittal to the FDA for approval. I have included a copy of the project abstract for your review.

Based on my previous research performed during my master's program at the Johns Hopkins University, I have created a prosthetic device that allows quadriplegic spinal injury patients to become more self-sufficient through the use of a surgically implanted robotic device. This device is activated by nerve impulses traveling throughout the patient's body. It may be adapted to serve as an auxiliary limb for most C5-L3 spinal patients; full research and testing will provide a basis for future development of this prosthesis.

You may address all correspondence to me at the address shown above. Thank you for your assistance.

Sincerely Yours,

Joel K. Fishbein, M.S.
Principal Researcher
Enclosures

CHAPTER SIX

COLLEGE AND UNIVERSITY DIRECTORY

COLLEGE AND UNIVERSITY DIRECTORY

If you need to contact any school in Florida, we have included the complete list of private and public Florida colleges and universities, along with their home pages on the web.

Community Colleges

BREVARD COMMUNITY COLLEGE
(Cocoa)
1519 Clearlake Road
Cocoa, FL 32922
321/632-1111
http://web2010.brevard.cc.fl.us/

BREVARD COMMUNITY COLLEGE
(Melbourne)
3865 N. Wickham Road
Melbourne, FL 32935
321/632-1111, EXT 5513
http://web2010.brevard.cc.fl.us/

BREVARD COMMUNITY COLLEGE
(Palm Bay)
250 Community College Parkway
Palm Bay, FL 32909
321/632-1111, EXT 5513
http://web2010.brevard.cc.fl.us/

BREVARD COMMUNITY COLLEGE
(Titusville)
1311 North U.S. 1
Titusville, FL 32796
321/632-1111, EXT 5050
http://web2010.brevard.cc.fl.us/

BROWARD COMMUNITY COLLEGE
(Center for Health Science)
3501 S.W. Davie Road, Building 8
Davie, FL 33314
954/201-6780
http://www.broward.edu/

BROWARD COMMUNITY COLLEGE
(Central)
3501 S.W. Davie Road
Davie, FL 33314
954/201-6500
http://www.broward.edu/

BROWARD COMMUNITY COLLEGE
(Commercial Boulevard)
1515 West Commercial Boulevard
Ft. Lauderdale, FL 33309
954/201-7800
http://www.broward.edu/

BROWARD COMMUNITY COLLEGE
(Downtown)
111 East Las Olas Boulevard
Ft. Lauderdale, FL 33301

954/201-7476
http://www.broward.edu/

BROWARD COMMUNITY COLLEGE
(North)
1000 Coconut Creek Boulevard
Pompano Beach, FL 33066
954/201-2240
http://www.broward.edu/

BROWARD COMMUNITY COLLEGE
(Pines)
16957 Sheridan Street
Pembroke Pines, FL 33331
951/201-3601
http://www.broward.edu/

BROWARD COMMUNITY COLLEGE
(South)
7200 Hollywood Boulevard
Pembroke Pines, FL 33024
954/201-8835
http://www.broward.edu/

CENTRAL FLORIDA COMMUNITY COLLEGE
(Citrus County)
3800 S. Lecanto Highway
Lecanto, FL 34461
352/746-6721
http://www.cfcc.cc.fl.us/

CENTRAL FLORIDA COMMUNITY COLLEGE
(Hampton Center)
1501 W. Silver Springs Boulevard
Ocala, FL 34475
352/732-7755
http://www.cfcc.cc.fl.us/

CENTRAL FLORIDA COMMUNITY COLLEGE
(Levy County Center)
114 Rodgers Boulevard
Chiefland, FL 32626
352/493-9533
Ocala, FL 34475
http://www.cf.edu/about/levy/

CENTRAL FLORIDA COMMUNITY COLLEGE
(Ocala)
3001 S.W. College Road
Ocala, Fl 34474
352/854-2322
http://www.cfcc.cc.fl.us/

CHIPOLA JUNIOR COLLEGE
3094 Indian Circle
Marianna, FL 32446
850/526-2761
http://www.chipola.edu/

DAYTONA BEACH COMMUNITY COLLEGE
1200 Volusia Avenue
P.O. Box 2811
Daytona Beach, FL 32014
386/254-4467
http://www.dbcc.cc.fl.us/

DAYTONA BEACH COMMUNITY COLLEGE
(Deland)
1155 County Road 4139
Deland, FL 32724
386/228-3090
http://www.dbcc.cc.fl.us/

DAYTONA BEACH COMMUNITY COLLEGE
(Flagler/Palm Coast)
3000 Palm Coast Parkway S.E.
P.O. Box 1271
Palm Coast, FL 32137
386/445-4030
http://www.dbcc.cc.fl.us/

DAYTONA BEACH COMMUNITY COLLEGE
(New Smyrna)
940 10th Street
New Smyrna Beach, FL 32168
386/427-3472
http://www.dbcc.cc.fl.us/

EDISON COMMUNITY COLLEGE
(Charlotte Center)
26300 Airport Road
Punta Gorda, FL 33950
941/637-5629
http://www.edison.edu/

EDISON COMMUNITY COLLEGE
(Collier County)
7007 Lely Cultural Parkway
Naples, FL 34113
239/732-3700
http://www.edison.edu/

EDISON COMMUNITY COLLEGE
(Hendry/Glades Center)
4050 Cowboy Way
Labelle, FL 863-674-0408
863/674-0408
http://www.edison.edu/

EDISON COMMUNITY COLLEGE
(Lee)
8099 College Parkway, S.W.
P.O. Box 06210
Fort Myers, FL 33906-6210
239/489-9300
http://www.edison.edu/

FLORIDA COMMUNITY COLLEGE
(Distance Learning Center)
601 W. State Street
Jacksonville, FL 32202
904/632-3116
http://www.distancelearning.org

FLORIDA COMMUNITY COLLEGE
(Downtown)
101 W. State Street
Jacksonville, FL 32202
904/633-8100
http://www.fccj.cc.fl.us/

FLORIDA COMMUNITY COLLEGE
(Kent)
3939 Roosevelt Boulevard
Jacksonville, FL 32205
904/381-3400
http://www.fccj.cc.fl.us/

FLORIDA COMMUNITY COLLEGE
(North)
4501 Capper Road
Jacksonville, FL 32218
904/766-6500
http://www.fccj.cc.fl.us/

FLORIDA COMMUNITY COLLEGE
(Open)
601 W. State St.
Jacksonville, FL 32202
904/633-8100
http://www.fccj.cc.fl.us/

FLORIDA COMMUNITY COLLEGE
(South)
11901 Beach Boulevard
Jacksonville, FL 32216
904/646-2111
http://www.fccj.cc.fl.us/

FLORIDA KEYS COMMUNITY COLLEGE
5901 College Road
Key West, FL 33040
305/296-9081
http://www.fkcc.edu/

FLORIDA KEYS COMMUNITY COLLEGE
(Middle Keys Center)
900 Sombrero Road
Marathon, FL 33040
305/743-2133
http://www.fkcc.edu/

FLORIDA KEYS COMMUNITY COLLEGE
(Upper Keys Center)
P.O. Drawer 600
89951 U.S. Highway 1
Tavenier, FL 33070
305/296-9081
http://www.fkcc.edu/

GULF COAST COMMUNITY COLLEGE
5230 West Highway 98
Panama City, FL 32401
800/769-1551
http://www.gc.cc.fl.us/

HILLSBOROUGH COMMUNITY COLLEGE
(Brandon)
10414 E. Columbus Dr.
Tampa, FL 33619
813/253-7802
http://www.hcc.cc.fl.us/

HILLSBOROUGH COMMUNITY COLLEGE
(Dale Mabry)
North Dale Mabry Highway
P.O. Box 30030
Tampa, FL 33630
813/253-7202
http://www.hcc.cc.fl.us/

HILLSBOROUGH COMMUNITY COLLEGE
(MacDill)
6 MSS/DPE STE 2
8119 Marina Bay Drive
MacDill AFB, FL 33621
813/672-519
http://www.hcc.cc.fl.us/

HILLSBOROUGH COMMUNITY COLLEGE
(Plant City)
1206 N. Park Road
Plant City, FL 33566
813/757-2100
http://www.hcc.cc.fl.us/

HILLSBOROUGH COMMUNITY COLLEGE
(Sunpoint)
3052 College Avenue E.
Ruskin, FL 33570
813/672-519
http://www.hcc.cc.fl.us/

HILLSBOROUGH COMMUNITY COLLEGE
(Ybor City)
P.O. Box 5096
Tampa, FL 33675
813/253-7602
http://www.hcc.cc.fl.us/

INDIAN RIVER COMMUNITY COLLEGE
3209 Virginia Avenue
Fort Pierce, FL 34981
772/462-4700
http://www.ircc.cc.fl.us/

INDIAN RIVER COMMUNITY COLLEGE
(Chastain)
2400 S.E. Salerno Road
Stuart, FL
772/283-6550
http://www.ircc.cc.fl.us/

INDIAN RIVER COMMUNITY COLLEGE
(Dixon Hendry)
2229 N.W. 9th Avenue
Okeechobee, FL 34972
863/763-8017
http://www.ircc.cc.fl.us/

INDIAN RIVER COMMUNITY COLLEGE
(Mueller)
6155 College Lane
Vero Beach, FL 32966
772/569-0333
http://www.ircc.cc.fl.us/

INDIAN RIVER COMMUNITY COLLEGE
(St. Lucie West)
500 N.W. California Blvd.
Port St. Lucie, FL 34986
772/879-4199
http://www.ircc.cc.fl.us/

LAKE CITY COMMUNITY COLLEGE
Route 19, Box 1822
Lake City, FL 32025
386/752-1822
http://www.lakecity.cc.fl.us/

LAKE-SUMTER COMMUNITY COLLEGE
(Leesburg)
9501 U.S. Highway 441 S.
Leesburg, FL 34788
352/787-3747
http://www.lscc.cc.fl.us/

LAKE-SUMTER COMMUNITY COLLEGE
(South Lake)
1250 N. Hancock Road
Clermont, FL 34711
352/243-5722
http://www.lscc.cc.fl.us/

LAKE-SUMTER COMMUNITY COLLEGE
(Sumter)
1405 CR 526A
Sumterville, FL 33585
352/568-0001
http://www.lscc.cc.fl.us/

MANATEE COMMUNITY COLLEGE
(Bradenton)
5840 26th Street West
P.O. Box 1849
Bradenton, FL 34207
941/752-5000
http://www.mccfl.edu/

MANATEE COMMUNITY COLLEGE
(Lakewood Ranch)
7131 Professional Parkway, E.
Sarasota, FL 34240
941/363-7000
http://www.mccfl.edu/

MANATEE COMMUNITY COLLEGE
(Venice)
8000 S. Tamiami Trail
Venice, FL 33595
941/408-1300
http://www.mccfl.edu/

MIAMI-DADE COMMUNITY COLLEGE
(Homestead)
500 College Terrace
Homestead, FL 33030
305/237-5555
http://www.mdcc.edu/homestead/

MIAMI-DADE COMMUNITY COLLEGE
(Medical Center)
950 N.W. 20th Street
Miami, FL 33127
305/237-4000
http://www.mdcc.edu/medical/

MIAMI-DADE COMMUNITY COLLEGE
(Mitchell Wolfson)
300 N.E. Second Avenue
Miami, Fl 33132
305/237-3000
http://www.mdcc.edu/wolfson/

MIAMI-DADE COMMUNITY COLLEGE
(New World)
300 N.E. 2nd Avenue
Miami, FL 33132
305/237-7007
http://www.mdcc.edu/nwsa/

MIAMI-DADE COMMUNITY COLLEGE
(North)
11380 N.W. 27th Avenue
Miami, FL 33167
305/237-1000
http://www.mdcc.edu/north/

MIAMI-DADE COMMUNITY COLLEGE
(South)
11011 S.W. 104th Street
Miami, FL 33176
305/237-2000
http://www.mdcc.edu/kendall/

NORTH FLORIDA JUNIOR COLLEGE
1000 Turner Davis Drive
Madison, FL 32340
850/973-1600
http://www.nflcc.edu/

OKALOOSA-WALTON COMMUNITY COLLEGE
100 College Boulevard
Niceville, FL 32578
850/678-5111
http://www.owcc.cc.fl.us/

PALM BEACH COMMUNITY COLLEGE
(Belle Glade)
1977 College Drive

Belle Glade, FL 33430
561/993-1167
http://www.pbcc.edu

PALM BEACH COMMUNITY COLLEGE
(Lake Worth)
4200 Congress Avenue
Lake Worth, FL 33461
561/868-3035
http://www.pbcc.edu

PALM BEACH COMMUNITY COLLEGE
(Palm Beach Gardens)
Edward M. Eissey Campus
3160 PGA Boulevard
Palm Beach Gardens, FL 33410
561/207-5340
http://www.pbcc.edu

PALM BEACH COMMUNITY COLLEGE
(South)
P.O. Box 3095
3000 Saint Lucie Avenue
Boca Raton, FL 33431
561/862-4313
http://www.pbcc.edu

PALM BEACH COMMUNITY COLLEGE
(West Palm Beach)
Count and Countess DeHoernle Historic Bldg.
812 Fern Street
West palm Beach, FL 33401
561/868-3300
http://www.pbcc.edu

PASCO-HERNANDO COMMUNITY COLLEGE
(Brooksville)
11415 Ponce De Leon Boulevard
Brooksville, FL 33573
352/796-6726
http://www.pasco-hernandocc.com/

PASCO-HERNANDO COMMUNITY COLLEGE
(Dade City)
2401 S. Highway 41 North
Dade City, FL 33525
352/567-6701
http://www.pasco-hernandocc.com/

PASCO-HERNANDO COMMUNITY COLLEGE
(Spring Hill)
11245 Spring Hill Drive
Spring Hill, FL 34609
352/688-8798
http://www.pasco-hernandocc.com/

PASCO-HERNANDO COMMUNITY COLLEGE
(West Campus)
10230 Ridge Road
New Port Richey, FL 34654
727/847-2727
http://www.pasco-hernandocc.com/

PENSACOLA JUNIOR COLLEGE
1000 College Boulevard
Pensacola, FL 32504
850/484-1000
http://www.pjc.cc.fl.us/

PENSACOLA JUNIOR COLLEGE
(Milton)
1130 Highway 90 West
Milton, FL 32570
http://www.pjc.cc.fl.us/

PENSACOLA JUNIOR COLLEGE
(Warrington)
5555 Highway 98 W.
Warrington, FL 32507
http://www.pjc.cc.fl.us/

POLK COMMUNITY COLLEGE
999 Avenue H, N.E.
Winter Haven, FL 33881
813/297-1010
http://www.polk.edu/

ST. JOHNS RIVER COMMUNITY COLLEGE
(Orange Park)
283 College Drive
P.O. Box 1748
Orange Park, FL 32065
904/272-6800
http://www.sjrcc.cc.fl.us/

ST. JOHNS RIVER COMMUNITY COLLEGE
(Palatka)
5001 St. Johns Avenue
Palatka, FL 32177
386/312-4200
http://www.sjrcc.cc.fl.us/

ST. JOHNS RIVER COMMUNITY COLLEGE
(St. Augustine)
2990 College Drive
St. Augustine, FL 332084
904/808-7400
http://www.sjrcc.cc.fl.us/

ST. JOHNS RIVER COMMUNITY COLLEGE
(Orange Park)
283 College Drive
Orange Park, FL 32065
904/276-6800
http://www.sjrcc.cc.fl.us/

ST. JOHNS RIVER COMMUNITY COLLEGE
(Ponte Vedra Center)
5150 Palm Valley Road
Ponte Vedra Beach, Fl 32082
904/280-1322
http://www.sjrcc.cc.fl.us/

ST. PETERSBURG COLLEGE
P.O. Box 13489
8580 66th Street, North
St. Petersburg, FL 33733

727/341-4772
http://www.spcollege.edu/

ST. PETERSBURG COLLEGE
(Allstate Center)
3200 34th Street S.
St. Petersburg, FL 33733
727/341-3600
http://www.spcollege.edu/ac/

ST. PETERSBURG COLLEGE
(Clearwater)
2465 Drew Street
Clearwater, FL 33733
http://www.spcollege.edu/clw/

ST. PETERSBURG COLLEGE
(Health Education Center)
7200 66th Street, N.
Pinellas Park, FL 33781
727/341-3687
http://www.spcollege.edu/Hec/

ST. PETERSBURG COLLEGE
(Tarpon)
600 Klosterman Road
Palm Harbor, FL 34683
http://www.spcollege.edu/tsc/

SANTA FE COMMUNITY COLLEGE
3000 N.W. 83rd Street
Gainesville, FL 32606
352/395-5000
http://www.santafe.cc.fl.us/

SANTA FE COMMUNITY COLLEGE
(Davis Center)
17500 S.W. Archer Road
Archer, FL 32618
http://archer.sfcc.edu/archer/

SANTA FE COMMUNITY COLLEGE
(Andrews Center)
209 W. Call Street
Starke, FL 32091
352/395-580
http://stk.sfcc.edu/stk/andrews/

SANTA FE COMMUNITY COLLEGE
(Charles L. Blount Downtown Center)
401 N.W. 6th Street
Gainesville, FL 32601
352/395-5645
http://dtc.sfcc.edu/dtc/blount/

SANTA FE COMMUNITY COLLEGE
(George G. Kirkpatrick, Jr. Criminal Justice Training
Center)
3737 N.W. 39th Avenue
Gainesville, FL 32609
352/334-0300
http://ips.sfcc.edu/ips

SEMINOLE COMMUNITY COLLEGE
100 Weldon Boulevard
Sanford, FL 32773
407/328-4722
http://www.scc-fl.edu

SOUTH FLORIDA COMMUNITY COLLEGE
600 W. College Drive
Avon Park, FL 33825
813/453-6661
http://www.sfcc.cc.fl.us/

TALLAHASSEE COMMUNITY COLLEGE
444 Appleyard Drive
Tallahassee, FL 32304
850/201-6200
http://www.tcc.cc.fl.us/

VALENCIA COMMUNITY COLLEGE
P.O. Box 3028
Orlando, FL 32802
407/299-5000
http://valencia.cc.fl.us/

VALENCIA COMMUNITY COLLEGE
(East)
701 N. Econlockhatchee Trail
Orlando, FL 32825
407/299-5000
http://valencia.cc.fl.us/

VALENCIA COMMUNITY COLLEGE
(Osceola Campus)
1800 Denn John Lane
Kissimmee, FL 34744
407/299-5000
http://valencia.cc.fl.us/

VALENCIA COMMUNITY COLLEGE
(West)
1800 S. Kirkman Road
Orlando, FL 32811
407/299-5000
http://valencia.cc.fl.us/

State Universities

FLORIDA AGRICULTURAL & MECHANICAL
UNIVERSITY
South Boulevard Street
Office of Admissions
Tallahassee, FL 32307
904/599-3000
http://www.famu.edu/

FLORIDA ATLANTIC UNIVERSITY
500 N.W. 20th Street
Boca Raton 33431
http://www.fau.edu/

FLORIDA ATLANTIC UNIVERSITY
(Boca Raton)
777 Glades Road
Boca Raton, FL 33431-0991
561/297-3000
http://www.broward.fau.edu/

FLORIDA ATLANTIC UNIVERSITY
(Broward/Davie)
2912 College Avenue
Davie, FL 33314
954/236-1000
http://www.broward.fau.edu/

FLORIDA ATLANTIC UNIVERSITY
(Commercial Boulevard)
1515 West Commercial Blvd.
Fort Lauderdale, FL 33309
954/229-4140
http://www.broward.fau.edu/

FLORIDA ATLANTIC UNIVERSITY
(Dania Beach)
101 North Beach Road
Dania Beach, FL 33004
954/924-7000
http://www.broward.fau.edu/

FLORIDA ATLANTIC UNIVERSITY
(Fort Lauderdale)
111 East Las Olas Blvd.
Fort Lauderdale, FL 33301
954/762-5200
http://www.broward.fau.edu/

FLORIDA ATLANTIC UNIVERSITY
(Jupiter)
5353 Park Side Drive
Jupiter, FL 33458
561/799-8500
http://www.fau.edu/northern/jupiter/

FLORIDA ATLANTIC UNIVERSITY
(Port St. Lucie)
500 N.W. California Blvd.

Port St. Lucie, FL 34986
772/873-3300
http://www.fau.edu/northern/psl/

FLORIDA GULF COAST UNIVERSITY
10501 FGCU Blvd. S.
Ft. Myers, FL 33965-6565
239/590-1000
http://www.fgcu.edu/

FLORIDA INTERNATIONAL UNIVERSITY
11200 S.W. 8th Street
Miami, FL 33199
305/348-2000
http://www.fiu.edu/

FLORIDA INTERNATIONAL UNIVERSITY
(Biscayne Bay)
3000 N.E. 151st Street
North Miami, FL 33181
305/919-5000
http://www.fiu.edu/

FLORIDA STATE UNIVERSITY
215 WM Johnson Building
Tallahassee, FL 32306
850/644-2525
http://www.fsu.edu/

FLORIDA STATE UNIVERSITY
(Panama City)
4750 Collegiate Drive
Panama City, FL 32405
507-341-0367
http://www.fsu.edu/~cppanama/

UNIVERSITY OF CENTRAL FLORIDA
4000 Central Florida Boulevard
Orlando, FL 32816
407/823-2000
http://www.ucf.edu/

UNIVERSITY OF FLORIDA
135 Tigert Hall
Gainesville, FL 32611
352/392-3261
http://www.ufl.edu/

UNIVERSITY OF FLORIDA
(Eglin Center)
P.O. Box 1918
Eglin Air Force Base, FL 32542
904/882-5614
http://www.ufl.edu/

UNIVERSITY OF NORTH FLORIDA
4567 St. Johns Bluff Road, South
Jacksonville, FL 32216

904/620-1000
http://www.unf.edu/

UNIVERSITY OF SOUTH FLORIDA
(Ft. Myers)
8111 College Parkway, S.W.
Fort Myers, FL 33919
http://www.usf.edu/

UNIVERSITY OF SOUTH FLORIDA
(Lakeland)
3343 Winter Lake Road
Lakeland, FL 33803
813/667-7000
http://www.lklnd.usf.edu/

UNIVERSITY OF SOUTH FLORIDA
(Sarasota)
5700 N. Tamiami Trail
Sarasota, FL 34243
941/359-4200
http://www.sarasota.usf.edu/

UNIVERSITY OF SOUTH FLORIDA
(St. Petersburg)
140 7th Avenue South
St. Petersburg, FL 33701
727/553-4USF
http://www1.stpt.usf.edu/

UNIVERSITY OF SOUTH FLORIDA
(Tampa)
4202 Fowler Avenue
Tampa, FL 33620
813/974-2011
http://www.usf.edu/

UNIVERSITY OF WEST FLORIDA
11000 University Parkway
Pensacola, FL 32514
850/474-2000
http://www.uwf.edu

Independent Colleges and Universities

AMERICAN FLYERS COLLEGE
1401 N.E. 10th Street
Pompano Beach, FL 33060-6517
954/772-7500
http://www.americanflyers.net/

ART INSTITUTE OF FORT LAUDERDALE
1799 S.E. 17th Street
Ft. Lauderdale, FL 33316
800/275-7603
http://www.aifl.edu/

BARRY UNIVERSITY
11300 N.E. 2nd Avenue
Miami Shores, FL 33161
800/756-6000
http://www.barry.edu/

BEACON COLLEGE
105 E. Main Street
Leesburg, FL 34748
352/787-7660
http://www.beaconcollege.edu/

BETHUNE-COOKMAN COLLEGE
640 2nd Avenue
Daytona Beach, FL 32115
386/481-2000
http://www.cookman.edu/

CLEARWATER CHRISTIAN COLLEGE
3400 Gulf-to-Bay Boulevard
Clearwater, FL 34619
727/726-1153
http://www.clearwater.edu/

COLUMBIA COLLEGE - Orlando Naval Training Center
2600 Technology Drive
Suite 100
Orlando, FL 32804
407/293-9911
http://www.ccis.edu/Orlando/

ECKERD COLLEGE
4200 54th Avenue, S.
St. Petersburg, FL 33711
800/456-9009
http://www.eckerd.edu/

EDWARD WATERS COLLEGE
1658 Kings Road
Jacksonville, FL 32209
888/898-9131
http://www.ewc.edu/

EMBRY-RIDDLE AERONAUTICAL UNIVERSITY
600 S. Clyde Morris Boulevard
Daytona Beach, FL 32114
800/862-2416

http://ec.db.erau.edu/

FLAGLER COLLEGE
74 King St.
St. Augustine, FL 32084
904/829-6481
http://www.flagler.edu/

FLORIDA BAPTIST THEOLOGICAL COLLEGE
5400 College Dr.
Graceville, FL 32440
904/263-3261

FLORIDA BEACON BIBLE COLLEGE
6900 142nd Avenue, N.
Largo, FL 34641
813/531-4498

FLORIDA CHRISTIAN COLLEGE
1011 Osceola Boulevard
Kissimmee, FL 34744
407/847-8966
http://fcc.edu/

FLORIDA COLLEGE
119 Glen Arven Avenue
Temple Terrace, FL 33617
813/988-5131
http://www.flcoll.edu/

FLORIDA INSTITUTE OF TECHNOLOGY
150 West University Boulevard
Melbourne, FL 32901
321/674-8000
http://www.fit.edu/

FLORIDA MEMORIAL COLLEGE
15800 N.W. 42nd Avenue
Miami, FL 33054
305/623-4100
http://www.fmc.edu/

FLORIDA METROPOLITAN UNIVERSITY
(Brandon)
3924 Coconut Palm Drive
Tampa, FL 33619
813/621-0041
http://www.fmu.edu/

FLORIDA METROPOLITAN UNIVERSITY
(Fort Lauderdale)
1040 Bayview Drive
Fort Lauderdale, FL 33304
954/568-1600
http://www.fmu.edu/

FLORIDA METROPOLITAN UNIVERSITY
(Jacksonville)
8226 Philips Highway
Jacksonville, FL 32256

904/731-4949
http://www.fmu.edu/

FLORIDA METROPOLITAN UNIVERSITY
(Lakeland)
995 East Memorial Blvd., Ste. 110
Lakeland, FL 33801
863/686-1444
http://www.fmu.edu/

FLORIDA METROPOLITAN UNIVERSITY
(Melbourne)
2401 N. Harbor City Blvd.
Melbourne, FL 32935
321/253-2929
http://www.fmu.edu/

FLORIDA METROPOLITAN UNIVERSITY
(North Orlando)
5421 Diplomat Circle
Orlando, FL 32810
407/628-5870
http://www.fmu.edu/

FLORIDA METROPOLITAN UNIVERSITY
(Orange Park)
805 Wells Road
Orange Park, FL 32073
904/264-9122
http://www.fmu.edu/

FLORIDA METROPOLITAN UNIVERSITY
(Pinellas)
2471 McMullen Booth Rd., Ste. 200
Clearwater, FL 33759
727/725-2688
http://www.fmu.edu/

FLORIDA METROPOLITAN UNIVERSITY
(Pompano Beach)
225 North Federal Highway
Pompano Beach, FL 33062
954/783-7339
http://www.fmu.edu/

FLORIDA METROPOLITAN UNIVERSITY
(South Orlando)
9200 South Park Center Loop
Orlando, FL 32819
407/851-2525
http://www.fmu.edu/

FLORIDA METROPOLITAN UNIVERSITY
(Tampa)
3319 W. Hillsborough Avenue
Tampa, FL 33614
813/879-6000
http://www.fmu.edu/

FLORIDA NATIONAL COLLEGE
4425 W. 20th Avenue
Hialeah, FL 33012
305/821-3333
http://www.florida-national.edu/

FLORIDA NATIONAL COLLEGE
(South)
11865 S.W. 26th Street, Unit #H-3
Miami, FL 33175
305/226-9999, EXT 3
http://www.florida-national.edu/

FLORIDA SOUTHERN COLLEGE
111 Lake Hollingsworth Drive
Lakeland, FL 33801
863/680-4131
http://www.flsouthern.edu/

FLORIDA TECHNICAL COLLEGE
(Orlando)
1819 North Semoran Boulevard
Orlando, FL 32807
888/678-2929
http://www.flatech.edu/

HARBOR BRANCH INSTITUTION
5600 Old Dixie Highway
Ft. Pierce, FL 34946
772/465-2400
http://www.hboi.edu/

HARID CONSERVATORY OF MUSIC
2285 Potomac Road
Boca Raton, FL 33431
561/997-2677
http://www.harid.edu/

HOBE SOUND BIBLE COLLEGE
P.O. Box 1065
Hobe Sound, FL 33475
800/881-5534
http://www.hsbc.edu/

**INTERNATIONAL ACADEMY OF
MERCHANDISING &
DESIGN - TAMPA**
5225 Memorial Highway
Tampa, FL 33609
http://www.academy.edu/

INTERNATIONAL COLLEGE OF NAPLES
2655 Northbrooke Drive
Naples, FL 34119
800/466-8017
http://www.internationalcollege.edu/

INTERNATIONAL FINE ARTS COLLEGE
1501 Biscayne Boulevard
Suite 100
Miami, FL 33132
800/225-9023
http://www.ifac.edu/

ITT TECHNICAL INSTITUTE
(Tampa)
4809 Memorial Highway
Tampa, FL 33634
813/885-2244
http://www.itt-tech.edu/

JACKSONVILLE UNIVERSITY
2800 University Boulevard, N.
Jacksonville, FL 32211
904/256-8000
http://www.ju.edu/

JONES COLLEGE
5353 Arlington Expressway
Jacksonville, FL 3221
904/743-1122
http://www.jones.edu/

KEISER COLLEGE OF TECHNOLOGY
1500 N.W. 49th Street
Ft. Lauderdale, FL 33309
800/749-4456
http://www.keisercollege.cc.fl.us/

LYNN UNIVERSITY/COLLEGE OF BOCA
RATON
3601 N. Military Trail
Boca Raton, FL 33431
561/237-7000
http://www.lynn.edu/

MIAMI CHRISTIAN COLLEGE
9775 S.W. 87th Avenue
Miami, FL 33167
305/595-5314
http://www.mcu.edu/

NOVA SOUTHEASTERN UNIVERSITY
3301 College Avenue
Ft. Lauderdale, FL 33314
800/541-6682
http://www.nova.edu/cwis/

PALM BEACH ATLANTIC UNIVERSITY
901 S. Flagler Drive
West Palm Beach, FL 33402
561/803-2000
http://www.pba.edu/

PENSACOLA CHRISTIAN COLLEGE
P.O. Box 18000
Pensacola, FL 32523
850/478-8496
http://www.pcci.edu/

PHILLIPS JUNIOR COLLEGE
1479 South Nova Road
Daytona Beach, FL 32114
904/255-1707

RINGLING SCHOOL OF ART & DESIGN
2700 N. Tamiami Trail
Sarasota, FL 34234
800/255-7695
http://www.rsad.edu/

ROLLINS COLLEGE
1000 Holt Avenue
Winter Park, FL 32789

407/646-2000
http://www.rollins.edu/

SAINT JOHN VIANNEY COLLEGE SEMINARY
2900 S.W. 87th Avenue
Miami, FL 33165
305/223-4561
http://www.sjvcs.edu/

SAINT LEO COLLEGE
33701 State Road 52
Saint Leo, FL 33574
352/588-8283
http://www.saintleo.edu/

SAINT THOMAS UNIVERSITY
16400 N.W. 32nd Avenue
Miami, FL 33054
305/625-6000
http://www.stu.edu/

SAINT VINCENT DE PAUL
REGIONAL SEMINARY
10701 S. Military Trail
Boynton Beach, FL 33436
561/732-4424
http://www.svdp.edu/

SCHILLER INTERNATIONAL UNIVERSITY
453 Edgewater Drive
Dunedin, FL 34698
727/736-5082
http://www.schiller.edu/

SOUTH UNIVERSITY
1760 North Congress Avenue
West Palm Beach, FL 33409
561/697-9200
http://www.southcollege.edu

SOUTHEASTERN COLLEGE OF THE
ASSEMBLIES OF GOD
1000 Longfellow Boulevard
Lakeland, FL 33801
800/500-8760
http://www.secollege.edu/

SPURGEON BAPTIST BIBLE COLLEGE
4440 Spurgeon Drive
Mulberry, FL 33860
863/425-3429
http://www.spurgeon.edu/

STETSON UNIVERSITY
421 North Woodland Boulevard
Deland, FL 32723
800/688-0101
http://www.stetson.edu/

TRINITY COLLEGE OF FLORIDA
2430 Welbilt Boulevard
Trinity, FL 34655
888/776-4999

http://www.trinitycollege.edu/

TROY STATE UNIVERSITY
(Florida Region)
81 Beal Parkway, S.E.
Fort Walton Beach, FL 32548
850/244-7414
http://www.tsufl.edu/

UNION INSTITUTE
16853 N.E. 2nd Avenue, Suite 102
North Miami Beach, FL 33162
800-486-7141
http://www.tui.edu/

UNIVERSITY OF MIAMI
P.O. Box 248006
Coral Gables, FL 33124
305/284-2211
http://www.miami.edu/

UNIVERSTY OF TAMPA
401 West Kennedy Boulevard
Tampa, FL 33606
813/253-3333
http://www.utampa.edu/

WARNER SOUTHERN COLLEGE
13895 Highway 27
Lake Wales, FL 33859
800/949-7248, EXT 7202
http://www.warner.edu/

WEBBER COLLEGE
1201 North Scenic Highway
Babson Park, FL 33827
800/741-1844
http://www.webber.edu/

WEBSTER COLLEGE
2127 Grand Boulevard
Holiday, FL
727/942-0069
http://www.webstercollege.com/